# Business Process Management: The Next Wave

"Let every eye negotiate for itself and trust its agents.
—Much Ado About Nothing, Act II, Scene I (adapted)

"Something is happening, but you don't know what it is,
do you, Mister Jones?" —Bob Dylan, Ballad of a Thin Man.

"Toto, I've a feeling we're not in Kansas anymore."
—Dorothy, the 1939 film, *The Wizard of Oz*

"We are at that very point in time when a 400-year old age is dying and another is struggling to be born—a shifting of culture, science, society, and institutions enormously greater than the world has ever experienced."
—Dee Ward Hock, founder of VISA

"The world has been reset. Today's uncertainty feels like the 'new normal.' We will not return to the relative tranquility of the pre-crisis world. Growth will be harder to come by, trends will be more volatile and constituent voices will be louder."
—Jeffrey Immelt, CEO, General Electric, March, 2010.[1]

"Strategy, as we knew it, is dead. It's now all about operational agility and how fast businesses can seize opportunities. If strategies and forecasts have to change daily or weekly, then so be it." —Walt Shill, former McKinsey and Accenture executive.

---

[1] http://www.reuters.com/article/idUSTRE6243OD20100305

## Landmark Books by Meghan-Kiffer Press

**BUSINESS INNOVATION IN THE CLOUD**
EXECUTING ON INNOVATION WITH CLOUD COMPUTING

**THE COO REVOLUTION**
REINVENTING CUSTOMER-FACING
PROCESSES FOR MOMENTS OF TRUTH

**ENTERPRISE CLOUD COMPUTING**
A STRATEGY GUIDE FOR
BUSINESS AND TECHNOLOGY PROFESSIONALS

**DOT CLOUD**
THE 21ST CENTURY BUSINESS PLATFORM

**THE BUSINESS PROCESS ECOSYSTEM**

**EXTREME COMPETITION**
INNOVATION AND
THE GREAT 21ST CENTURY BUSINESS REFORMATION

**SAMURAI BUSINESS:**
THE WAY OF THE WARRIOR IN THE DIGITAL CENTURY

**THE BUSINESS PROCESS ECOSYSTEM**

**BPM BOOTS ON THE GROUND**
HOW TO IMPLEMENT STRATEGIC PROCESS MANAGEMENT

**MASTERING THE UNPREDICTABLE**

**BUSINESS ARCHITECTURE**
THE ART AND PRACTICE OF BUSINESS TRANSFORMATION

**MORE FOR LESS:**
THE POWER OF PROCESS MANAGEMENT

**BUSINESS PROCESS MANAGEMENT: THE THIRD WAVE**

**THE POWER OF PROCESS:**
UNLEASHING THE SOURCE OF COMPETITIVE ADVANTAGE

**IT DOESN'T MATTER:**
BUSINESS PROCESSES DO

**POWER IN THE CLOUD**
HOW TO BUILD SYSTEMS AT THE EDGE OF CHAOS

**THE REAL-TIME ENTERPRISE:**
COMPETING ON TIME

**THE DEATH OF 'E' AND
THE BIRTH OF THE REAL NEW ECONOMY**

**THE GREATEST INNOVATION SINCE THE ASSEMBLY LINE**

# Business Process Management: The Next Wave

## Harnessing Complexity with Intelligent Agents

Jim Sinur
James Odell
Peter Fingar

MK
Meghan-Kiffer Press
Tampa, Florida, USA, www.mkpress.com
*Advanced Business-Technology Books for Competitive Advantage*

Publisher's Cataloging-in-Publication Data

Jim Sinur, James Odell, Peter Fingar
Business Process Management: The Next Wave / Jim Sinur, James Odell, Peter Fingar, - 1st ed.
p. cm.
Includes index and appendices.
ISBN 978-0929652-22-1 (paperback : alk. paper)

1. Business Process Management 2. BPM 3. Agent 4. Agent-based Technology 5. Intelligent Process. 6. Complex adaptive systems. I. Sinur, James. II. Odell, James III. Fingar, Peter

| | |
|---|---|
| HD58.87.S548 2013 | 2013947326 |
| 658.4'063–dc21 | CIP |



**Published by Meghan-Kiffer Press**
310 East Fern Street — Suite G
Tampa, FL 33604 USA



MK
Meghan-Kiffer Press
Tampa, Florida, USA
*Advanced Business-Technology Books for Competitive Advantage*

Printed in the United States of America. SAN 249-7980
MK Printing 10 9 8 7 6 5 4 3 2 1

# Table of Contents

# Foreword by Thomas H. Davenport

Decades ago, in 1990 to be precise, I coauthored an article, "The New Industrial Engineering: Information Technology and Business Process Redesign," in the *Sloan Management Review.* A little later that same year, another (more revolutionary and not surprisingly, more popular) article by Michael Hammer, "Reengineering Work: Don't Automate, Obliterate" appeared in the *Harvard Business Review.* These writings seeded a new wave of process innovation and radical business process reengineering (BPR) that led to a movement in which companies downsized, rightsized, outsourced and restructured their work—all with some help from information technology.

But BPR was only one shot in a broader wave of business transformation. In 2003, Howard Smith's and Peter Fingar's book, *Business Process Management: The Third Wave* put IT at the core of business process change. It announced a new era of business process management (BPM) that gave greater control over IT-driven process change to business people, changing the role of the IT organization. The third wave was built to optimize change, and even today there are few higher goals of organizations today than achieving agility.

Much of my work since the BPR focus has involved applying technology to knowledge management and analytics. Indeed, as Sinur, Odell, and Fingar note in this book, "Technology marches on." The complexity of business processes has grown exponentially, the amount and complexity of data has grown even faster, and new technologies are needed to master this environment.

We need to connect the dots among BPM, knowledge management, and analytics, especially in a world in which mobile and social technologies have transformed how people work and live. The authors argue that *intelligent agent technology* is now needed to manage the new complexities going forward.

I agree that agent technology holds great potential. It embeds smart decision-making into the core of business processes, and allows the efficiency, flexibility, and customization that customers want from organizations today. I believe the authors are setting the stage for the next wave of BPM a wave that you cannot afford to miss. Go forth and learn to surf it!

**Thomas H. Davenport**
Distinguished Professor of IT and Management, Babson College
Co-Founder and Research Director, International Institute for Analytics
Research Fellow, MIT Center for Digital Business
Senior Advisor to Deloitte Analytics

# Preface

*How We Organized This Book.* We open the book by examining the major trends in the world outside of business that include globalization as the greatest reorganization of the world since the Industrial Revolution, and the Internet as the greatest revolution in human communication since the advent of the telephone. We now live in a world of *exponential change*, and businesses will feel the full impact of that change.

With the context set, we move on to describe the major waves of business process management (BPM) over the past 30 years and set the stage for the next wave, agent-oriented BPM. Next we explore agent technology, the evolution of business systems and programming, the uses of agent technology, complexity, and emergence. Then we move on to the organization and coordination of work, followed by a case study. The final chapter provides strategies and action items for architecting and implementing agent-oriented BPM in business.

For the more technically oriented reader, we have included Technical Appendices to take a deeper dive into agent communication, agent interaction, security, architecture and standards. For those less interested in the technical details, the book is designed to be a quick 215 page read.

*Who Should Read This Book?* The book has been written for C-level executives and technology leaders. We do not shy away from technical terminology, but we have strived to explain technical topics in lay language, for in today's world technology and business are inseparable. The book builds on the groundbreaking book, *Business Process Management, The Third Wave*, but is not a substitute for that seminal work that spells out the shift from data processing to *process processing* and the advent of the business process management system (BPMS) that places *process* center stage in the world of business automation. If you haven't already read *The Third Wave* we highly recommend it as a corequisite for this book.

This book strives to provide insights and outline strategies for transforming current BPM approaches and technologies by harnessing the revolutionary business platform, the Cloud, and the disruptive technologies of mobile, social, big data and predictive analytics.

*Ask the right questions if you're going to find the right answers.*
—Vanessa Redgrave

No one can provide you "pat answers," to the challenges we all face, but we want to help you ask the right questions. Our goal is to provide a starting point that will help you know what is coming, how to think about addressing it and suggest some places to get started.

We wish you great success in your journey ahead, doing the work of pushing the envelope in your organization. After all, it's *how* you do what you do that matters in the current world of unpredictable change.

Jim Sinur
James Odell
Peter Fingar
August 2013

The authors would like to acknowledge Dr. David Greenstein (dgreenst@tir.com) for his providing a comprehensive description of his agent-based AMIS case study. James Odell would like to thank CSC for a grant to organize his existing material on agent-oriented technology into a cohesive form.

# 1. Preamble: The Future Ain't What It Used to Be

*The Scream*
Is this Edvard Munch's 1893 Painting, or a portrait of today's CEO contemplating exponential change and complexity?

*The future ain't what it used to be.*
—Legendary Baseball Player and Coach, Yogi Berra

Though it's not requisite reading for this book, we've included this brief preamble and suggest a quick skim to set the *context* for the main body of the book.

---

Going one step beyond most current business process management (BPM) technologies, intelligent agents are poised to transform the way we model the enterprise and build information systems. But before we can properly discuss the changing role of agent technology as an enabler of business process innovation, we need to set the *context* of what's happening in the larger socioeconomic world *outside* of business, what's happening in our world as a result of dramatic advances brought about by the global hyper-connectivity of the Internet and the accelerating advance of technology. For example, watch how today's technology can remix Van Gogh's classic, *Starry Night* into something new. Not only are we moving from atoms to bits, we are also moving from bits to atoms with things like 3-D printing—the current revolution in manufacturing.

tinyurl.com/cal2wtw

## Today's State of the Business

What strikes fear in the hearts of business leaders these days? Globalization and commoditization. We are not on the brink of a new world economic order; we've already crossed that threshold. With three billion new capitalists from China, India and the former Soviet Union ready to engage your company in extreme competition, you'll have to make deep structural changes in the very ways you operate your business, the very ways you do what you do—and that's what Extreme Competition is all about. Operational innovation—where you forge new relationships across the globe to form extreme supply chains, pursue extreme innovation and collaborate with extreme specialists—is the next true source of competitive advantage.

Prior to the beginnings of Internet-based e-commerce, the computer was essentially a filing cabinet, handling the affairs of the back office, programmed under the file clerk metaphor: capture, storage, and retrieval of records. Today, however, we are not only seeing Sun Microsystems' vision that *the network is the computer*, now we can observe that *the network is the business!*

To participate in the digital economy, the business tasks we must ask of computers move from back-office record-keeping to the frontline *operations of the business*. We are automating very different *kinds of things*: business processes and workflows that are human, knowledge-based phenomena; and opening our core business systems for direct interaction with customers, suppliers, and sometimes with competitors (i.e., the airlines industry). New forms of pervasive communications have allowed forward thinking business people to blur industry boundaries and create virtual corporations, whose core competencies are information and knowledge management, taking much of the operational information once in workers' heads and codifying it into executable software.

The new realities of business have created new imperatives for business information systems. Today's business systems must provide enterprise (and inter-enterprise) reach so that islands of disparate information can be integrated into a meaningful whole. They must be able to cope with the overwhelming complexity of distributed technology and an inter-enterprise information base. They must be open to survive a network-centric ecosystem. Rapid applications development goes without saying, and applications must be designed to embrace constant change. Business systems must be knowledge-based (not just information-based) if they are to cope with the incompleteness and ambiguity of real business processes and workflows. And they must be adaptive to meet the needs of the moment and bring productivity to an increasingly overwhelmed business user and self-service to our customers. That's what is being asked of CIOs today, a very tall order.

## Full Steam Ahead!

Well, thanks to Larry Roberts and other Internet pioneers, the authors of this book had the opportunity to work with TCP/IP (the Internet) in 1969! We were full of excitement and wonder, as described in this *must-watch* one-minute clip by futurist Arthur C. Clark in 1974, long before the Internet revolution.

Watch the Youtube: http://goo.gl/viVXV

Oops. Nothing seems to happen as soon as it's "invented," so we had to wait until Jeff Bezos "Amazoned" the retail industry before the Internet became the backbone of eCommerce. Amazon is a marvel of a "virtual company," one that taps intelligent agent technology including *Eyes and Ears*, to deliver services that once before only humans could deliver.

Today we are witnessing a seismic shift in information technology. It's called the Cloud, and cloud computing is set to unleash a perfect storm in business, especially in today's dire economy. But unlike the retail industry that got *Amazoned*, the Cloud will affect *every industry* and go beyond enabling a virtual company and on to multi-company virtual business networks and ecosystems. And don't forget to add in social platforms, Mobile/Smart devices, Big Data, and predictive analytics that live in the Cloud. And it won't involve just a single Cloud. Just as the Internet is a network of interoperating networks of computers, the "Intercloud" will be an interoperating network of Clouds: private, public and hybrid. Complexity will grow exponentially, and tools and methods are desperately needed to build businesses that are *complex adaptive systems* capable of bringing order out of the chaos (charodic systems).

That's why it is now time for agent technology, a technology that's been around for years, to take center stage in the world of business in general, and specifically in the world of BPM, for intelligent business processes are how work gets done in the emerging

Cloud economy.

Think this is a bunch of hype? Think it will be years and years before such systems affect the marketplace? Think it will take quantum computing to implement? Think again, for in many ways the future is already here; it's just not evenly distributed.

How big is the need for agent technology? Let's turn to *Science World Report*, "What is Industry 4.0? The term 'Industry 4.0' was coined, similar to Cloud Computing, to have a short and symbolic keyword describing the smart factories, intelligent machines and networked processes that facilitate and result from the 4th industrial revolution that is now beginning. This will be one of the major trends shaping the first half of the 21st century."

"To put this into perspective, the first industrial revolution started around 1780 with the first mechanical manufacturing facilities and especially the invention and widespread use of the steam engine and coal for energy. The second phase set in around 1900 with electricity and the development of large capital goods industries like steel and oil which enabled mass-manufacturing. The microchip, computers and globalization ushered in the third industrial revolution in the 1970s, which expanded highly efficient production on a global scale and scope never seen before, all on the foundation of automation. This trend now matured and is still growing, with multi-national consumer good corporations like Volkswagen planting highly automated factories on all continents. It will over the next years be supplemented by the fourth industrial revolution that merges the existing vast industrial infrastructure with the Internet of Things and Cloud Computing, creating a direct and real-time interface between the virtual and physical world: The birth of Cyber-Physical Systems!" (Read the full report here: http://bit.ly/142z18F )

## Exponential Change

Executives are concerned, rightly so, that their operations will not be able to change fast enough to maintain their organizations edge in a rapidly changing world. This implies that the processes and the resources that service the operations will not be able to change with the agility needed to deliver the existing and desired business outcomes. At the same time, these same executives will have to deal with the resistance to change represented in the brittleness in business processes and the actual resources getting the work completed. We are at a critical time where one cannot wait for the evolution of BPM over a long period of time to pick up wider scopes and deeper levels of complexity.

*Episodic Change.* Jeralean Talley, who lives in Detroit, was four years old when the Wright brothers took their first powered flight. Just think of the *episodic* changes she has see so far in her life (Electrification, Wright Brothers flight, 1903; the Benz automobile, 1908, Henry Ford's mass production). But there's another kind of change, *exponential* change that is now upon us in many realms on this earth. In short, "We ain't seen nothing yet!"

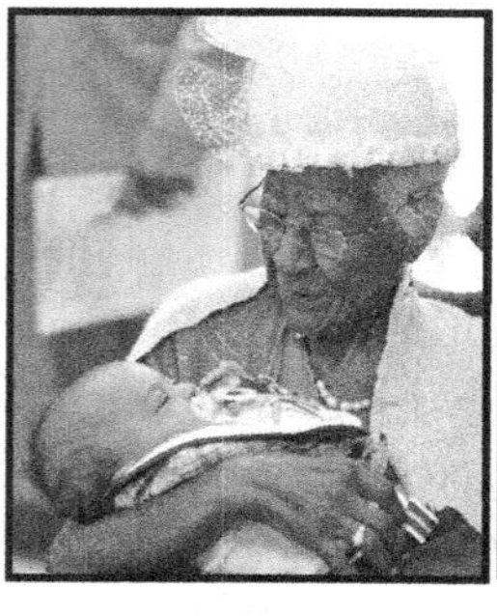

As shown in the figure below, in 1981, coauthor Peter Fingar met the man who invented the electronic digital computer, Dr. John Vincent Atanasoff.

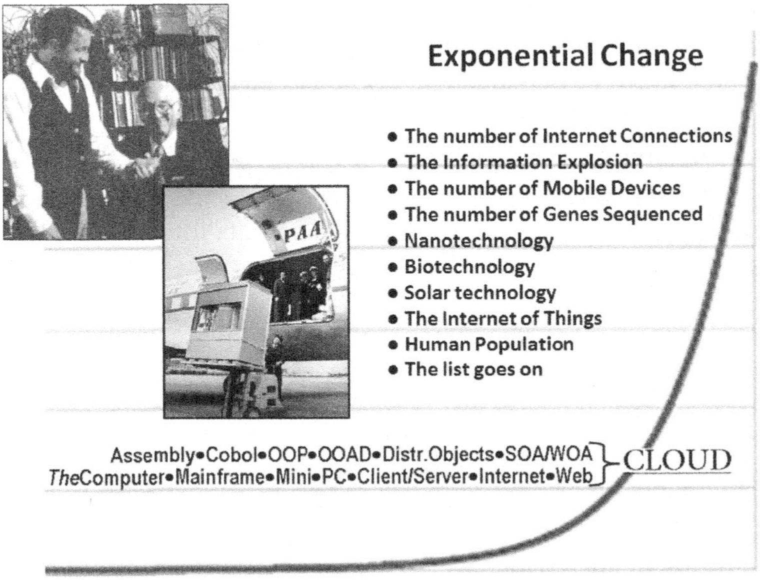


It's *AMAZING* the amount of change the authors of this book have experienced in our lifetimes so far. Just check out that 1956 photo of a whopping 5 megabyte hard drive being delivered to be installed in IBM's first supercomputer the IBM 305 RAMAC. You could say we've seen it all from the very beginning. So we don't pay much attention to the constant stream of hype that comes from the IT industry. But now and then, something game-changing comes along and we devote our full attention. For example, the minicomputer in the 1970s, the PC in the 1980s, and the Internet in the 1990s, just to name a few.

At their start, exponential curves appear to be linear or a straight line rising gradually. We humans understand and like that kind of predictable change. But after a certain point, the pitch of the curve takes off like a rocket. It's time to wake up, to buckle up and get ready for the ride ahead. Let's face it, we've reached the knee of the exponential curve and are switching from a linear existence to a world of exponential change and we're completely unprepared because we have no prior frame of reference.

In addition to the current mega-patterns of technology (Social platforms, Mobile/Smart devices, Big Data, predictive analytics and the Cloud), there are a myriad of point technologies that extend the impact of change into countless facets of our lives. A partial list would include:

- miniaturization of nearly every device type,
- extremely low cost sensors,
- services architectures for software and data interchange,
- in-memory processing,
- virtualization,
- cognitive computing,
- affective computing,
- services avatars,
- persona management systems,
- augmented reality,
- fractal business architecture,
- sentiment analysis,
- ... and a host of others.

Suffice to say that the exponential pace of change has no end in sight, and what it portends for business challenges our comprehension.

## Complexity, Complexity

Businesses have evolved quickly from dictating products and services to providing products and services that customers demand—pull versus push. Organizations will have to continue to react to this basic change and will need to be proactive to intercept business patterns before they overwhelm an organization's ability to change. Changing business outcomes are going to be the norm, going forward. New business models will have to be considered and played out before changes are implemented. This adds a tremendous level of complexity in businesses.

In addition, the scope of process is going to widen beyond traditional and artificial organizational boundaries to large-scale business networks. The dynamic nature of these business networks will accelerate, thus contributing to the complexity that organizations will need to address. Add to all of this that the convergence and extension of technologies applied to BPM (social, mobile, big data, analytics, Cloud) is further complicating the alternatives for business process owners. There will be a big shift from purely reactive approaches, as we have seen for decades, to proactive behaviors that enable a more adaptive enterprise that can really manage change, sometimes centrally and sometimes at the point of local impact where customer "moments of truth" dictate real-time actions. To make such a shift, intelligent software will be essential, and that's where intelligent agent technologies come in to bridge together BPM, knowledge management, and predictive analytics.

With the advent of highly distributed clouds of processing and the emergent Internet of Things, information systems based on intelligent agent technology are inevitable, even though the tasks of conceiving, designing, and building them are not trivial. As we turn our attention to these tasks, we will benefit from keeping the fundamental question in mind, "How can we conceive, design, and build adaptive, multi-enterprise-scale information systems and business processes?" Intelligent agent technology is an enabler of such systems, but is not an end unto itself. When combined with the maturing disciplines of object technology and BPM methods, their synergy, embodied in *agent-oriented BPM* (aoBPM), can take us to a new level in the search for the prize of harnessing complex business ecosystems and multi-company business networks.

Now is the time to get ready to *master complexity and the unpredictable.* And as Thomas H. Davenport wrote in the Foreword, "I believe the authors are *setting the stage* for the next wave of BPM, a wave that you cannot afford to miss." This book won't provide you *how-to, cookie-cutter* answers, but does provide the concepts and information you'll need to ask the right questions for starting your journey ahead.

> *Asking the right questions takes as much skill as giving the right answers.*
> —Robert Half

# 2. Technology Marches On

*Digitization represents a revolution that may be the greatest opportunity for growth that our company has ever seen.*

—GE, Key Growth Initiatives 2002.

Although we have witnessed great progress in the theory and practice of business process management, deployments have so far been mostly tactical. Reviewing the case studies that abound at BPM vendors' Web sites in 2013, many business processes have been revamped and there are ROI stories to tell. That's good; but typical BPM deployments to date have been limited in scope, applying to improvements in specific business functions. And it's not always clear what the case studies mean by BPM. Is it streamlining administrative processes, building composite applications, simplifying application integration, or deploying configurable templates to deal with specific needs such as Sarbanes-Oxley compliance? Sure, ROI can be demonstrated and departmental performance improved, but where's the breakthrough that can help the company win in the brave new world of globalization and extreme competition?

As long as BPM deployments remain tactical, BPM is likely to become just another technique for squeezing out costs and making incremental performance improvements in functional departments. Today, however, what executive wants to settle for small internal gains in Department X or Department Y, when there's a battle for survival raging? The full potential of BPM is about 'enterprise business processes' and 'value-chain business processes' not technical improvements here or there, or streamlining individual functions in the company.

Tactical BPM only offers a way of improving what a company already does, which, though good, can mean clinging to the past. BPM's full potential offers a *strategic* capability for achieving breakout competitive advantage through process innovation. For that to happen, the scope and complexity increases exponentially as companies progress from point-solution BPM, to enterprise BPM where cross-functional processes are taken on, and on to value-chain BPM where totally new cross-company processes emerge and must be managed. The shortcomings of the many current flavors of BPM solutions (EAI/BPM, Workflow/BPM, Business Rules/BPM, and federations of these approaches) will appear as a company moves beyond the tactical solutions and on to the value chain.

Today, competition is about setting the pace of innovation in your industry. It's about forming new multi-company alliances (sometimes even with competitors) to innovate new value delivery systems that span your suppliers' suppliers and your customers' customers. It's about competing for the future in the new era of extreme competition, where the customer is no longer King, the customer is now a Dictator that demands you go to the ends of the earth to provide cheaper, better, faster products and services. This is the stuff of strategic deployments of BPM.

## Focusing on Strategic BPM

To move on to strategic BPM, *the next generation,* five capabilities will become the focus: (1) the BPMS, (2) Process-Oriented Architecture and Methods, (3) Human Interaction Management, (4) Complex Event Processing, and (5) Agent Technology.

### The BPMS

In order for BPM to continue its impressive growth rates, it will need to demonstrate the ability to manage innovative and intelligent processes that span wider scopes and deeper levels of complexity. While there is a strong trend towards *smart* processes that incorporate big data, predictive analytics, social platforms, mobile smart devices, and cloud computing, the challenge will be to manage these new and more complex processes over wide scopes and in business transformation contexts.

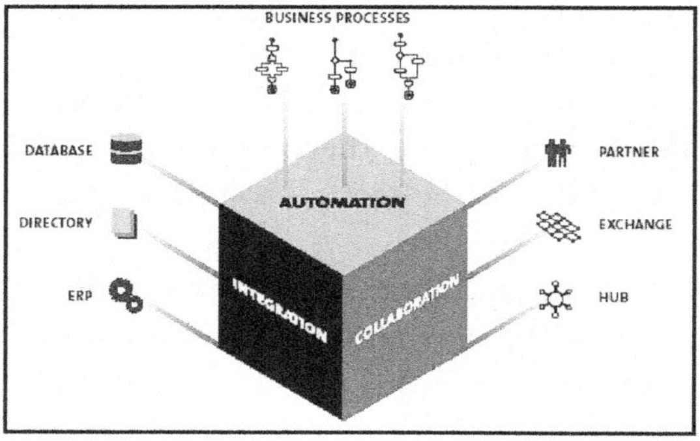

Many BPM suites today are just that, *suites* of workflow, rules engines and EAI technologies federated into a process *tier*. In *Business Process Management: The Third Wave*, a different vision calls for a universal "engine of process," the Business Process Management System (BPMS), that fuses and extends those preexisting technologies, and treats *process processing* in a way that a DBMS treats *data processing* so that business processes can be managed in a far more holistic manner. When processes get pushed into a federated tier, you no longer have an engine executing them; you have any number of engines executing any number of processes, some built into legacy applications or pulled from Web services.

This scenario quickly becomes unwieldy, for the end-to-end process becomes splintered. What you will ultimately need is the capability to directly build and manage *whole processes* that interact with applications rather than building composite applications that interact with scattered processes. The process, not the application, should be the grand orchestrator, and the BPMS its single platform for modeling, deployment and management.

The BPMS is based on a "design-driven" versus a "model-driven" architecture. This means that the process model is directly executable by the BPMS without translation through a software development cycle as required in a model-driven architecture. Think of a spreadsheet. When you design a spreadsheet you just execute it; you don't use it as a model to front-end a systems development lifecycle. Ditto the BPMS. Round-trip integration between process modeling and execution engines attempt to close the gap between the two worlds of modeling and execution.

## Process-Oriented Architecture and Methods

Clearly, process conception, analysis, and development represent a different set of artifacts and constructs than those found in traditional software development, which is aimed at *information management*, not *process management*. In his landmark book, *Business Process Management: A Rigorous Approach*, Martyn Ould, explains, "The key thing about a paradigm shift is that old ways of thinking just won't work in the new world.

"If your engineers have only had mud to work with in the past, their ways of specifying and designing buildings will be fine for mud buildings but they won't make a lot of sense when the steel girder appears on the scene. Today's dedicated follower of fashion in information system development is likely to be speaking UML and using one of the various development approaches based on the UML. [But] we cannot view business process management systems as just another sort of information system."

Information-oriented languages and information-oriented methods have evolved around a world of storing, retrieving, and updating information, not the dynamic world of process. Ould elaborates, "Simply extending our information-based methods simply won't work – they don't have the necessary concepts at their heart. We're moving from the Information Age to the Process Age. We need purpose-built methods for working with processes to replace our methods for working with information."

The process-managed enterprise demands that the center of automation be shifted from *information processing* to *process processing*. Ould continues, "The traditional paradigm views organisations as things that work with information, so our systems have been about looking after information. In the past we have specified our information systems in terms of what data they will store and how we can access it and change it and move it around. And we have designed our information systems in terms of data representations and operations on data."

Processes need an architecture and a paradigm of their own, not a data-oriented information systems paradigm. Further, just as spreadsheets are placed directly in the hands of business people without the need for a cadre of support technicians, BPMSs must be turned over to business analysts. While new "service-oriented" techniques for software development offer flexible, loosely-coupled approaches to computing, these advances, while good, are aimed at technical people who build and manage information systems, e.g., programmers, not business analysts who want to build and manage business processes.

There aren't enough programmers in the world to design and code the needed process-oriented systems using conventional software development, even with the aid of service-oriented software techniques. So, think of Web services and Service-Oriented Architecture (SOA) as an underlying *technical operating system* for the Process-Oriented Architecture (POA) and the BPMS. The new paradigm of business process management needs new methods for thinking about *collaborative* processes in ways that build on the concepts of *collaboration, evolution,* and *business context,* not program calls, WSDL and SOAP. To this end, a long-established modeling framework called Role Activity Theory and Role Activity Diagramming (RAD) techniques, in line with Ould's concepts of process-oriented architecture, are needed to supersede mechanistic information-oriented approaches to process modeling and analysis. This shift from the Information Age to the Process Age in terms of architecture and methods will serve as the cornerstone of BPM, the next generation.

## Human Interaction Management

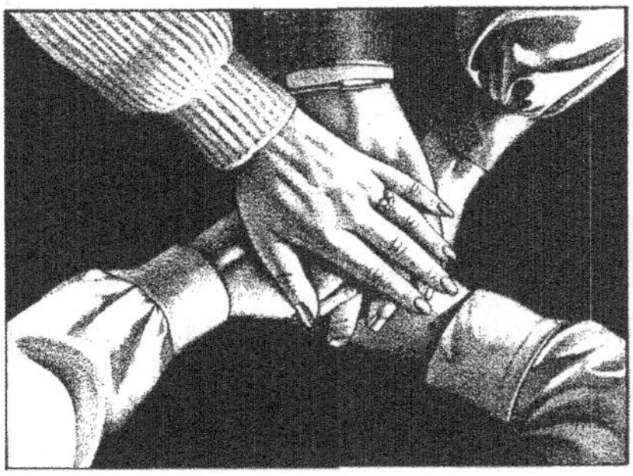

Most of today's BPM solutions can take care of 80% of the mechanistic, predetermined system-to-system scenarios with predefined workflow and inter-application transaction management. Such capabilities are needed to help a company put its "house in order" with application integration. However, when you consider *collaborative* activities and the fact that, as Xerox's former Chief Scientist, John Seely Brown, explains, "processes don't do work, people do," BPM's missing link is made visible.

There's no doubt that what's now needed isn't more and more software for animating computers; it's software for animating *human interactions* across end-to-end business processes, where work teams may be scattered across the globe. While interwoven with mechanistic processes, human-driven processes span your suppliers, your suppliers' suppliers, your employees, your customers and your customers' customers, forming the DNA of a complete value delivery system.

It's now time to shift the BPM spotlight onto those human-driven processes. That means fusing traditional collaboration and information tools (groupware, knowledge management, workflow and system-to-system BPM) and *extending* them with a complete theory of human work if we are to build systems that can support the way people *actually* work, versus treating them as cogs in an information machine.

The Human Interaction Management System needs formal foundations—and these include role-activity theory, formal activity specifications, mobile processes built on a Pi calculus foundation, intelligent agent technology, first-order (and higher order) predicate logic, the computer science of speech acts and conversations for action, autopoeisis, and other principles drawn from cognitive theory, psychology, learning theory, biology and social systems theory. Phew!

For the business user, this level of detail is, of course, overkill—and such underpinnings must be completely hidden in daily use of a Human Interaction Management System. However, they are essential to its ability to handle the true dynamics of human collaborative activity. In short, a *complete* theory of how humans actually work must underpin Human Interaction Management. In a groundbreaking work, *Human Interactions: The Heart and Soul of Business Process Management,* Keith Harrison-Broninski, wrote, "We must find a way of thinking about human-driven processes that allows *controlled management of change*—something that is innate in all interaction work, as human-driven work processes evolve continuously throughout their lifetime."

With the rise of social media of the likes of Facebook and Twitter and various forms of corporate social networks (e.g., Yammer) and wikis, it's all too easy to think that collaboration, inside and outside the company is now widespread. But is it? Most social media can be classified as *implied* collaboration. Sure they provide vast new channels of communication, but they also provide huge amounts of random chatter and noise. What's needed is *explicit* collaboration that's goal oriented; and that's precisely where the human interaction management system comes in.

## Complex Event Processing

All modern information systems are event-driven, where an event can be as simple as clicking a mouse button. According to Gartner research, event-driven business applications can be sorted into four categories: 1. Simple event-driven (or message-driven) applications where application programs explicitly send and receive messages directly to and from each other. 2. Event-driven applications that are mediated by integration brokers that transform and route simple event messages according to logical rules. 3. Event-driven applications that are directed by business process management (BPM) engines that manage the end-to-end flow of a multistep process using special, BPM-oriented types of events. 4. Complex event processing (CEP) applications, where a sophisticated event manager logically evaluates multiple events to enable decoupled, parallel, asynchronous processing or business activity monitoring (BAM).

Complex event processing is most effective when event messages carry information relating individual events with other events along with causal information on how an event came about. As described in the landmark book on complex event processing, *The Power of Events*, by Stanford professor, David Luckham, some CEP messages may not even carry business data swapped between applications. Instead, they contain information about low-level events that, when aggregated into patterns, can reveal high-level business intelligence.

As an everyday example consider how the intelligence agencies filter low-level noise among terrorist groups to derive meaningful information used to set terrorist alert levels for law enforcement agencies. In a business context, Luckham asserts that low-level events that occur in "the cloud" of network-based business interactions can yield valuable business intelligence. By using complex event processing for business activity monitoring, CEP can close the loop between BAM and the business process management system that, in turn, can act on the business intelligence. As companies extend BPM outside their walls and on to the complex business ecosystem across the value chain, the value of CEP becomes an obvious lynchpin for business activity monitoring and real-time process analytics.

Eight years later, Opher Etzion and Peter Niblett (from IBM's research lab) have taken CEP one step further by specifying the underlying event technology that is being used by software professionals. *Event Processing in Action* is a ground-breaking book that demonstrates how to use, design, and build event processing applications. It follows a detailed example to present the concepts and show you the how-tos of both architecture and implementation. The book introduces the leading free and commercial tools available, along with several language implementations and many examples. manning.com/etzion

Using agent technology, the authors describe how event-processing apps collect, analyze, and react to events as they occur. They recognize event patterns—from the obvious to the complex, even predicting outcomes such as power shortages or customer dissatisfaction—and respond to them accordingly. In some applications, such as financial trading, fast reaction times are a must.

## Agent Technology

To manage the inherent complexity in enterprise or value-chain business processes, smart companies will demand smart processes that go far beyond today's typical business rules engines. But "smart" doesn't mean some Orwellian thinking machine; it means agent technology.

What's an agent? Backing away from technology for a moment, the everyday term, agent, provides a starting definition: "one who acts for, or in the place of, another." A *software agent* is a software package that carries out tasks for others, autonomously without being controlled by its master once the tasks have been delegated. The "others" may be human users, business processes, workflows or applications. A basic software agent stands on three pillars, three essential properties: autonomy, reactivity, and communication ability. The notion of autonomy means that an agent exercises exclusive control over its own actions and state. Reactivity means sensing or perceiving change in their environment and responding. And, even the most basic software agents have the ability to communicate with other entities: human users, other software agents, or objects.

Add to this definition the ability to plan and set goals, to maintain data and data models (often called "belief models" in academic literature) to reason about the actions of itself and other agents (including humans), and the ability to improve its knowledge and performance through learning, you then have the core ingredients of an "intelligent agent." An intelligent agent represents a distinct category of software that incorporates local knowledge about its own and other agents' tasks and resources, allowing it to operate autonomously or as a part of a community of co-operative problem solvers (including human users), each agent having its own roles and responsibilities. (Chapter 4 will discuss *intelligence* in detail—particularly in terms of processing. Because an agent is "something that acts," it is fundamentally about processing—as well as enabling the processes of others.)

Agents can be integrated into BPM frameworks that contain, in one package, specific problem-solving functions, data, and control. Intelligent agents support a natural merging of BPM and knowledge-based technologies.

Intelligent agents can facilitate the incorporation of reasoning capabilities (e.g., encapsulation of business rules within agents). They permit the inclusion of learning and self-improvement capabilities at both infrastructure (adaptive routing) and application (adaptive user interfaces) levels. Intelligent user interfaces (supporting task-centered user interfaces and intelligent assistance to end-users) can be a boon to productivity in a complex world of multi-company business processes. With the complexity of tasks inherent in multi-company business processes, we will certainly need a little help from our knowledgeable friends, software agents.

## Complexity Busters

As the business world moves beyond the tinkering phase with tactical BPM point solutions and on to multi-enterprise process management for true process and value-chain innovation, complexity will explode. Thus BPM, the next generation, will require the complexity buster of the BPMS, which, in turn, incorporates process-oriented architecture and methods, human interaction management, complex event processing and agent technology. No, this isn't some mad computer scientist's dream; it's what's required by the messy and complex real world of business. Don't be surprised to find skunk works in progress among the leading BPM vendors who are successfully selling tactical solutions today, but know what's required for BPM to become a true source of strategic competitive advantage.

## Competing for the Future

The importance of agent technology is now widely recognized in several industries, especially defense, telecommunications, and manufacturing, as well as standards bodies such as the Object Management Group. These and other leading organizations have recognized the business and technical benefits:

- Increased productivity of business computer users and self-service customers in a network-centric business.
- A combined information and knowledge model of the business and information systems that makes rapid development in a complex environment a reality.
- Bandwidth efficiency so necessary in a network-centric computing environment.
- An enabler for rapid scaling for large organizations.

Not only do they recognize the benefits, some companies are already deploying intelligent agent technology as a competitive weapon—today! They turn Web hits into business relationships. They use smart technology to plug suppliers and customers directly into their core business systems. They profile their constituents and search for new patterns in their data warehouses to better meet ever changing needs. Is your company ready to compete with them?

With careful planning and armed with a solid understanding of the current limitations of intelligent agent technology, powerful business information systems can be developed that exploit the Internet and distributed objects and services to gain strategic business advantage. Although the tasks of designing and building them are not trivial, information systems based on intelligent agent technology are inevitable. Learning to harness this technology should be a top priority of today's business and technology leaders. Companies can go it alone but those that face immediate mission critical requirements will be well advised to seek outside assistance from those who have gone before.

# 3. BPM–The Next Wave

*What is needed is a relativistic theory, to give up altogether the notion that the world is constituted of basic objects or building blocks. Rather one has to view the world in terms of the universal flux of events and processes.*
—David Bohm

Process is nothing new, but the capability to manage end-to-end processes has progressed through three technology-enabled waves over the past several decades—and we are now on the cusp of another wave.

Before going through the waves, let's get some definitions out of the way. Throughout this book we use the terms BPM (a management discipline for a process-managed enterprise) and the BPMS (a technology enabler for BPM). So, let's turn to Gartner to define these terms for readers unfamiliar with them.

"*Business process management (BPM)* is the discipline of managing processes (rather than tasks) as the means for improving business performance outcomes and operational agility. Processes span organizational boundaries, linking together people, information flows, systems and other assets to create and deliver value to customers and constituents."

"*Business process management suites (BPMSs)* are the leading application infrastructures to support BPM projects and programs. A BPMS supports the entire process improvement life cycle — from process discovery, definition and design to implementation, monitoring and analysis, and through ongoing optimization. Its model-driven approach enables business and IT professionals to work together more collaboratively throughout the life cycle than is possible with other approaches to solution delivery."

## The First Wave: TQM

It's doubtful that the pyramids in Giza, Egypt, were built without "management." So the very idea of management isn't new. In a sense, the roots of *modern management* began with the arrival of *scientific management* in the 1920s and was dominated by Fredrick Taylor's, theory of management recorded in his 1911 monograph, *The Principles of Scientific Management.* Back then processes were *implicit* in *work practices* and not automated. In Peter Drucker's, description, "Frederick W. Taylor was the first man in recorded history who deemed work deserving of systematic observation and study. On Taylor's 'scientific management' rests, above all, the tremendous surge of affluence in the last seventy-five years which has lifted the working masses in the developed countries well above any level recorded before, even for the well-to-do. Taylor, though the Isaac Newton (or perhaps the Archimedes) of the science of work, laid only first foundations, however. Not much has been added to them since – even though he has been dead all of sixty years."

After WWII, applying science to *process* became front and center as W. Edwards Deming and Joseph Juran taught the Japanese about the power of quality management. Their work and the work of others triggered a wave of total quality management (TQM), spurred on by the publications of Deming and Juran in 1982 as shown below. The emphasis was not so much on the design of new processes, but on statistical measurements as a means of improving existing work practices and quality.

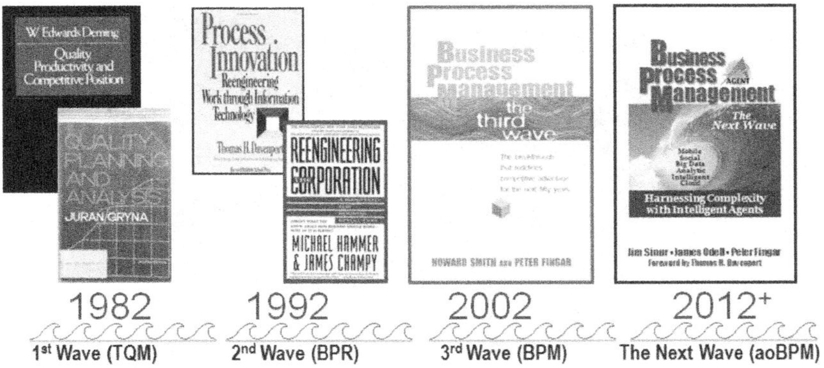

## The Second Wave: BPR

Then a decade later, the 1992 blockbuster books, *Process Innovation* and *Reengineering the Corporation,* hit corporate board rooms, and reengineering work through information technology took off. In this second wave of business process management, processes were manually *reengineered*, and through a one-time, big-bang activity, cast in concrete in the bowels of today's automated Enterprise Resource Planning (ERP) and other packaged systems. Although "downsizing" is the moniker most remembered from Business Process Reengineering (BPR), it was technological enablement—including office automation—that allowed companies to tear down internal silos and reengineer end-to-end business processes that spanned individual functional departments (silos).

Historically, ERP solutions had all the flexibility of wet concrete as they were configured and installed, then all the flexibility of dry concrete after installation. Even with document-centered workflow added to ERP, such systems only took up discrete roles as participants in processes; rarely did they provide business management control over the processes. Those that did only did so for sub-processes and were generally limited in their capability.

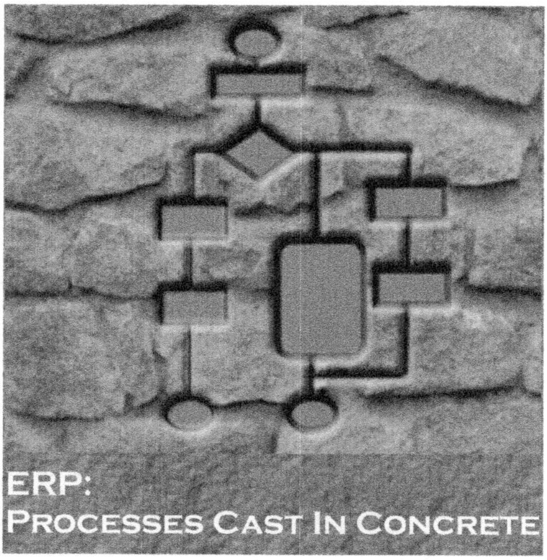

## The Third Wave: BPM

In the third wave of process management, the business process was freed from its concrete castings and made the central focus and basic building block of automation and business systems. Processes became first-class citizens in the world of automation. *Change* was the primary design goal because in the world of business process management: *the ability to change is far more prized than the ability to create in the first place.* It is through agile business process management that end-to-end processes can be monitored, continuously improved and optimized. Feedback of results, agility and adaptability are the bywords of the third wave.

### The Emergence of BPM

Before we continue, let's reflect on the evolution of Business Process Management (BPM). In the mid-nineties, BPM meant business process modeling where processes were documented and analyzed for improvement opportunities. This form of process work was an alternative to the rigorous and statistics-driven six sigma methods prevalent in the ERP era. Since there was no real process management as performed by actions, per se, Gartner changed the name to BPA meaning business process analysis. This market persists to this day for organizations that are trying to understand what processes are in effect, but has been augmented with automated business process discovery (ABPD) to measure the *actual process versus the modeled process.* There are significant benefits to analyzing the processes in effect and adjusting them even without an integrated process execution technology to perform the processes like a BPMS.

In the early 2000s BPM was defined as a management practice and a discipline, according to Gartner. BPM is a management practice that treats processes as corporate assets in order to attain the goal of improving business agility and operational performance while staying compliant with industry practices and government regulations. BPM is a discipline that employs methods, rules, metrics, practices and software tools to manage and continuously optimize an organization's activities and processes in light of its management strategies, decisions, policies, goals and tactics. The BPM execution technologies needed to perform the modeled processes expanded and split into to two major camps.

One camp centered on light-weight human workflow, usually surrounding content and cases. This was a data-driven approach that provided and continues to provide efficiency benefits. The other camp focused on system and data integration where transactions that spanned systems were orchestrated to completion. This was generally very system centric and left the human element out of the picture, but there were, and continue to be, efficiency benefits to glean for organizations. Then processes began to span both human and systems activities and the traditional BPMS was born.

This new wave was ushered in by a seminal book, *Business Process Management: The Third Wave.* Although feedback of results, agility and adaptability were the bywords of *The Third Wave*, the question was, however, how can such noble goals be attained? And the answer came in the form of a Business Process Management System (BPMS). Unlike an ERP system with data and applications at its core, the BPMS puts the abstract data type of *process* at the core. In lay terms, the BPMS places the notion of *process* center stage in the world of technological enablement for business change.

2012 was its 10th anniversary of *The Third Wave* book. But instead of celebrating the "Tin" Anniversary, it is somewhat disheartening to see that the "M" in BPM has often been ignored. As process luminary Andrew Spanyi famously asked, "How has BPM actually changed the behavior of leadership?" Such questions go straight to the heart of true business transformation.

In some cases the BPMS has been used for little more than a newer version of enterprise application integration (EAI) or traditional workflow. While such approaches can improve back-office efficiencies, where's the competitive advantage beef? As we'll explore, the word "enterprise" has to be prefixed to the term BPM. For that to have meaning, companies must cross over from "organization management" of people to process management that supersedes organization management and spans multiple organizations—*Enterprise BPM*. Politics and inertia are the high-barrier obstacles, and companies must navigate these obstacles to harness the true value of process management, *strategic* BPM. That is all about *people and change in human behavior*, not BPM technology.

As we look at what passes for BPM these days, it keeps coming to mind that we don't seem to have moved much beyond the ideas of Rummler and Brache in 1990. The end of BPM history, however, didn't happen in 2003 with *The Third Wave*. This may sound over the top, but it seems that the universe continues to evolve under certain immutable laws. These laws apply to everything: biology, physics, and social systems that, in turn, include these things we call an enterprise and BPM.

Okay, your organization has made the big leap to Enterprise BPM. But that doesn't signal the beginning of the end of your BPM journey; it signals the end of the beginning of a much more challenging journey. Now what?

Both BPM technology and agent paradigms focus on addressing *change* and *complexity*. Intelligent agent technology is the next logical step in moving the BPM technology paradigm forward and overcoming some of its shortcomings. Both technologies have been around for quite a while but only now are they being repurposed for business in response to a rapidly changing world.

The time has come where agents aren't just possible—they are *needed* to manage the growing chaos. In short, many companies will hit the wall if they stick to using conventional BPM Suites. Agents are necessary to scale—and "manage chaos."

**The Analyst's Perspective**

Traditional BPM then started including highly integrated software tools to address the many resources that could be managed by a process (people, systems, services, integrations, data, events, goals, rules, tolerances, work lists, dashboards, tolerances etc.). At the same time a process life cycle from Gartner became quite ubiquitous as shown in Figure 3.1.

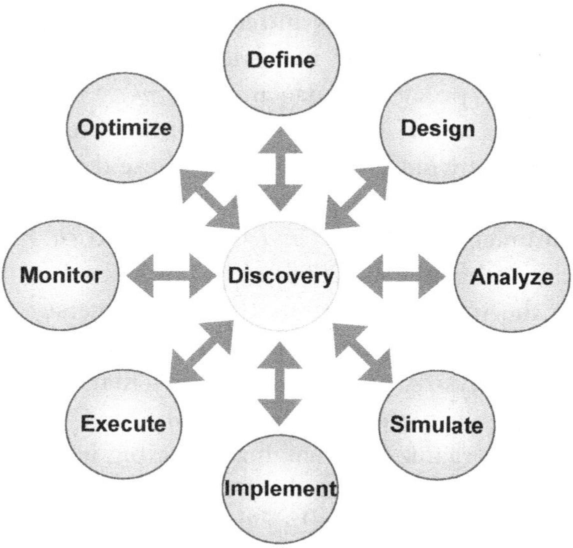


Figure 3.1 Process Life Cycle

Advanced BPM-focused organizations also established process Centers of Excellence (COE) that were expected to build BPM-foundational domains. An example from Gartner follows in Figure 3.2.

| Management Procedures | Organizational Governance | Information Technology | Expertise and Experience | Partnerships and Services |
|---|---|---|---|---|
| ▪ Discover<br>▪ Define<br>▪ Model<br>▪ Simulate<br>▪ Deploy<br>▪ Execute<br>▪ Monitor<br>▪ Analyze<br>▪ Optimize | ▪ Culture<br>▪ Structure<br>▪ Roles<br>▪ Responsibilities<br>▪ Policies and rules<br>▪ Incentives<br>▪ Procedures<br>– Compliance/ audit<br>– Change management<br>– Quality improvement | ▪ Architectures<br>▪ Application platforms<br>▪ Web services<br>▪ Portals<br>▪ Processing engines<br>▪ EAI<br>▪ Advanced technologies<br>▪ Middle ware connectivity<br>▪ Communications<br>▪ Mobile and wireless<br>▪ Storage/ repositories | ▪ Skills<br>▪ Training<br>▪ Education<br>▪ Certification<br>▪ Research<br>▪ Business acumen<br>▪ Intellectual capital<br>– Frameworks<br>– Templates<br>– Methodologies<br>– Standards | ▪ Consulting<br>– Strategy<br>– Business process<br>– Technology<br>▪ Implementation<br>– Design<br>– Build<br>– Manage<br>▪ Business process outsourcing |

Figure 3.2 Domains

The dominant technology for processes from about 2006 on was and continues to be the BPMS as defined by a number of the research firms. Below in Figure 3.3 is the definition according to Gartner that supports the full life cycle of BPM activities.

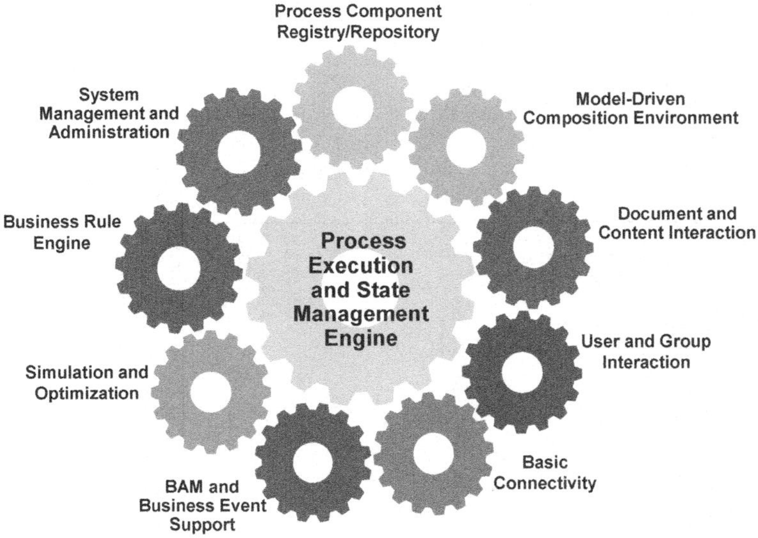


Figure 3.3 Core BPMS Components

The BPMS was tweaked over the next five years and became the market dominant BPM technology; but something happened that caused a change in what was really needed for BPM. As process scopes grew and the sophistication of the processes that organizations wanted to implement grew, there was a need for more *intelligent processes* to handle the ever changing and demanding business conditions. Intelligent Business Operations (IBO) are difficult without a significant amount of intelligence being built into business processes. This requires a level of intelligence that is not found in the typical BPMS.

Organizations also got stuck in their maturity journey and could not get to dynamically goal-driven and optimized processes. Most organizations get stuck on the politics of cross-boundary process management without seeking *innovation*-laden processes (see the sample Gartner maturity model) in Figure 3.4.

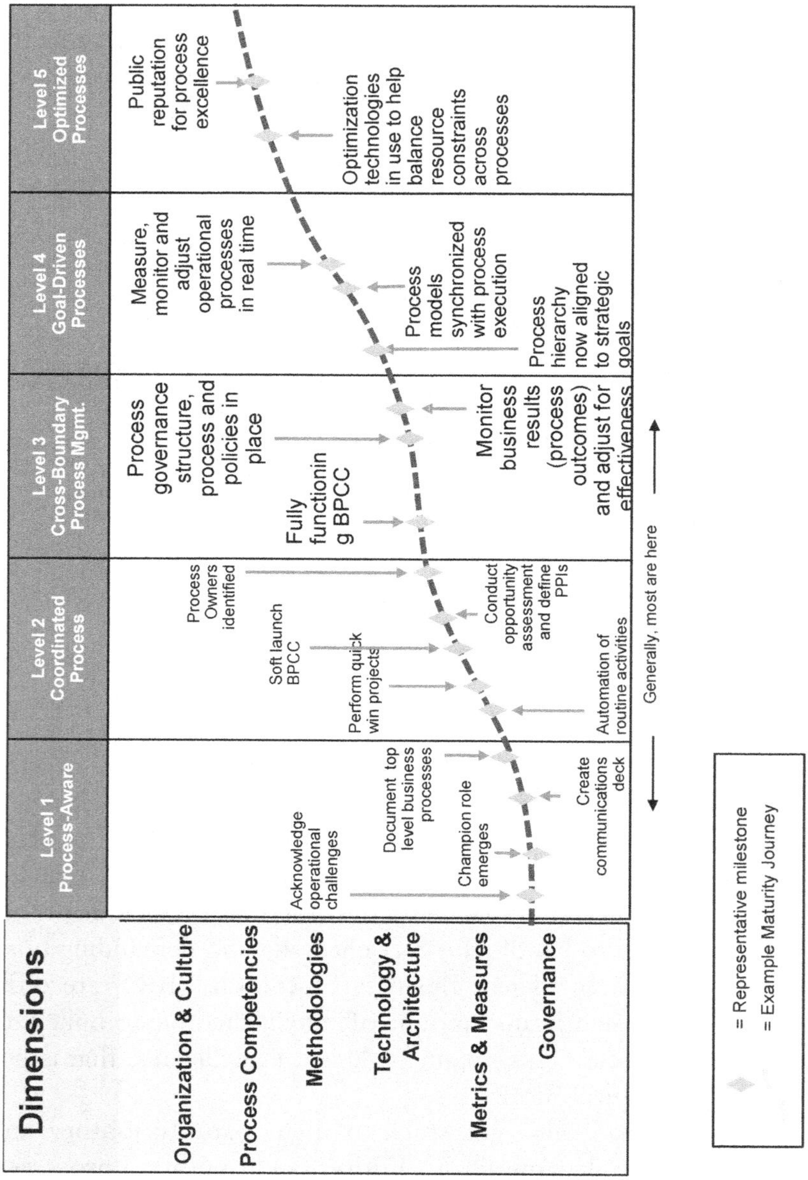


Figure 3.4 Sample Maturity Model (Gartner IT Score for BPM)

## Conclusion

Each wave of process management doesn't supersede the previous waves; it builds on them. TQM and Six Sigma approaches to quality are still valid and deployed throughout modern organizations. BPR and its manifestations in today's ERP systems are still core to enterprise information systems that span silos *inside* the enterprise. The third-wave BPMS is still the engine for driving the next wave that we label as agent-oriented BPM (aoBPM), as we'll explain in the following chapters. Because technology marches on, organizations must build on the foundations that came before. The BPMS must be refocused from back- and middle-office deployment and on to the new customer-driven realities brought about via social, mobile, analytic and Cloud technologies that are changing how we interact and transact. To cope with this new world, organizations will demand "smarter processes."

So, before we tie BPM and agent technology together as the *next wave,* the following chapter will walk us through the evolution of increasing intelligence for BPM (iBPM).

# 4. The Era of Smart Processes

Because BPM and the BPMS delivered significant benefits and process activity started to spread quickly, the scope of processes expanded along with the complexity of the resources being deployed. In addition, most BPMS technologies deliver a new kind of agility not offered before, thus enabling faster change cycles. These levers of change need to be watched for patterns of interest inside even fully modeled processes. Now that processes are change enabled, we need help to manage the processes in a holistic fashion.

Add the fact that the fastest growing process sectors have forms of collaborative, unstructured and self-evolving behavior for knowledge workers, the need to add intelligence is evident. This is more than most business process owners, directors, and managers can do, without some assists from the processes themselves. Because of this need, features needed to be added to the BPMS to make it more intelligent. The three major areas of intelligence revolve around pattern and event recognition; modeling decisions and alternatives; and smart responses and actions. In order to support these three major areas of functionality and new advances in visualization, mobile behavior, social interactions, Cloud sharing, big data analytics, and new media types, the *intelligent* BPMS (iBPMS) was established as the new process platform. See Figure 4.1 for Gartner's definition of the iBPMS.

## Core iBPMS Components

When one compares the core component chart of a BPMS (Figure 3.3) with the core components of an iBPMS (Figure 4.1), the differences are subtle visually. There is, however, a significant change in the way the components interact and the breadth and the depth of the features that are needed to make a process *intelligent.*

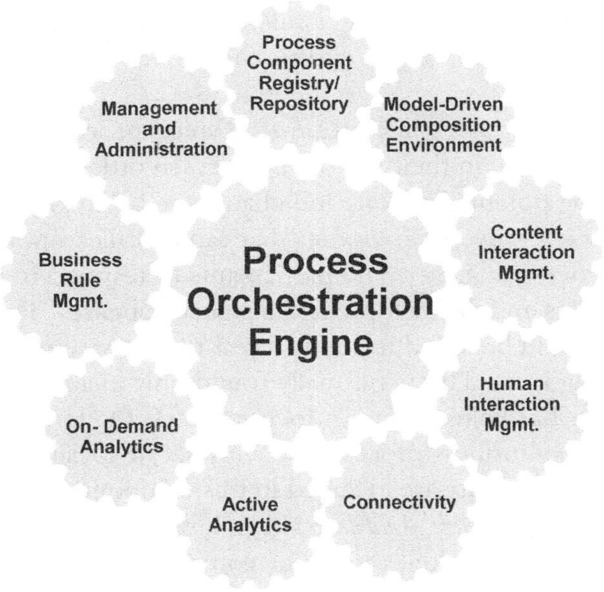


Figure 4.1 Core iBPMS Components

Some components shown in the figure have expanded greatly and others have added key features. These include:

- *Change to Rich Outcome and Goal-Directed Processes:* One of the major differences with an intelligent process is that it can seek out business outcomes and suggest or automatically make changes to stay on track or respond to business changes. This implies that processes have knowledge of conflicting outcomes and can dynamically balance them, with or without the assistance from a process manager or participant, to attain blended and dynamic outcomes. This can be accomplished through static or dynamic goal models in an iBPMs.
- *Change to Rich Policy and Business Rules Management:* Traditional processes can deal with small scale rule changes to enable agility, particularly around navigation, work environments, dashboards, and work load assignments. However, sophisticated, coordinated and managed change around business policies and scenarios can only be supported by distributed rules

management not just *a* single rules engine alone. Rules management that impacts the end-to-end processes is the hallmark of an iBPMS.

- *Change to Rich On-Demand Analytics:* Typical processes have been quite restricted in their use of analytics. In order to deal with modeling potential actions and changes in behavior, processes must possess deep *poly-analytics* that can be called upon by business process managers and participants to respond to changing conditions and difficult process instances or cases. These analytics should be tuned to run in a real-time environment leveraging Big Data. This is normally found only in an iBPMS or a separate, but linked decision focused stack. Quite often an automated business process discovery set or social network analytics capability are included in this component.
- *Change to Rich Active Analytics:* This is a brand new area for process suites. This includes real-time complex event recognition running in an "always on" fashion sniffing for expected and unexpected events and patterns. This approach usually leverages rules and poly-analytics for complex patterns, but there is room to also sense simple events. The iBPMS is typically event sensitive, but may be completely event driven.
- *Change to Rich Social and Collaborative Human Interactions:* Intelligent processes must enable great knowledge worker collaborations. Process instances or cases, emerging patterns, decisions, and potential actions all can use assistance from technologies such as complex event processing, business rules, analytics and goals, but optimally leveraging human resources is the key to intelligent processes. Skills and knowledge-driven approaches are helpful, but so are better practice-pattern discovery and analysis capabilities that are typically a part of an iBPMS.

## Measuring Process Intelligence for BPM

You can see there are any number of components and features that contribute to an intelligent process, but how do you know how smart a process is or can be? Are there patterns of intelligence? Should anyone care? The answer is yes, because your business is only as smart as your processes. Yes, we should come up with a way to measure the intelligence of processes. Businesses are no longer lucky enough to stand pat on predictable operations, for innovation is the table stakes in today's world. This means that businesses need processes that are smart, and growing smarter over time. This will require processes that are intelligent, social, collaborative, agile, and autonomous.

- *Raw Intelligence:* Business professionals that are working with processes must be focused on making them *smarter* in order to keep pace with exponential change. Making processes smarter may be as simple as notification of new conditions or it could be as savvy as suggesting changes in policy and resource allocations. The idea of intelligent process is in its infancy, but we expect a large demand for more intelligence in processes emerging over time. In fact, many of the new features in processes that pursue changing business outcomes will depend on intelligence. Today intelligence is aimed at reaction, but the future will require *pro-action* and *incremental learning* in order to deliver alternative success scenarios.
- *Social and Collaborative:* Business professionals working with knowledge intensive processes need to design appropriate collaboration opportunities and capture evolving better practices for future improvements in business outcomes. The level and scope of collaboration will be encouraged by *goals* and guided by business constraints. Dynamic and extended collaboration patterns will allow for knowledge-intensive problem solving. Today, collaboration is growing rapidly as specialization must be leveraged and process participants are being asked to expand their skill bases. People will have to learn new work patterns that deliver successful outcomes in an ever changing world.
- *Agility:* Business professionals need agility features built into their processes in order to respond to changes. This may mean proactive planning for flexibility points in a fixed process or reactive ways of tweaking goals, flow sequences, resources, tolerances, rules, exceptions and business services. Making all these lever points explicit and external for last-second change is a

great way to deal with the demand for change. Good analysis of change patterns will lead to learning opportunities for future responses to emerging patterns.

- *Autonomy:* Business professionals need look to events, agents, constraints and dynamic goals to allow autonomous process-smart snippets to converge, just in time, to accomplish or contribute to desired business outcomes. This means that portions of a process are "always on" looking for conditions to respond to in near real time to a dedicated or complex set of programmed outcomes. Snippets are likely to flock to patterns needed to deal with proposed business outcomes. These patterns can be learning experiences for scenario planning.

BPM is fast moving into the "Era of Smart Processes," so it would be good to get out in front of the trend and establish some good watermarks for intelligence. A good place to start is to consider how we measure people.

We measure people's raw intelligence with IQ (intelligent quotient) (http://bit.ly/XUYPk9), so we should be able to come up with something on the IQ of a process. This would correlate to the ability of a process to sense patterns, then analyze and act on them.

We measure people's ability to *get along* with EQ (emotional quotient aka emotional intelligence) (http://bit.ly/anZCG), so we should be able to come up with something that measures relationship behavior. This would correlate to the Social interaction ability of a process.

We can also measure how well people *accept and embrace change.* There are various mechanisms for measuring the ability to change, so we should be able to come up with something that measures agility. This would correlate to the flexibility a process can exhibit.

We can measure the levels of freedom we give people to attain business outcomes on their own without micro management. So we should be able to come up with something that measures delegation levels. This would correlate to a process snippet's autonomy to act on its own in seeking single or multiple goals.

## Cumulative Process Intelligence Quotient (CPIQ)

This section drills down into a cumulative process intelligent quotient (see Figure 4.2). To understand the individual contributing factors to the cumulative intelligence spider diagram, we provide the explanations of each vector in the diagram.

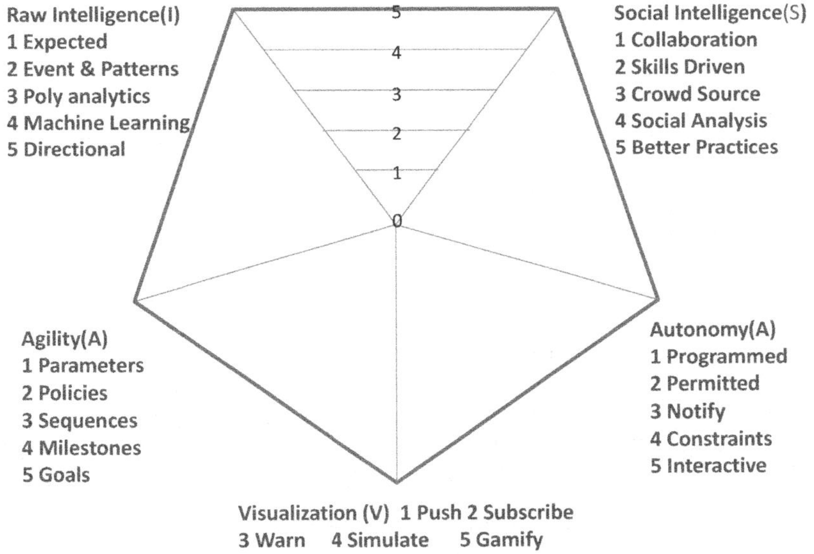


Figure 4.2 Cumulative Process Intelligence Quotient

## Measuring Levels of Raw Intelligence in Your Processes

There are definite levels of raw intelligence that processes can possess. As we will all have to learn how to utilize various levels of intelligence over the coming years, we propose the following five levels of raw intelligence that build on each other (Figure 4.3):

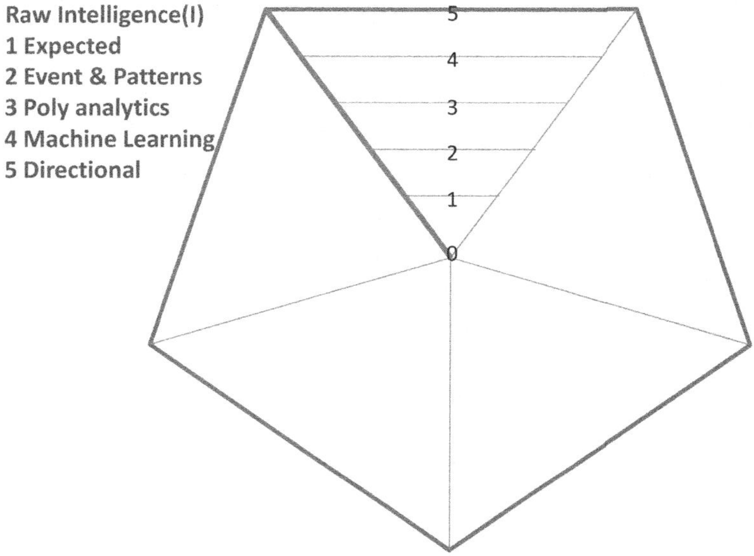


Figure 4.3 Five levels of *raw* intelligence

- *Handling Expected Business Logic:* The policies and rules of expected traditional conditions and actions typically are handled by a pre-planned process, leveraged sets of orchestrated applications, and services. This is typical of traditional ensconced best and standard practices. This is action-oriented intelligence that is burned-in base intelligence that can change from time to time.
- *Recognizing Emerging Events and Patterns:* Processes that can recognize events of opportunity or threat are a step above processes that can just act on normal conditions and expected exceptions. Once an emerging event or pattern of events is recognized, a smarter process can notify in cases where no action logic exists, and interact with pre-planned responses. Quite often exceptions, opportunities, and threats can be taken advantage of in a real-time fashion to the benefit of a business.
- *Analyzing Alternatives with Poly-Analytics:* Processes that can analyze emerging patterns, either on demand or in line, are a step above processes that can just recognize situations that may require attention and action. Processes that have several kinds of

analytics built-in, to run in real time, will have a better chance to anticipate and determine the next best action for processes in-flight. Processes instrumented with multiple (poly) analytics are simply smarter.

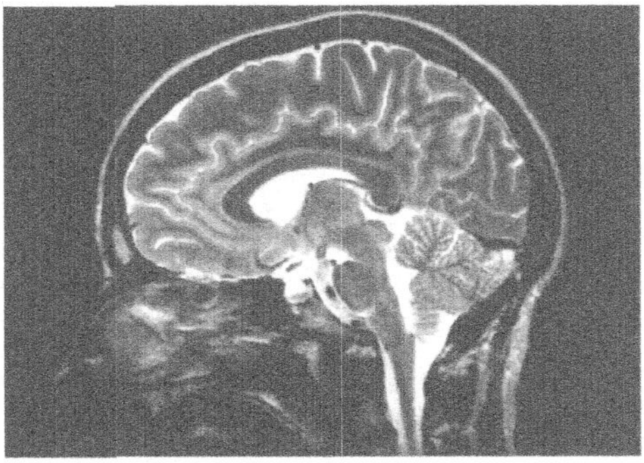

- *Machine Assistance and Learning:* Processes that can suggest the right analytics to use in the right combination, based on goals that are set at the moment, are a step above processes that can just analyse what has happened (rear-view mirror). Based on its own analysis, a process that can suggest actions to process participants will be invaluable for situations were great agility is required.
- *Digital Direction:* Processes that can think and act on their own within predetermined constraints are the ultimate in intelligent processes. These constraints could be goal models that are either static or dynamically calculated and assisted by intelligently balanced analytics or heuristics. Constraints can also be used as boundaries that are not to be crossed. This fully empowered process will require great care in setting up constraints.

## Measuring the Social Intelligence of Your Processes

There are definite levels of social intelligence that processes can enable. We all will have to learn how to utilize various levels of social interactions over the coming years. We propose the following five levels of social intelligence that build on each other (Figure 4.4).

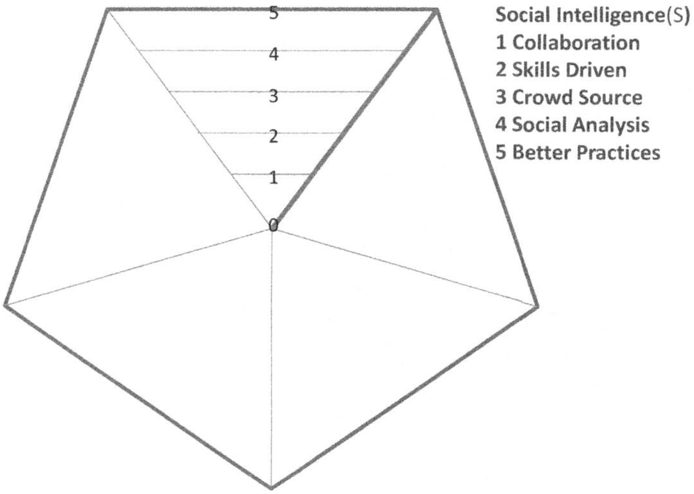


Figure 4.4 Five levels of *social* intelligence

- *Basic Collaboration:* Leveraging the minds of multiple knowledge workers on difficult cases and process instances is essential when there are specialized skills, high levels of knowledge gaps, and complex decisions that require a team effort. Quite often there is shared content such as forms, images, and video to work with and comment on in completing a given case or process instance.
- *Skills Driven Collaboration:* Collaboration can become smarter when the best available resources are assigned dynamically to cases at certain milestones and steps. This approach generally leverages a skills and knowledge inventory and analytics that can measure the work load of a resource for the best outcome of a case. This means that there is a fine balance between skills and availability that needs to be sorted out in the context of an overall existing or anticipated workload.
- *Crowd Sourcing:* When all of the resources may not be under the command of the process manager, then the notion of dynamically finding and putting activities up for bid is an intelligent way of managing dynamic and difficult work streams. This may mean some of the resources may work outside of your organi-

zation in organizations that may be in your value network, but can contribute. This may require certain levels of certification over time, but crowd sourcing allows for better results in terms of timing and quality. This requires more intelligence to measure and manage, so that crowd sourcing doesn't result in noise.

- *Social Network Analysis:* When social interactions are wide, varied analyses of these interactions are invaluable, especially when tied to goals and outcomes. Interactions can be analyzed for compliance, efficiency, customer satisfaction and various other desired business outcomes. These social interactions can be analyzed in-flight or after the fact, as appropriate.
- *Ranked Better Practices:* When social interactions are analyzed for best pairings and sequencing, additional intelligence can be applied to ranking best collaboration and interaction patterns. This way, in-flight case and process instances can be guided through choices between multiple successful best practices. Participants can pick from successful patterns and even evolve new approaches (*next practices*). This is a great paring of machine and human intelligence for maintaining excellent outcomes in a rapidly changing environment.

## Measuring the Real Time Intelligence of Your Process Via Agility

There are definite levels of change intelligence that processes can enable. We all will need to learn how to utilize various levels of change agility over the coming years. We propose the following five levels of process agility that build on each other (Figure 4.5).

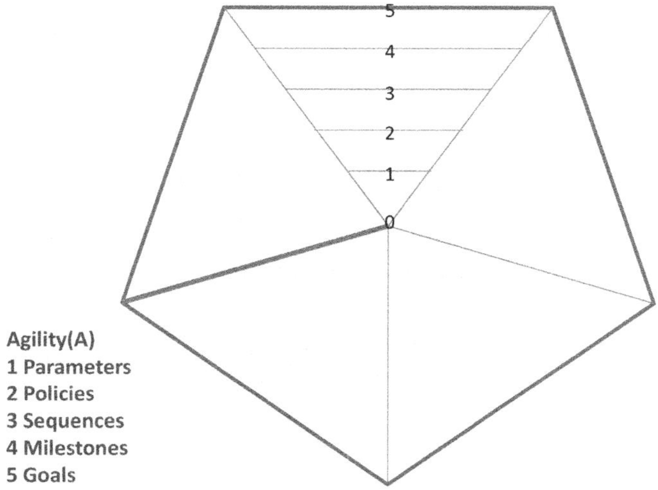


Figure 4.5 Five levels of *agility* intelligence

- *Explicit Parameters:* Where process and logic volatility can be planned ahead of time and represented by external data, explicit parameters can be leveraged. The parameters are usually bound into the logic at the very last second allowing for up to the last second change (explicit). This allows for a basic level of agility and can be handed over to business professionals for change (usually via forms and screens).

- *Explicit Policies and Rules:* Where process and logic volatility can be planned ahead of time and be represented by decision tables, decision trees, visual logic flows or linguistics forms, business rules can be leveraged. The rules are bound into the logic at the very last second. In some instances the rules can be used to not only induce, but to deduce logic. This is a higher level of intelligence and agility that generally leverages a business friendly development environment.

- *Dynamic Sequencing of Services (logic):* While adding agility within a fixed process model is a good start, not all process paths can be modeled. In this situation, sequencing work and process activity can be dynamically arranged and completed. While common patterns can be identified and modeled over time, this approach is aimed at variable work sequences. This can be accomplished by aggregating fixed process snippets (small, modeled sub-processes) guided by rules or case management guided by milestones (mini completion points).
- *Dynamic Milestones:* In completely unstructured processes that are milestone driven, changes in priorities can be accomplished by changing the milestones, in flight. This approach is particularly useful for cases that have emerging new outcomes to handle and where the work sequences are highly variable. This is often leveraged by adaptive case management technologies and human interaction management systems.
- *Goal Directed:* The ultimate in gaining agility is where processes reconfigure themselves around a new set of goals or goal weightings. This can be accomplished by having goal models that can change through a business-friendly development environment or the dynamic real-time setting of goals and weightings by leveraging predictive and prescriptive analytics. These kinds of processes generally are getting real-time feedback from the Internet of Things (IoT) or other real-time sensors.

## Measuring the Autonomous Intelligence of Your Process Via Freedom Levels

There are definite levels of autonomous intelligence that processes can exercise. We all will need to learn to utilize various levels of autonomy over the coming years. We propose the following five levels of process autonomy that build on each other (Figure 4.6).

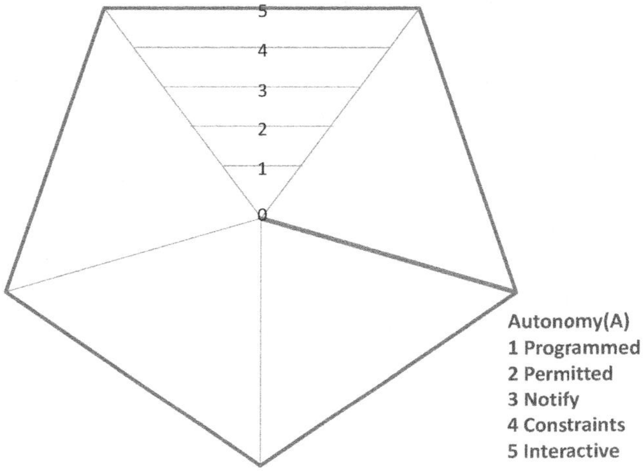


Figure 4.6 Five levels of *autonomy* intelligence

- *Programmed Behavior:* A process can be completely prescribed with some levels of agility, but the permutations and combinations are preplanned. This way, control is exercised by the process participants and there is a high dependence on a command and control approach. This is a proactive approach, but quite rigid.
- *Permitted Actions:* Process can suggest alternative actions for process managers or ask permission to act in a way that was not expected. This requires a level of intelligence capable of pointing out emerging patterns and suggesting proper responses. Nothing happens without some level of permission.
- *Act First, Then Notify:* A process can watch and learn and then take action based on some proactive anticipation. In this case the process manager is notified in a timely manner of the process's decision and action. A process manager can then take appropriate actions, if the process is wrong, or lower the level of freedom for this kind of process instance or case.
- *Act with Constraints and Goals:* On its own, a process can be goal seeking in nature and call in the proper analytics to self-adjust

goals to reach optimum outcomes based on static or dynamic weightings of goals. Processes or appropriate process snippets can be kept away from out-of-bounds conditions through constraints. This creates a balance between freedom and negative boundary conditions.

- *Interactive Independent Action:* Processes or process snippets can interact with other process snippets or the Internet of Things (IoT) to create a dynamic response that requires automated collaboration of analytics and measures. These snippets can systematically flock temporarily or permanently to deal with emerging patterns.

## Visually Measuring the Cumulative Intelligence of Your Processes

Having several guides for process intelligence is a great idea, but none of the ratings mean anything without a visual way of grokking that intelligence. You can't harness and guide intelligence without some great ways of visualizing the business outcomes and creating better alternatives proactively. In other words, "You can't manage what you can measure and visualize." There are definite levels of visualization that processes can exercise reactively or proactively. We all will need to learn how to utilize various levels and layers of visualization over the coming years. We propose the following five levels of visualization that build on each other (Figure 4.7).

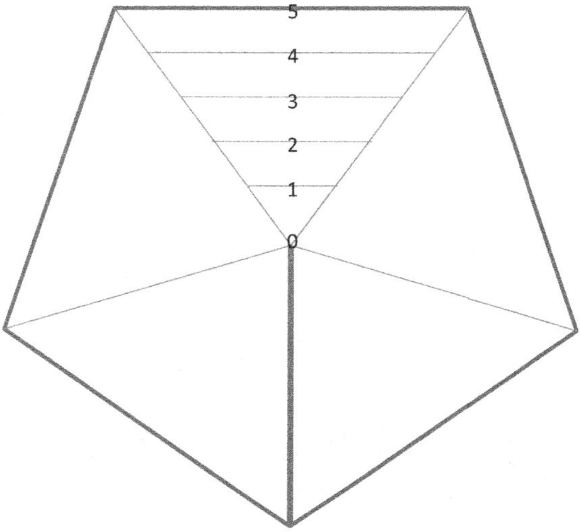


Figure 4.7 Five levels of *visualization* intelligence

- *Push Visualization:* Many business outcome visualizations are designed by others to be used for specific roles. These are generally in the form of multi-panel dashboards that have some minor personalization and viewing options. These are good for "keeping your eye on the ball" for desired and known business outcomes. There are usually specific views for process owners, process managers, and others that are supporting the process. This is a typical visualization approach for a process.
- *Custom, Subscribed Visualization:* When individuals are able to assemble dashboard components, snippets, and feeds to meet their specific needs within a visualization pallet that they chose themselves, then this is known as a subscription model. This visualization model allows for optimum performance as an individual process participant considers both local and end-to-end business outcomes. It also allows for dynamic changes and alternative views of a process worker's workbench.
- *Warning and Notification:* Even when events or exceptions occur, there are mechanisms for capturing the attention of crucial re-

sources and process managers. It may be simple blinking lights when important preplanned events or business patterns occur. These mechanisms are aimed at asking for human intervention by an operator or a decision maker. Notification of unplanned patterns or events must also employ unique attention capturing techniques and mechanisms.

- *Simulation Driven Visualization:* Moving up to proactive visualization will require ways of showing the effect of changes in process action and decisions surrounding possible actions. This is where scenario planning and visualizing outcome differences become essential for adjustments in process behavior. This can be a separate sandbox with safe test data or real data under new scenarios without actual implementation. Scenarios can actively be pre-planned with the ability to dynamically switch in and out, depending on process conditions and outcomes. Visualization of such actions needs to be quite interactive and dynamic in nature.
- *Gamification:* The ultimate in interactive and dynamic business direction would be combining human resources, machine resources, multiple roles, multiple organizational units, and multiple partners in social interactions in a massively multiple online (MMO) gaming fashion to reach desired outcomes in either a "training simulator" mode or in an actionable real-time mode. Watch the following examples:

bit.ly/1bamZzE

SCM Globe: Supply Chain Simulation and Design

bit.ly/12M5ptm

INNOV8 2.0 BPM Gameplay

## Traditional Business Operations

Intelligent Business Operations are underway and organizations are deploying smarter and smarter processes. The CPIQ will allow organizations to visualize the intelligence in their processes. This is important, but the business outcomes that these intelligent processes deliver for organizations are even more important. What follows are examples of processes that make a difference in terms of business outcomes for specific organizations, the results, and a rating on the CPIQ chart. Before we do that, it would be good to rate traditional applications, traditional BPM, and a hybrid process-driven application with advanced features.

## Traditional Applications Intelligence

Traditional applications, whether they be hand-crafted legacy applications or best practice application packages, do not show the kind of process intelligence that will be required to meet the changing business needs that face us today and in the foreseeable future. It was not a great surprise that these applications did not fare well on the CPIQ spider chart. Applications augmented with additional technologies like rules engines would fare better. Unless a traditional application has extended or surrounded itself with advanced technologies or process technologies, it shows up minimally on the CPIQ and requires significant effort to update and change (see the black rating dots at the center of Figure 4.8).

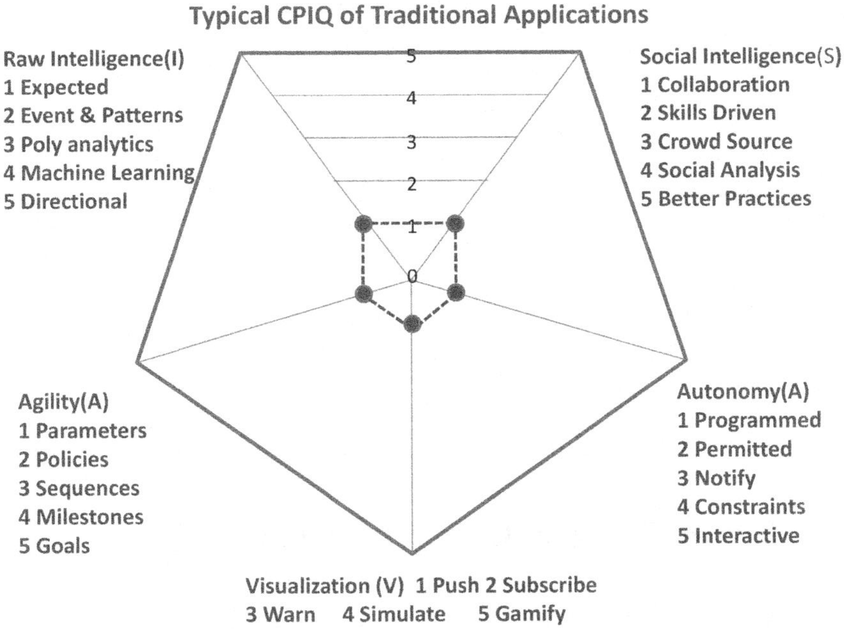


Figure 4.8 Typical CPIG of traditional applications

## Traditional BPM Intelligence

Traditional BPM bumps up the visualization and agility over typical applications and employs explicit flows, rules and services, tipping the CPIQ up a notch closer to average intelligence. Early process efforts with BPM did not exercise the kind of intelligence that would be necessary in the business environments evolving today. While there were significant improvements in visualization and dynamic navigation with simple rules and event engines, this would not be enough to compete in a change-prone world (Figure 4.9).

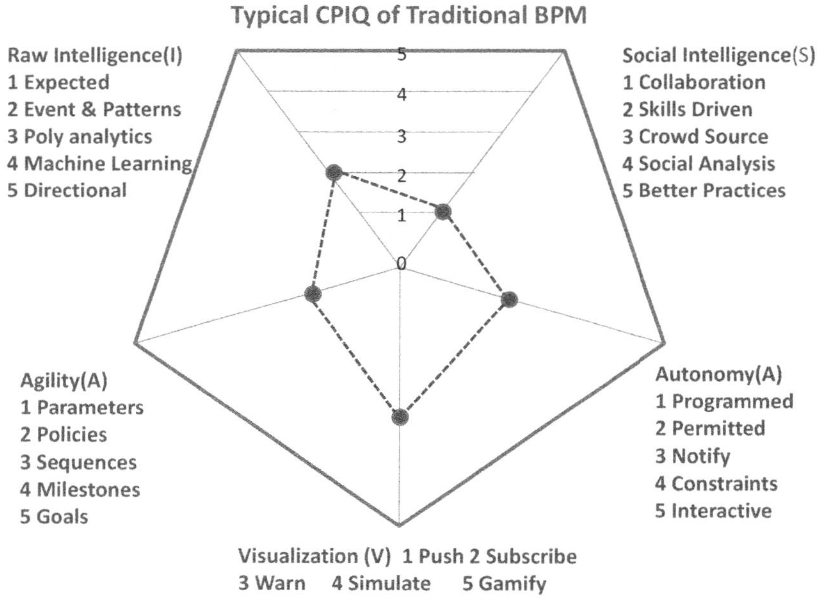


Figure 4.9 Typical CPIQ of traditional BPM

## A Hybrid Process-Driven Application

Before BPM became a software category, coauthor Jim Sinur had the opportunity to write a process and rule-driven underwriters workbench. His team had to create a dynamic work-list workbench and provide a high-end collaboration environment for work specialties to share an emerging life insurance policy. High-risk cases were shared among specialty roles within the organization with rule driven services applied as needed. It was ahead of its day, but still not intelligent enough for today's world (Figure 4.10).

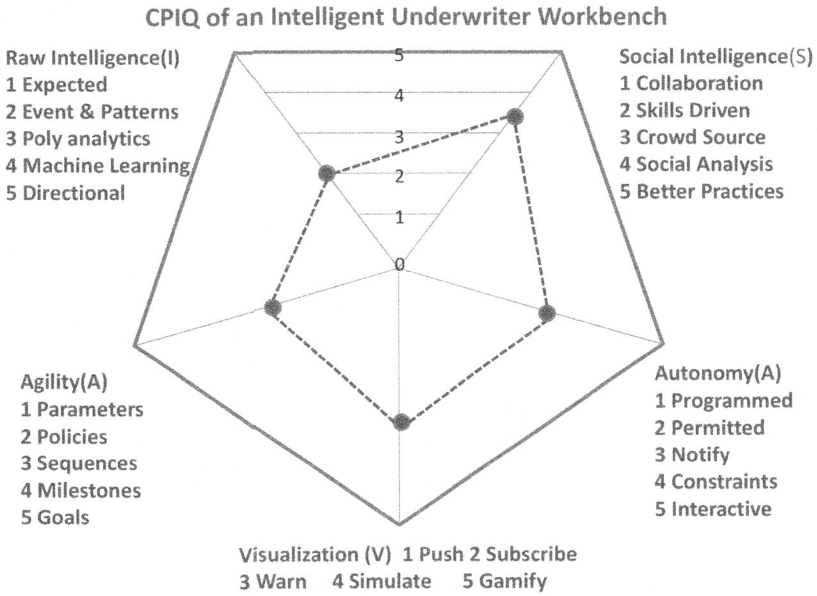


Figure 4.10 CPIQ of an intelligent underwriter workbench

## Smart Medical Process Rated on the CPIQ

This is an example of an intelligent process that manages an outpatient surgical center.

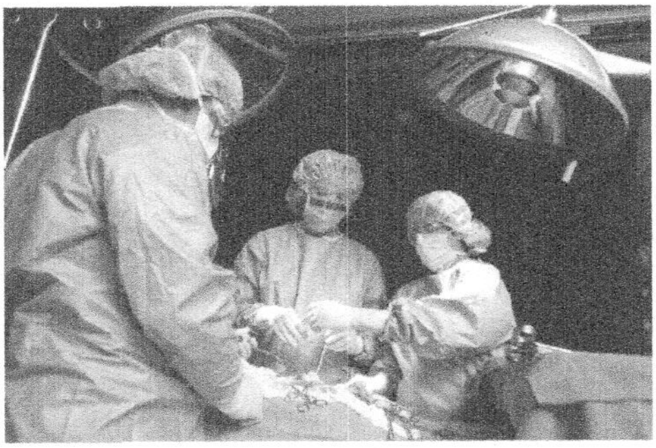

- *The Challenge:* This organization wanted to find a balanced optimization that leveraged resource utilization with the best patient care. Quite often one suffers at the expense of the other. In fact, this organization defined an extended patient care approach that gave the people accompanying the patient visibility into progress in near real time.

- *The Solution:* Each resource was tagged with sensors that were readable throughout the facility. This included patients, relatives, friends, medical personnel, and equipment. A visual simulation was run to show optimal throughput and positive outcomes. Once a goal, among many, was sensed to be in jeopardy, a re-simulation with adjusted goals was run with a new visual dashboard representing the new goal balance. There are many reasons for optimal goal balances to be in jeopardy, including medical personnel getting interruptions, equipment not being ready, late patients, slower than expected recoveries and so on, but this process was smart enough to deal with rebalancing and real-time visibility. You can visually see where the intelligence of this process is more advanced (Figure 4.11).

### How Smart is this Process Measured by the CPIQ?

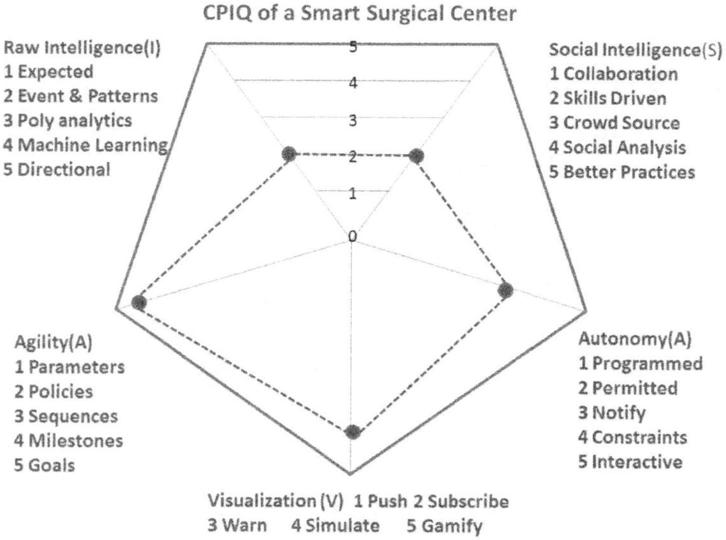


Figure 4.11 CPIQ of a smart surgical center

This is a highly summarized and anonymous case study provided by Bosch Software Innovations.

## Smart Retail Process Measured on the CPIQ

This is another example of an intelligent process that manages the retail therapy experience:

- *The Challenge:* Create a highly individualized shopping experience for customers while keeping inventory levels and special situations in mind. For clients in the area of the store with registered cell phones, invite them in with specials that relate to the client's potential needs and wants leveraging known information.
- *The Solution:* Determine the physical location of the customer and push offers related to the location. For instance, if the client is in the men's department looking at ties, offer a coupon for shoes or men's cologne. In the case where the mobile opportunity is not available, print related offers on the back of the receipt of current purchases. This has increased revenue, reduced inventory, and pushed slower lines into the fast lane. This is an impressive business solution that leverages process. You can visually see where the intelligence of this process is more advanced (Figure 4.12).

**How Smart is this Process Measured by the CPIQ?**

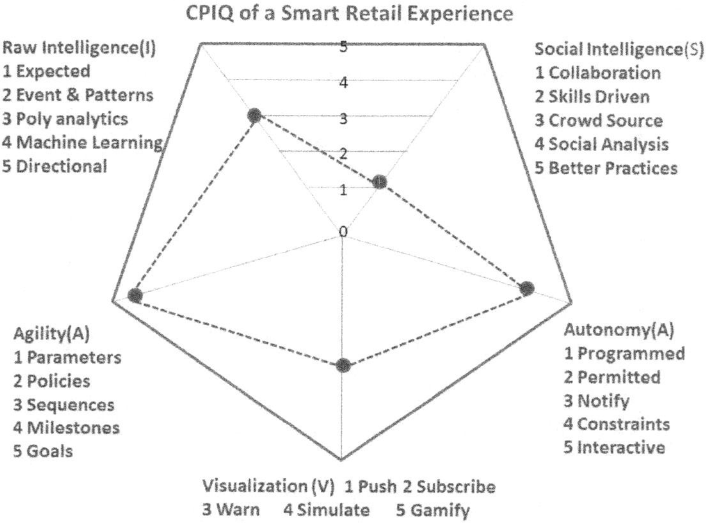


Figure 4.12 A highly summarized and anonymous case study provided by Tibco

## Tomorrow's aoBPM

Even though there are a variety of processes emerging today, the real promise of BPM occurs when intelligence is applied in all resources that a process touches, orchestrates, triggers, or choreographs. This is a natural outgrowth of extending intelligence to many facets of large-scoped and complex processes.

Many organizations have realized that although they have employed BPM to improve their internal efficiency, the business processes *between and among* organizations and consumers have not been clearly described and streamlined. Furthermore, the execution of business processes, techniques, and methods can no longer scale to meet the global requirements of many organizations. This leads to the misunderstanding of responsibilities, blocking coordination, slowing reaction times to changing markets, and ineffective monitoring of rules and regulations.

In the next evolution of BPM implementations, these and

other shortcomings will be addressed. As we will explore in the next chapter, aoBPM promises to provide efficient ways to model and control the complex business processes within and among organizations. By also employing intelligent agent technology, the benefits of aoBPM include explicit process definitions, quick reaction to changing environments, and easier tracking of operations.

While BPM focuses on managing the process logic, it needs to be integrated with an agent-based approach to fully control a given business process, such as activity assignment, resource allocation, and complex event processing (CEP). In short, the agent-oriented approach has both BPM and BPMS aspects. When we discuss aoBPM, we imply that an agent computing environment is also present in the iBPMS (see Appendix D for more information on the agent environment). With the conventional "one central command" approach of BPM among large distributed organizations, business processes have no way to be managed. The independent companies across the value chain network make their own decisions on how to process their pieces of business activities. As such, agent technology provides support for BPM in a more flexible, distributed, scalable, timely, integrative, proactive, reactive, and *intelligent* manner—*intelligent processes.* In the "Measuring the Cumulative Intelligence Quotient (CPIQ) of a Process" (see Figure 4.2 above) intelligent agents can optimize any and all of five CPIQ levels on the five continuum lines.

## Taking Agents to the Edge Incrementally

While agents greatly enhance and in some cases subsume and leverage processes, most organizations will take agents on in a phased approach. The first phase supercharges existing processes and acts somewhat independently, and agents are controlled by a master process of sorts. While there will be local intelligence to augment the master intelligence in the process, there is a hub someplace managing the end-to-end process. In more advanced applications, the agents themselves will control the BPM processes—without the need for central control. The aim, then, is to apply the notion of "intelligence" described in this chapter for agents as well as BPM. Such agents can be called *intelligent agents,* where each employs degrees of raw intelligence, social intelligence, agility, autonomy, and visualization (see Figure 4.2). The level of each of these dimensions, therefore, determines the degree and type of agent's intelligence.

Growing complexity and exponential rates of change are going to create a need for more dynamic processes that self-configure based on agent bidding, systems dynamics models, and agent models that leverage business simulations. These are some of the base disciplines that surround complexity theory, and they are ideal for supporting an agent-based process that leverages snippets of traditional processes.

# 5. The Next Wave: Agent-Oriented BPM

*Let every eye negotiate for itself and trust its agents.*
—Much Ado About Nothing, Act II, Scene i (adapted)

Process is nothing new. Over the past several decades, the capability to manage end-to-end processes has progressed through three technology-enabled waves. We are now on the cusp of a fourth wave.

## Applying Agent Technology to BPM

Applying agent technology to BPM is called *agent-oriented BPM* (aoBPM) and includes such benefits as:

- *Distributed system architecture*: In traditional BPM software, only one central process engine exists that controls all the activities. For multiple BPM activities and systems, agent technology enables a loosely coupled distributed system structure for integrating and federating distributed BPM.
- *Automation*: The inherent autonomy of software agents can start a workflow based on event triggers, or a more complex reaction to environmental changes. Agents can also be designated and empowered to represent humans—and, therefore, may substitute for humans in certain cases.
- *Interaction*: Software agents can interact with each other, sending semantic (machine understandable) messages. Agents can also enable organizations to interact with each other, normally through semantic message exchanges. In fact, groups of agents can act as organizations in their own right where their members can coordinate, cooperate, and even compete. In short, agents can collaborate socially both as individuals and as groups.
- *Resource management*: Agents can represent resources. Task assignments and resource allocations are done through negotiation among these agents. Agents can therefore act on behalf of a resource and even be embedded in the resource.

- *Reactivity and proactivity*: Agents react to changing circumstances and have the ability to generate alternative execution paths. In addition, agents can be proactive, anticipating a future situation, rather than just reacting to it. In short, agents can take control and make things happen, rather than adjust to a situation or await an event. Proactive agents are anticipatory, change-oriented, and employ self-initiated behavior in situations. An agent may be reactive, proactive, or both.
- *Interoperation among heterogeneous systems*: When agents assume multiple roles or types, they are *heterogeneous*. For example, a Stock Broker agent may play the roles of buyer and seller, where each role has its own specialized services, rules, data and so on.. The interactions rely on semantic Agent Communication Language (ACL) [1,2] messages that contain machine understandable syntax and ontologies—making agent-style interoperation more feasible than API calls.
- *Intelligent processing*: In the CPIQ (mentioned in the previous chapter), agents can accomplish any, or indeed, even all five CPIQ levels on the five continuum lines.

Agent-Oriented BPM can be applied in two ways: as basic, *agent-enhanced BPM*, or in a more advanced form, *agent-based BPM*.

## Basic Agent-Enhanced BPM

Agent-enhanced Business Process Management is the basic form for applying agents to BPM, as depicted in Figure 5.1. The order processing in this diagram is fairly simple. It begins with an Accept Order process. Once the order is accepted, it is assembled. Then—in any sequence (e.g., in parallel)—the order is shipped and the invoice and payment are processed. Eventually, the order is closed after *both* the order is shipped and the payment is processed. (Note: Simultaneous, parallel processes are best handled in an *agent-based* process flow—particularly where cross-communication among simultaneous processes occur. The business world is not so sequential and agents are small and autonomous. As a result agents can act in a socially interactive manner—just like organisms in the real world.)

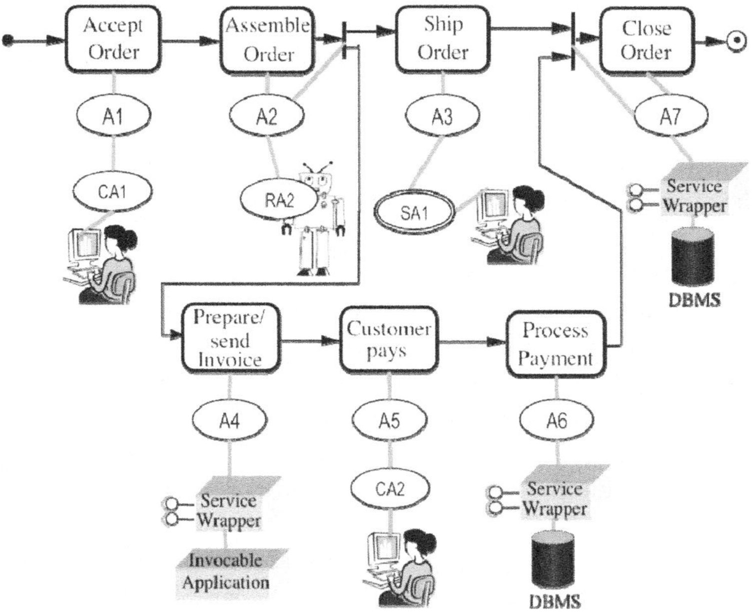


Figure 5.1 Basic Agent-Enhanced Business Process Flow

As mentioned earlier, traditional BPM software has only one central workflow engine that controls all activities. With an agent-enhanced approach each time a BPM process is invoked, the process has an agent that is generated to support it. The agent is eliminated when no longer needed by the process. For example, each time the Accept Order process is invoked for a given order, a specifically assigned agent is generated to support the acceptance process of that order.

Each generated agent is autonomous (has its own thread of control), interactive (can communicate with others), and adaptive (makes its own choices using rules, goals, learning, and so on). (Agents are described more fully in the next chapter.) Using agents, then, enables us to achieve the following enhanced process capabilities:

- *Human interface*: The business process provides a human interface for its workplace environment. In Fig. 5.1, A1 is a specialized agent that requests the items that are being ordered via a user-friendly interface; that validates the items that are requested by the customer; and that performs other order-taking interactions with the customer. A1 might also verify that it is interacting with a person who is a customer-in-good-standing with A1's company; take into account the customer's status level (e.g., Silver, Gold, Platinum, etc.); know the customer's order-related preferences; and so on.

Human customers have the option of using an agent to represent them (CA1) for a variety of functions. These can include acquiring work items, receiving reminder events, notifying the system of work-related events that the human has completed, sort email, and so on. In the case of the order placement, agent CA1 could "know" what items the customer needs and automatically place an order for them on behalf of the human. CA1 might even be able to negotiate prices and terms with A1—making agents A1 and CA1 *designated representatives* that are empowered to represent the supplier and customer, respectively. Such interactions can occur in a distributed (non-centralized) manner and without direct and real-time involvement of humans at either end of the process.

- *Machine Interface:* This is the part of the business process that provides interactions with machines, such as robots, equipment, embedded devices, sensors and sensor nets, and other physical-world intelligent interfaces. In this example, The Assemble Order process has an agent specialized differently than A1. In this situation, A2 assembles the particular order's items as per the customer's request.

  In the real world, this process could be executed by people, machines, or both. If humans were used, each would have an agent representing him or her, as discussed in the Human Interface, above. If machines were used, each would have an agent assigned to monitor, command, and control activities. For example, you might have a robot (represented by agent RA1) that assembles the order in coordination with the process agent A2. While this example only uses a single robot, multiple robots could be employed—with the "oversight" of agent A2.

A2, then, could even consider among multiple robots, choosing ones that are available and that have the right set of properties for the assembly process. In this scenario, A2 could send out a Request for Proposal (RFP) to multiple robot agents and each could "bid" on doing the work. A robot that is already engaged in filling another order would bid differently than a robot that is immediately available or one that is not fully functional. The bidding could also take into account "rush" and priority orders (e.g., VIP orders). By employing a marketplace-like selection technique, the assembly process does not need to employ a complex centralized planning system that assigns machine resources. Furthermore, if one machine breaks down, the order assembly line does not suffer a large *re*-planning exercise; the marketplace mechanism is still in place to find the next available robot.

- *Software Interface*: In this aspect of the workplace environment, the business process interfaces with external software applications or databases. Software agents employ technology that is more complex than traditional software. Because of this, an "impedance mismatch" can exist in the communication between agents and conventional applications and databases. The technology differences, however, can be synchronized by employing relatively straightforward techniques. For example, to enable an agent to communicate with a software application, a *service wrapper* can be constructed. Here, the application is "wrapped" so that its interface can meet the requirements of the agent. The wrapper can simply act as a translator between the agent and application; or it could go further by making the conventional application appear to interact and function as though it were, itself, an agent. More advanced wrappers, for example, could include wrappers as transform agents and AI techniques. For example, agent A4 (assigned to Prepare/Send Invoice) interfaces with a service wrapper that enables A4 to connect with an invoicing application using semantic-based, two-way communication. The main benefit of using the wrapper approach means that: (1) your system can benefit immediately from agent technology, and (2) agents will be able to work with existing software—rather than having to rewrite entire systems.

Similarly, agents A6 and A7 need to interface with existing databases. Again, the wrapper approach can be used; obtaining the benefits of an agent approach and enabling reuse of existing databases.

- *Community-based interface*: In this part of the workplace environment, the business process interfaces with a complex group of agents that collaborate and act as a group or social unit. A *community* can be ad hoc groups, assigned teams, coalitions, markets, organizations, composites of other community-based groups (e.g., an organization chart configuration or a network configuration), institutions, and any other agent grouping that is useful to the system.

  For example, agent SA1 is a community agent (symbolized by the two concentric ovals) that consists of agents that can appropriately enable the shipment of a given order. Thus SA1 consists of agents that play various roles. For example, multiple agents can collaborate to select the most appropriate delivery time, route, shipper, and price. The agents can use techniques such as route-optimizing routines, marketplace-style negotiation for the cheapest shipper, and so on. Once determined, a packing agent can prepare its assigned order for shipping by employing robots or people. Another agent can ensure that an order is loaded onto the correct vehicle for shipment. Lastly, a tracking agent can monitor an order to ensure that it remains on schedule and is delivered to the correct customer.

  The Shipping Agent (SA1) is not "one central process" controller for the entire community of agents. Rather, it is the initial point of communication for a shipping organization of agents. Internally, the agents organize themselves. Some are specialized so that they handle a task for a *particular* order (e.g., track a specific order); others have roles for computing shipping routes or vendor selection for the order. In other words, agent SA1 is a distributed grouping of collaborative, coordinative, and competitive agents that requires no centralization—only virtual collaboration that can self-organize itself for some given purpose.

So, why have agent communities? Imagine unleashing thousands or millions of agents in a system. Is it reasonable to expect all these individual agents to coordinate in some manner? Just like humans, agents need to be organized into communities. From organizational theory, we know that community structures can be defined to include roles that have processing capabilities that can, to put it in IT terms, maximize cohesion and minimize coupling. Each community: (a) comprises multiple agents playing multiple roles; (b) can interact with other communities; (c) is an agent in its own right; and (d) can be self organizing. In this way, *communities as social structures* reduce the danger of combinatorial explosion of agent interaction. They provide, instead, a structured scheme for focusing and enhancing the coordination of agent activities, making richer, more complex structures possible—while hiding unnecessary details. In short, they enable scalability for large populations to tangibly produce significant deliverables. Additionally, they encourage resource sharing, promote internal coordination, and establish common supervision. (For additional reading on communities, see Appendix C.)

## Agent-based BPM

The preceding section discussed a basic realization of aoBPM called *agent-enhanced BPM*. A more comprehensive level of aoBPM is the *agent-based BPM*. An agent-oriented BPM system is a distributed system consisting of multiple agents. These agents are independent and each is responsible for the *actual execution* of a business process. Furthermore, a process agent can consist of other processes—where each sub-process can be assigned to the same or different agent (Figure 5.2). In this scenario, the whole business process is formed by the hierarchies of sub-networks within those agents. The process logic is embedded in the agents, rather than being explicitly represented elsewhere. (Note that there are other kinds of agents that can handle business rules as well as various aspects of a BPM system.)

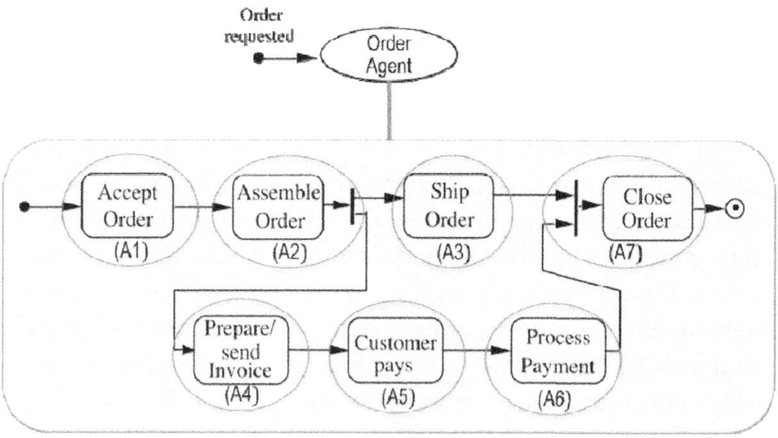


Figure 5.2 Agent-based Business Process Flow

In today's world, the business process can span multiple business units within a company or even several companies. Thus, in a large (or even global) operation, one central BPM engine *cannot* manage an entire business process in a timely manner. A common solution is to federate multiple process engines residing in multiple organization units. Here, agent interaction via semantic message communications is the normal technique for "big data" and "big process."

In agent-based BPM, agents take full responsibility for a distributed BPM system, which means agents (together with other technologies) have all the means to analyze, automate, integrate, and inspect business processes.

Agents in this scenario (Figure 5.3) are much more complex than in the first scenario. The main features include: autonomy, communication, consistency, goal-orientation, and reaction to the environment. Other high-level features, such as learning and negotiation, are also benefits.

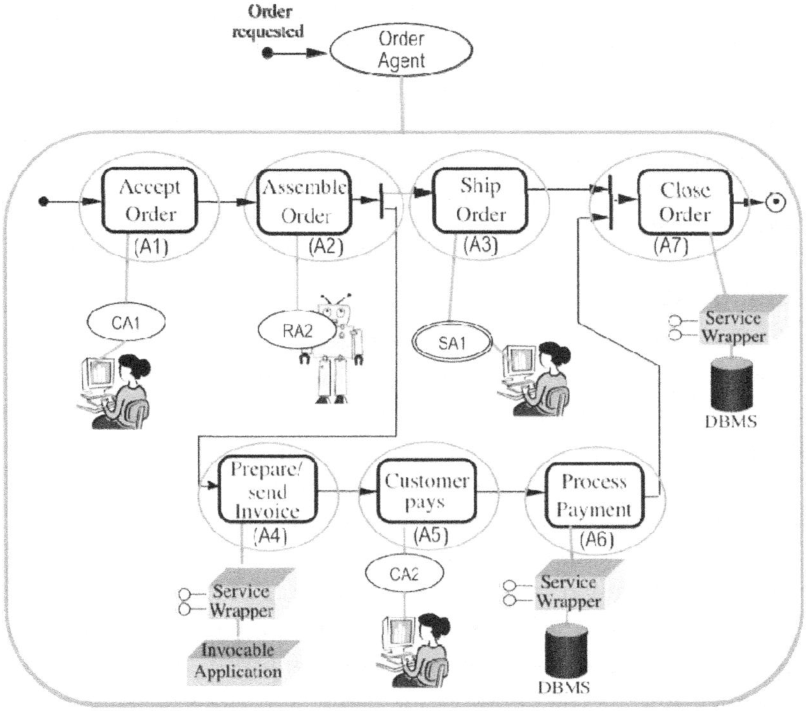


Figure 5.3 Agent-based Business Process Flow
Redrawn for Order Processing

The usage of agents in this scenario benefits process technology in the following ways:

- Enables distributed system architectures that can be federated.
- Employs standards-based communication languages using semantic messages. These are called agent communication languages (ACL). The two prominent ACLs are FIPA ACL and KQML. These languages can enable the interoperation of BPM systems, especially for the heterogeneous ones.
- Provides automation behavior. Each agent has the ability to execute tasks on its own without human involvement. The task can be pre-defined business process scenarios, or the agent can dynamically construct processes on-the-fly. This depends on such requirements as goals, context, existing (or changing)

conditions, business rules, local policies, and machine learning. (Note: Living Systems Process Suite can dynamically construct processes on-the-fly to some extent. See www.whitestein.com)

- Reacts to the environment. An agent can adjust itself based on what it has learned and can then form new activities and new routings. This means that the business processes can be modified at runtime depending on the dynamics of business events.

## Intelligent aoBPM

The agent-enhanced BPM approach has already been adopted by some commercial vendors; while the agent-based BPM systems are still in prototypes in research laboratories. However, the agent-based BPM systems are attracting more and more attention for studying the interaction of multiple BPM systems, which are required by the next generation deployment of BPM systems.

Agents can help to automate the management of business processes to a much greater degree than has been possible before. The potential benefits include enabling straight-through processing (STP), corporate-actions processing, automated reconciliation, thread-of-process tracking—while using semantics understandable by humans and machines. These advances can reduce the need for human intervention, which in turn lowers the overall cost of managing business processes. Response time to changes in the working environment is reduced. Interoperability is improved and intelligent processing among heterogeneous systems is enabled—all by employing *intelligent agents.* (Intelligent agents are agents that employ degrees of raw intelligence, social intelligence, agility, autonomy and visualization (Fig 4.2). The level of each of these dimensions determines the degree and type of an agent's intelligence.)

## References

[1] Foundation for Intelligent Physical Agents (FIPA), FIPA ACL Message Structure Specification, http://www.fipa.org/specs/fipa00061, 2000.

[2] Foundation for Intelligent Physical Agents (FIPA), FIPA Communication Act Library Specification, http://www.fipa.org/specs/fipa00037, 2000.

# 6. Agent Technology Overview

In the last chapter we discussed the evolution of business process management. Here we begin an exploration of agent technology: what it is and how it can be used. Later, we'll tie back to the role of agents in business process management.

## What is an Agent?

Imagine sitting in the park on a nice summer day and a flock of birds sweeps the sky. One moment they are circling, another they dart to the left or drop to the ground. Each move is so beautiful that it appears choreographed. Furthermore, the movements of the flock seem smoother than those of any one bird in the flock. Yet, the flock has no high-level controller or even a lead bird. Each bird follows a simple set of rules that it uses to react to birds nearby. When Craig Reynolds of DreamWorks developed his simulation, each individual bird's behavior was based on the following rules (http://www.red3d.com/cwr/boids/):

- Maintain a minimum distance from other objects, including other birds.
- Be sociable (i.e., try to match velocities with other birds if they are nearby, and move toward the perceived center of their group).

The flock is organized without an organizer, coordinated without a coordinator. Flocks of birds are not the only things that work like this. Beehives, ant colonies, freeway traffic, national and global economies, societies, and immune systems are all examples of patterns that are determined by local component interaction instead of a centralized authority.

In the world of IT applications, similar examples of decentralized coordination of activity can be found in order processing, supply chain, shop-floor control, inventory management, message routing, multiple database management, operating systems, and self-healing middleware. In other words, a decentralized approach is particularly suitable for agents and should be considered where local components have some degree of control—*instead* of limiting your approach solely to the centrally organized one traditionally employed by IT. After all, if New York City can maintain a two-week supply of food with only locally made decisions, why can't a supply chain system perform in a similar manner? Agents *can* be designed to behave in a hierarchical manner. However, the strength of agents is that they can employ *both* hierarchical and collaborative-network approaches; whereas, conventional IT systems lack this kind of flexibility and scalability.

Few in IT have not heard of software agents. Thanks to the dramatic growth of the Web, computing literature is replete with discussions of software agents. Like many technology terms, however, the diverse idioms for software agents are now weary from overuse and misuse. Various names have been used: bots, knowbots, softbots, personal assistants, software agents, intelligent agents. And various layman definitions have been offered: software that thinks, software with a head, smart object, and a smart computer program.

Backing away from technology for a moment, the everyday term, *agent*, provides a starting definition: "something that acts—often for, or in the place of, another." *A software agent is a software package that carries out tasks for others, autonomously without being controlled by its master once the tasks have been delegated. The "others" may be human users, business processes, workflows, applications, or other agents.* If you use a word processor such as Microsoft Word, you are a user of autonomous agent technology—the spelling and grammar checkers are carrying out those tasks for you, autonomously, as you type.

## The Basic Properties of Agents

Let's expand on the above. An agent does not have to be just software. It can be a person, a machine, a piece of software, or a mixture of these and a variety of other things. The basic dictionary definition of agent is *something that acts.* However, for developing business and IT systems, such a definition is too general. While a definition of agent is in the process of being standardized, most agree that agents deployed for IT systems are not useful without being autonomous, interactive, and adaptive. These properties are defined in the following manner:

- *Autonomous:* is capable of acting without direct external intervention. Agents have some degree of control over their internal state and can act based on their own experiences. They can also possess their own set of internal responsibilities and processing that enable them to act without any external choreography. As such, they can act in reactive and proactive ways. When an agent acts on behalf of (or as a proxy for) some person or thing, its autonomy is expected to embody the goals and policies of the entity that it represents. In UML terms, agents can have classifier behavior that governs the lifecycle of the agent.
- *Interactive*: communicates with the environment and other agents. Agents are interactive entities because they are capable of exchanging rich forms of messages with other entities in their environment. These messages can support requests for services and other kinds of resources, as well as event detection and notification. They can be synchronous or asynchronous in nature. The interaction can also be conversational in nature, such as negotiating contracts, marketplace-style bidding, or simply making a query. In the Woodridge-Jennings definition of agency, this property is referred to as social ability.
- *Adaptive*: capable of responding to other agents and/or its environment. Agents can react to messages and events and then respond in a timely and appropriate manner. Agents can be designed to make difficult decisions and even modify their behavior based on their experiences. They can even learn and evolve. In the Woodridge-Jennings definition of agency, this property is referred to as reactivity and proactivity.

Based on this approach, a basic working definition is:

> An *agent* is an autonomous entity that can adapt to and interact with its environment. [1, 2]

## Degrees of Autonomy, Interactivity, and Adaptivity

As illustrated in Figure 6.1, agents can be autonomous, interactive, and adaptive to some degree. It is not an all-or-nothing proposition.

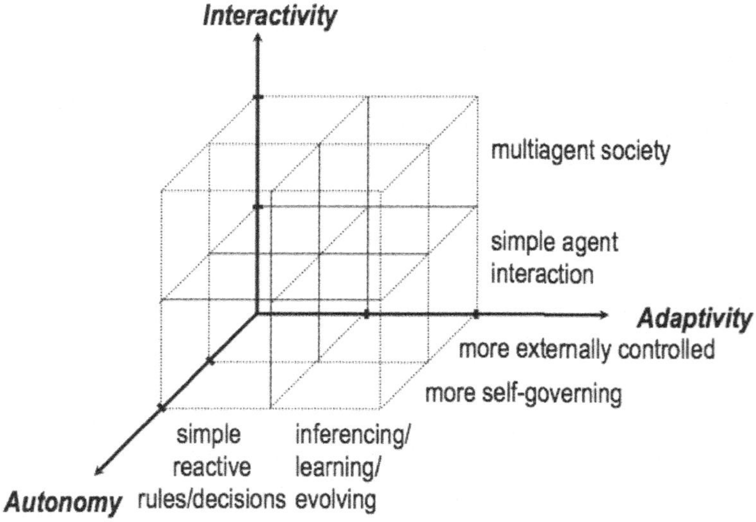


Figure 6.1 Agents have various degrees of autonomy, interactivity, and adaptivity.

In the next few sections, these three key agent properties will be discussed in more detail.

*Agents are Autonomous:* Agents can be thought of as autonomous because each is capable of governing its own behavior to some extent. Autonomy is best characterized by degrees. At one extreme, an agent could be completely self-governing and self-contained. However, an agent that does not require the resources of, or interaction with, other entities is very rare—primarily because it would be unmanageably large and unnecessarily complex for any common role. At the other extreme, an agent that is barely able to perform the simplest self-management is of limited use in complex systems. Even traditional objects have some degree of autonomy within their methods.

An agent's level of autonomy can be designed depending on its role. For example, in Figure 6.2, conventional objects are not completely dependent on outside resources—having some state and behavior of their own. However, they are traditionally simple in that they are far from being completely independent.

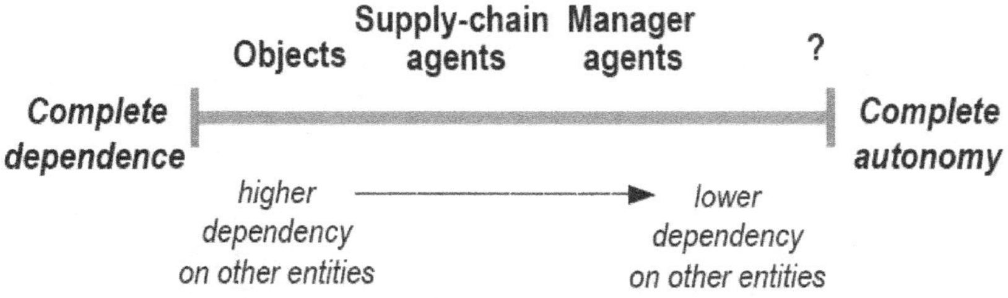


Figure 6.2 Degrees of Autonomy

Because a "supply-chain agent" is able to reach certain conclusions and make decisions on its own, it has more autonomy than an "object." By their very nature, supply-chain agents require interactions with other entities to enable a fully functional supply-chain system—one agent can not adequately support an entire organization's supply-chain processing. Autonomous interactions are also a characteristic for the class of agents called event-processing agents (EPA). Even more autonomous are manager agents, because their roles can involve a high degree of internal decision making through activities such as monitoring and delegation, which depend on outside resources.

Two major aspects of an agent's autonomy involve its capacity to be dynamic, as well as its ability to make decisions. As depicted in Figure 6.3, autonomy can be considered on two axes. On one axis, the dynamic aspect of an agent's autonomy can range from being simply passive in its action to entirely proactive. On the other axis, an agent's decision-making aspect ranges from being limited to simple decisions to being capable of making complex decisions.

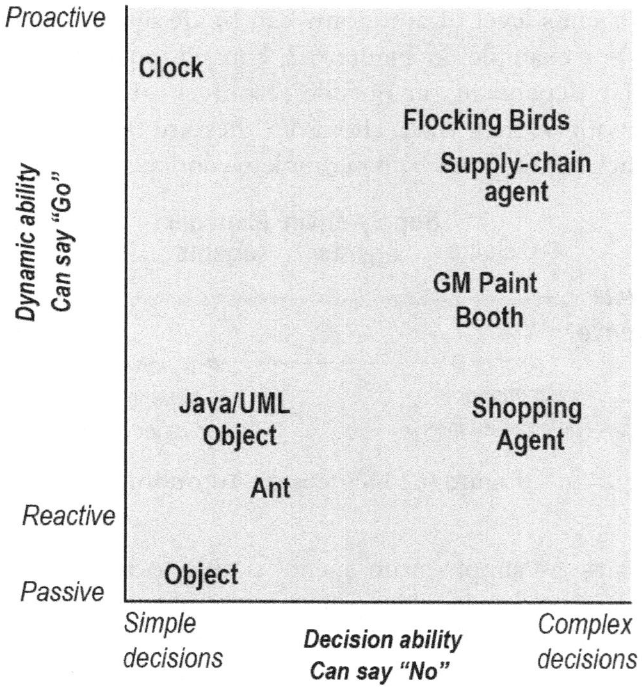


Figure 6.3 Two Aspects of Autonomy

*Dynamic Autonomy:* Agents can react not only to specific method invocations, but to observable events within the environment. Proactive agents will actually poll the environment for events and other messages to determine what action they should take. To compound this, in multiagent systems, agents can be engaged in multiple parallel interactions with each other—magnifying their dynamic nature. In short, an agent can decide when to say "go."

For example, the agent-based GM paint booths, described later in Chapter 8, had both reactive and proactive features. Information about an unpainted car or truck coming down the line was posted in an automated form accessible to all paint booths. When a paint booth had nearly completed its current job, it basically said, "Hmmm, I'm running out of work, I'll look over at the jobs posted." If the booth was applying the color of paint required by an upcoming job, it would bid more for the job than would a booth having a different color. Other bidding criteria could include how easy or important the job was. In other words, the booth was reactive in whether to bid on a paint job, but proactive in that it would check the paint job list and determine what to do.

Objects, on the other hand, are conventionally passive—with their methods being invoked under a caller's thread of control. The term autonomy barely applies to an entity whose invocation depends solely on other components in the system. However, UML and Java have recently introduced event-listener frameworks and other mechanisms for allowing objects to be more active. In other words, objects now have some of the dynamic capability of agents.

*Decision Autonomy:* Agents can be designed to make a few simple decisions. However, the more decisions an agent is capable of making and the more complex they are, the more autonomous the agent appears. A completely autonomous agent will do whatever it wishes.

For example, an ant that is wandering around looking for food can appear to be taking a random walk. However, once pheromones or food are detected, the choices for its behavior are predetermined. In contrast, the GM paint booth can decide on how much to bid based on the booth's ability to efficiently take on a new paint job. Certainly the choices are limited for a paint booth, but the ant has no choice on how to act when food is found. In contrast, shopping agents can have very complex criteria for selecting a gift for a specific individual. In fact, the agent might return empty handed because it decided no gifts were considered appropriate. A contract-negotiation agent may decide the contract is not worth pursuing for a number of reasons. In other words, the agent can also say "no" to performing a requested service.

Conventional objects certainly have the ability to make decisions. However, the typical usage and direct support with OO languages tends toward a less complicated approach to decision making. For instance, when a message is sent to an object, the method is always invoked. The contract-negotiation agent could refuse to invoke a requested Bid method, the object cannot. Yes, an object may determine whether or not to process the message and how to respond if it does. In common practice, however, the refusal of an object to execute its method is typically considered an error situation. With agents, this is not the case. Manager and quality assurance agents are good examples of agents who can say "no."

Object classes are usually designed to be highly predictable in order to facilitate buying and selling reusable components. Agents are commonly designed to determine their behavior based on their individual goals and states, as well their contexts within ongoing conversations with other agents. While OO implementations can certainly be developed to include nondeterministic behavior, this is common in agent-based thinking.

**Agents are Interactive:** Interaction implies the ability to communicate with the environment and other entities. As illustrated in Figure 6.4, interaction can also be expressed in degrees.

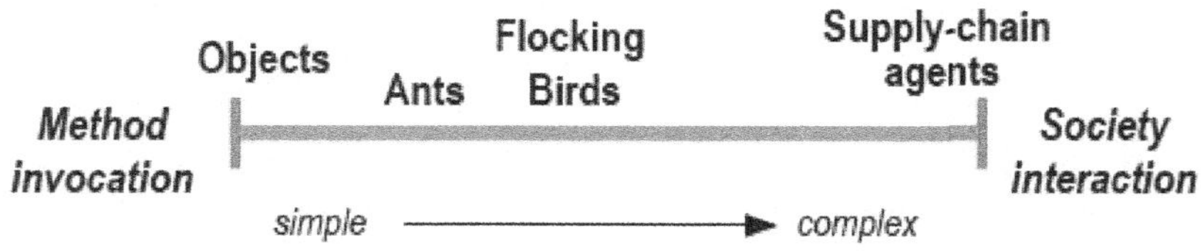


Figure 6.4 Degrees of Interaction.

On one end of the scale, object messages (method invocation) can be seen as the most basic form of interaction. A more complex degree of interaction would include those agents that can react to observable events within the environment. For example, food-gathering ants do not invoke methods on each other. Their interaction is indirect through the direct physical effects of their pheromones on the environment. Even more complex interactions are found where agents derive information — complex events — from multiple events over time. Here agents begin to act with "intelligence." And then there are multiagent systems (MAS) where agents engage in multiple, parallel interactions with other agents. Here agents begin to act as a society.

Finally, the ability to interact becomes most complex when systems involving many heterogeneous agents can coordinate cooperatively and/or competitively through such mechanisms as negotiation and planning.

While we can conceive of an agent that cannot interact with anything outside of itself, the usefulness of such an entity for developing agent-based systems is questionable.

*Agents are Adaptive:* An agent is considered *adaptive* if it can respond to other agents and its environment. Entities that fail to adapt to the ever-changing world become extinct—organisms die, companies go out of business, and so forth. For an organization, adaptation enables the system to react effectively to changes in areas such as the market and business environment. For IT systems, adaptation enables systems to react appropriately to enable such effects as system balancing, integrity assurance, and self-healing. The goals and motivations for adaptation are around remaining competitive and useful, and deriving value. When designed properly, individual parts of systems can be empowered to change based on their environment and market conditions.

*Simple Reaction Rules:* At a minimum, this means that an agent must be able to *react* to a simple stimulus—to make a direct, predetermined response to a particular event or environmental signal. Such a response is usually expressed by an IF-THEN form. Thermostats, robotic sensors, and simple events can fall into this category.

From atoms to ants, the reactive mode is quite evident. A carbon atom has a rule that states in effect, "If I am alone, I will only bond with oxygen atoms." An ant has a rule that if it finds food, it should return the food to its colony while leaving a pheromone trail. Simple reactions can also include business decision rules—such as event-condition-action (ECA) rules.

*Inference Rules:* Beyond the simple reactive agent is the agent that can appear to *reason* by following chains of rules. For example, agents can react by making inferences and include patient-diagnosis agents, certain kinds of data-mining agents, and identifying complex events. Such inferences are computed by following a chain of inference rules that can be described as goal-directed or data and event-driven.

Business process engines can use a similar approach. Here, libraries of processes are maintained that indicate the circumstances under which a particular process might be appropriate. Each step within a process would act as a service request, invoking the business process engine to choose the appropriate set of steps that should be executed. The choice would be based on the current context of the process. For example, a request to compute the sales task would trigger the engine to locate the appropriate set of steps that needs to be executed for a given location. The taxes in Michigan would be computed differently than in Brussels.

Rules do not change in and of themselves. Instead, change can come through other mechanisms such as learning and evolution. Without learning and evolution, ants and atoms are still able to support complex "societies." With learning and evolution, however, the rules can be changed based on experience—resulting in new and perhaps improved results.

*Learning:* Learning is change that occurs during the lifetime of an agent and can take many forms. Popular learning techniques employ reinforcement learning such as "credit assignment," Bayesian and classifier rules, and neural networks. Examples of learning agents would be agents that can approve credit applications, analyze speech, or recognize and track targets.

For example, in a basic bidding system, a bid could be selected simply on the basis of bid price. However, other considerations might also be appropriate, such as the bidder's ability to deliver its goods in the quantity, quality, and time frame requested. Over time, a *purchasing agent* can learn to choose from reliable *vendor agents* instead of just choosing the lowest bid. If a vendor's performance improves (or declines), the purchaser's decisions are modified accordingly. In other words, the agent *continues* to learn. Popular learning techniques that employ reinforcement learning include credit assignment, Bayesian and classifier rules, and neural networks. Examples of learning agents are agents that can approve credit applications, analyze speech, or recognize and track targets.

*Evolution:* Evolution is change that occurs over successive generations of agents. A primary technique for agent evolution usually involves genetic algorithms and genetic programming. Here, agents can literally be bred to fit specific purposes. For example, operation plans, circuitry, and software programs can prove to be more optimal than any product that a human can make in a reasonable amount of time.

## Other Agent Properties

In the sections above, three key agent properties were discussed: autonomy, interactivity, and adaptivity. These properties are important because they are *essential* for agents deployed by IT systems. However, agents may possess various combinations of other properties whose usefulness depends on the application requirements and the agent designer. Here, agent characteristics may include being:

- *Sociable:* interaction that is marked by friendliness or pleasant social relations, that is, where the agent is affable, companionable, or friendly.
- *Mobile:* able to transport itself from one environment to another.
- *Proxy*: may act on behalf of someone or something, that is, acting in the interest of, as a representative of, or for the benefit of some other entity.
- *Intelligent*: agents that employ degrees of raw intelligence, social intelligence, agility, autonomy and visualization (see Figure 4.2). The level of each of these dimensions determines the degree and type of agent's intelligence. (Note: The notion of process intelligence is described in Chapter 4. It applies to agents, because an agent is "something that acts"—i.e., it is an entity that carries out processes.)
- *Rational:* able to choose an action based on internal goals and the knowledge that a particular action will bring it closer to its goals.
- *Temporally continuous:* is a continuously running process.
- *Credible:* believable personality and emotional state.

- *Transparent and accountable:* must be transparent when required, yet must provide a log of its activities upon demand.
- *Coordinative:* able to perform an activity in a shared environment with other agents. Activities are often coordinated via plans, workflows, or some other process management mechanism.
- *Cooperative:* able to coordinate with other agents to achieve a common purpose; non-antagonistic agents that succeed or fail together. (*Collaboration* is another term used synonymously with cooperation.)
- *Competitive:* able to coordinate with other agents except that the success of one agent implies the failure of others (the opposite of cooperative).
- *Rugged:* able to deal with errors and incomplete data robustly.
- *Trustworthy:* adheres to Laws of Robotics and is truthful.

## Agent Anatomy

Figure 6.5 depicts a commonly employed structural pattern for an intelligent agent. (See Appendix A and B for more information regarding agent anatomy.) An agent has both "transient" (the active workspace) and "permanent" knowledge (permanent means intrinsic in this context; it stays stable from one execution cycle to the next). It has a controller (representing its head) which can be given alternative behavioral characteristics (e.g., stimulus-response-like, actor-like, or blackboard-like). An intelligent agent performs tasks that have both declarative and procedural components. (For definition of *intelligent agent,* see "intelligent", above, in the section entitled Other Agent Properties.) It can use alternative reasoning strategies, including belief management. An agent's repertoire of tasks represents its capabilities. Each task can have its procedural "how to do" component represented as rules, knowledge sources (rule sets), or methods.

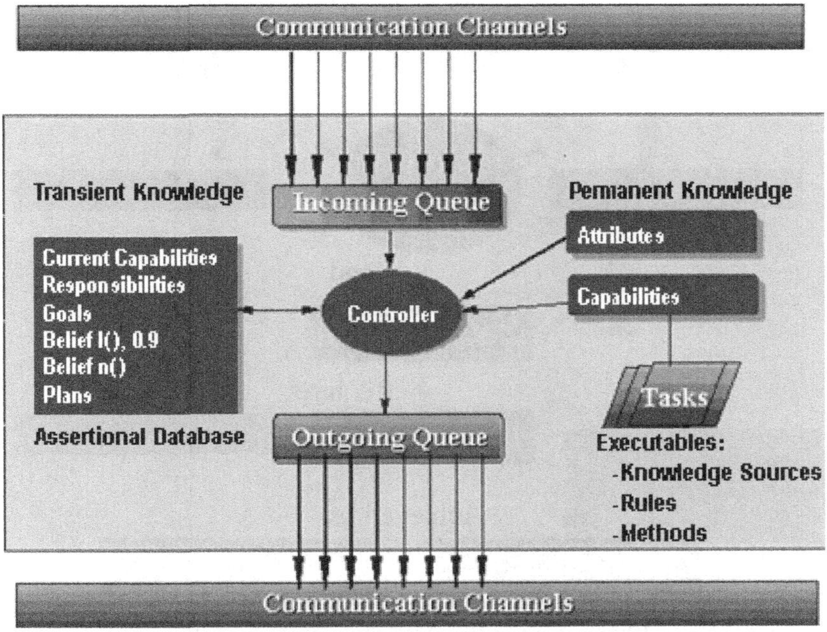


Figure 6.5 A common form of Intelligent Agent Anatomy

Figure 6.6 shows some of the key components of multiagent problem solving. To achieve common goals agents need coordination. Effective coordination requires cooperation, which in turn can be achieved through communication and organization. So in the process of developing agent-based systems we need answers to several fundamental questions:

- What are appropriate agent architectures for different classes of problem solving?
- How does an agent acquire its knowledge and how should it be represented?
- How does a complex task get decomposed and allocated to different agents?
- How should agents cooperate and communicate with each other?
- Can an intelligent agent be trusted?

Figure 6.6 Multiagent Problem-Solving

Many popular software agents bill themselves as intelligent when in fact they are basic software agents. Intelligent agent technology is a sub-field of Distributed Artificial Intelligence (DAI). DAI is concerned with issues arising out of problem-solving by a collection of smart entities and systems and concurrency of computation at different levels. Some of the basic tenets of problem-solving by intelligent agents are:

- Each agent may have different knowledge, capabilities, reliability, resources, responsibilities or authority.
- Different agents may perceive the same event or object differently.
- Agents may specialize in or focus on different problems and sub-problems.
- An important goal is convergence on solutions despite incomplete or inconsistent knowledge or data.

Going beyond today's business objects, Web services, and

Cloud services, *intelligent business agents* are the next higher level of abstraction in model-based solutions to business problems. By building on the distributed object foundation, intelligent agent technology can help bridge the remaining gap between flexible design and useable applications. Intelligent agents support a natural merging of object orientation and knowledge-based technologies. They can facilitate the incorporation of reasoning capabilities within the application logic (e.g., encapsulation of business rules within agents or modeled organizations). They permit the inclusion of learning and self-improvement capabilities at both infrastructure (adaptive routing) and application (adaptive user interfaces) levels. Intelligent user interfaces (supporting *task centered* user interfaces and intelligent assistance to end-users) can be a boon to productivity in a network-centric world.

On the technology side, intelligent agents solve run-time operations bottlenecks inherent in network-centric computing. Management of enterprise-wide objects in a run-time environment becomes more difficult using pre-programmed control objects. For example, as the size of a distributed system grows, the number of messages between objects grows non-linearly and "controller objects" themselves need to be coordinated or they can become performance bottlenecks. Unlike objects, intelligent agents can participate in high-level dialogues through the use of interaction protocols in conjunction with built-in organizational knowledge. In many cases, the need for communication is greatly reduced, as within these high-level dialogues, complex packets of procedural and declarative knowledge as well as state information may be exchanged in the form of mobile agents.

Figure 6.7 shows an example of an intelligent agent specializing in supporting risk management. It shows that such an agent would use its knowledge of risk assessment, its role in supporting this process, and historical data to examine various data feeds in order to compose a risk exposure picture.

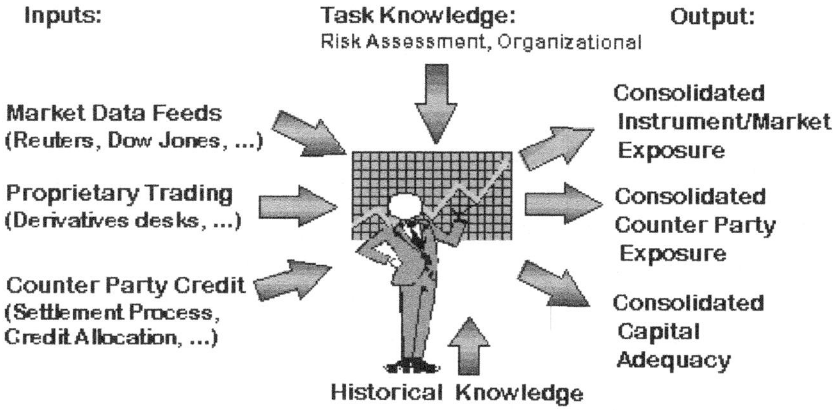


Figure 6.7 Risk Management Application of Intelligent Agents

Figure 6.8 illustrates a community of intelligent agents, including a Risk Assessment Agent, supporting a financial trader.

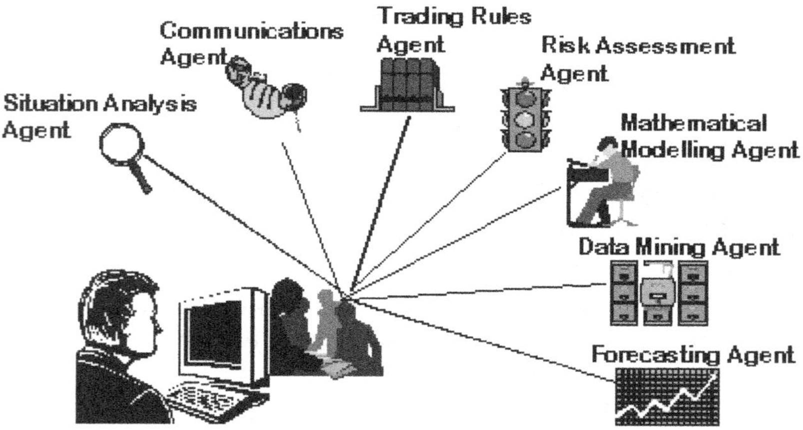


Figure 6.8 Intelligent Agents as
Personal Assistants to a Financial Trader

## To Use Agents or Not

Before James Odell develops agent-based systems, Figure 6.9 illustrates one way he considers whether or not to employ an agent approach. One axis represents the level of adaptability and agility required of an application. If your business application is both predictable and stable and its processes are centralized and scalable for the foreseeable future, it is low on this axis and adopting an agent-based approach is probably not necessary. The other axis represents the level of complexity that will be involved in the application.

Here, complexity refers to the amount of interaction among a number of different kinds of processing units. Complexity is high when many different kinds of processing units must interact with many others in a variety of ways. For example, the complexity would be high for a distributed system that federates hundreds or thousands of distributed service registries and databases. If such a system also required it to be agile in adapting to changes in properties, such as size, interaction, data, metadata, and rules, then an agent-oriented approach would be necessary. Conventional approaches cannot handle this requirement and still be responsive in a timely manner.

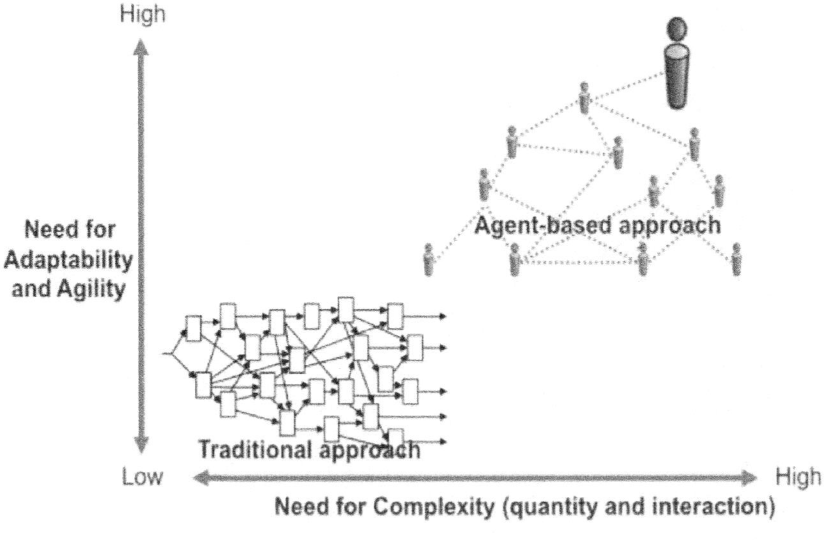


Figure 6.9 When to use an agent approach—or not.

Organizations all over the world are employing agent technology in their systems and products—to some extent. Some are simple server agents, others are "search bot" agents; but now large organizations (e.g., NASA, US Army, DOD, IBM, HP) are employing agents to simulate and manage complex systems in a dynamic and scalable manner. Organizations of all sizes should be leveraging agent technology and enabling their customers to deploy adaptive, competitive solutions to challenging, real-world problems.

## Collaborate, Collaborate

By the year 2000, people realized that they were in touch with people with whom they had never been in touch, and they were being challenged by people who had never challenged them. Our competitors were new and our collaborators were new. We were doing things as individuals that we had never dreamt of doing before. In what journalist Thomas Friedman referred to as the *flat world*, this phenomenon has caused, enabled, and empowered small groups and individuals to collaborate and compete globally.

Keep in mind, though, that adopting any new technology is disruptive, and agent technology is no exception. Yet, early-adopter companies are already finding that agent technology can provide one or more of the following benefits:

- Faster return on investment (ROI)
- Lower maintenance
- Higher productivity
- Leverage existing infrastructure
- Reuse of processes and services
- Foundation for future projects
- Reduction of time to market
- Increased agility to respond to business needs

However, is an agent-based approach useful for every application and usage? Does it always provide the benefits listed above? It certainly does not.

If your business is predictable and stable, and your processes are centralized and scalable for the foreseeable future, adopting an agent-based approach is not necessary. However, for those applications that must support complexity and change in a scalable and timely manner, agents will likely be a necessary technology. The typical organization probably has both of these situations in one form or another, and the savvy organization will have a mixture of technologies: object-oriented (OO), relational, *and* agent-oriented. OO and relational technologies enable a top-down and centralized solution to business applications. Agents provide one more tool that conventional IT shops do not have: a bottom-up and distributed approach. The real benefit, then, comes when an organization can choose the appropriate mix of technologies for a given application—providing a balance of both centralized and distributed approaches.

As journalist Thomas Friedman wrote, [1] we need "a global, Web-enabled platform for multiple forms of collaboration. This platform enables individuals, groups, companies, and universities anywhere in the world to collaborate – for the purposes of innovation, production, education, research, entertainment, and, alas, war-making – like no creative platform before. This platform now operates without regard to geography, distance, time, and, in the near future, even language. Going forward, this platform is going to be at the center of everything."

This emergence of new business processes is resulting in new IT practices and approaches—where the two mutually reinforce each other. Now that individuals, groups, companies, and universities are interacting on a global scale, IT must not forget its supporting role. Agents are a key ingredient in IT globalizing itself.

## References

[1] Friedman, Thomas L., *The World is Flat,* New York, Farrar, Straus and Giroux, 2006.

# 7. The Evolution of Business Systems and Programming Approaches

Agent technology is now necessary to reduce costs, to improve efficiency and effectiveness, and to support the requirements of individuals, groups, companies, and universities as they collaborate globally. More importantly, it will enable us to create and support a whole class of IT applications and approaches that we previously could not have developed.

## Evolution from Monolithic to Agent Programs

We are no longer in the era of mainframe computing, when both companies and applications were typically command-and-control oriented and organized in vertical silos. With the combination of the Internet, fiber optics, and PCs, the business and technology playing field has been flattened. No longer primarily top down, it has changed to more side-by-side—as individuals, small groups, and organizations interact around the world. As a result, organizations are now demanding and cultivating new business practices that encourage less command and control and more *horizontal connecting*, *collaborating*, and *competing*.

Agent technology is a primary enabler to support this new era. In fact, *without* agent technology, our current technology will not scale to support the ever-increasing global interaction.

Even non-technology-oriented business people can benefit from knowing how the role of computing technology has changed and how that change has progressively changed the game of business. The first electronic digital computer, the Atanasoff-Berry-Computer, built in 1939, had no stored program. The first programmable computer, the ENIAC, was built in 1946 using the Von Neumann architecture. It utilized procedural programming, also called imperative programming. In short, a program is list of instructions telling a computer, step-by-step, what to do, usually having a linear order of execution from the first statement to the second and so forth with occasional loops and branches. Programming early computers was done at a machine-level of abstraction with symbolic machine instructions. Zero business language, just machine-level abstraction.

Figure 7.1 Remington Rand employees, Harold E. Sweeney (left) and J. Presper Eckert (center) demonstrate the U.S. Census Bureau's UNIVAC for CBS reporter Walter Cronkite (right).

The first computer bought for commercial use was in 1951 when the U.S. Bureau of the Census purchased the Univac I computer. (Fig. 7.1) We've come a long way since 1951. Human-oriented, versus machine-oriented, languages began to emerge such as Fortran (formula translation) and COBOL (common business oriented language). But the languages continued to be procedural and ultimately translated into machine language through compilers or interpreters. What they were used to program were essentially computers as tabulating machines. Today, however, chunks of computer programs encapsulate business functionality and are rendered as services that other programs call on to get business tasks done. The level of abstraction has risen to a business level and services can be made available to anyone or anything in the Cloud.

| | Monolithic Programming | Modular Programming | Object-Oriented Programming | Agent Programming |
|---|---|---|---|---|
| Unit Behavior | Nonmodular | Modular | Modular | Modular |
| Unit State | External | External | Internal | Internal |
| Unit Invocation | External | External (CALLed) | External (message) | Internal (rules, goals) |

Figure 7.2 Evolution of programming approaches.

Figure 7.2 illustrates one way of thinking about the evolution of programming languages. Originally, the basic unit of software was the complete program where the programmer had full control. The program's state was the responsibility of the programmer and its invocation determined by the system operator. The term modular did not apply because the behavior could not be invoked as a reusable unit in a variety of circumstances.

As programs became more complex and memory space grew, programmers needed to introduce some degree of organization to their code. Modular programming employed smaller units of code that could be reused under a variety of situations. Here, structured loops and subroutines were designed to have a high degree of local integrity. While each subroutine's code was encapsulated, its state was determined by externally supplied arguments and it gained control only when invoked externally by a call statement. This was the era of procedures as the primary unit of decomposition. In contrast, object orientation added to the modular approach by maintaining its segments of code (or *methods*) as well as by gaining local control over the variables manipulated by its methods.

What is an "object?" Prior to the notion of object-oriented programming, computer programs contained procedures or code, but the data they operated on were totally separate from and outside the program (Fortran, COBOL, etc.). Objects encapsulate data and the operations on them so that only the operations are publicly accessible via an interface and internal details of the data structures are hidden. Other programs call on the object with a request and the object responds, but the requestor has no access to the internals of how the object does what it does. This request-respond approach greatly simplifies the construction of large, complex programs and is the basis of most contemporary computer programming languages (e.g., C++, Java). Think of objects as actors on a stage, calling upon one another to get things done. Object-oriented programming emerged in the 1960s (Simula and Smalltalk) and has advanced through many phases including distributed object computing; and the granularity has increased from primitive objects to components that package *business services*; and the request-respond interface has moved on to Web services, and now on to Cloud services, both using a service-oriented architecture (SOA).

However, in traditional OO, objects were considered passive because their methods were invoked only when some external entity sent them a message. Once invoked, they execute their method and go back to "sleep" until the next message. A current trend in many systems is to design objects that both react to events in their environment and are proactive. These are known as *active objects*; or in the agent community, they are known as a simple version of agents.

Just how different—or the same—are objects and agents? Some developers consider agents to be objects, except with more bells and whistles. Others see agents and objects as different even though they have many things in common. Both approaches, however, envision using objects and agents together in the development of software systems. In other words, objects and agents are two distinct notions—each having its own particular place in software development. The important point here is that the agent-based way of thinking brings a useful and important perspective for system development that is different from—while similar to—the object-oriented way.

Software agents have their own thread of control, localizing not only code and state but their invocation as well. Such agents can also have individual rules and goals, making them appear like "active objects (or active components) with initiative." In other words, the agent can determine when and how it acts.

An agent-based approach is employed when a particular situation requires that processing be decentralized and self-organized, instead of centrally organized. Savvy organizations, then, will employ a mixture of technologies in their applications: object orientated (OO), component-enabled, relational, *and* agent-based. OO, components, and relational technologies enable a top-down and centralized solution to business applications. Agents provide one more tool that conventional IT shops do not have; that is, a bottom-up and distributed approach. The real benefit comes when an organization can choose the appropriate mix of technologies for a given application—providing a balance of both the centralized and distributed approaches.

## Services Everywhere

Organizational involvement on a geographically broad level is the new-normal way of doing business (Figure 7.3). For an organization to operate and compete, it needs to consider a boundaryless approach to collaboration, cooperation, and competition.

This talk of "tearing down the walls and silos" is not new, and it has been a hot topic, particularly in recent years. So, what is different now? Increasingly, we find that we must pull together services from other organizations to form a collaborative team for just one consumer. This hybridized solution can create value for the consumer that does not exist in any one application or service or from any one organization. The underlying effort must support fine-grained, individualized resources and be able to address concerns on the personal, as well as organizational, levels. For this to scale, it must be automated. How can this be accomplished?

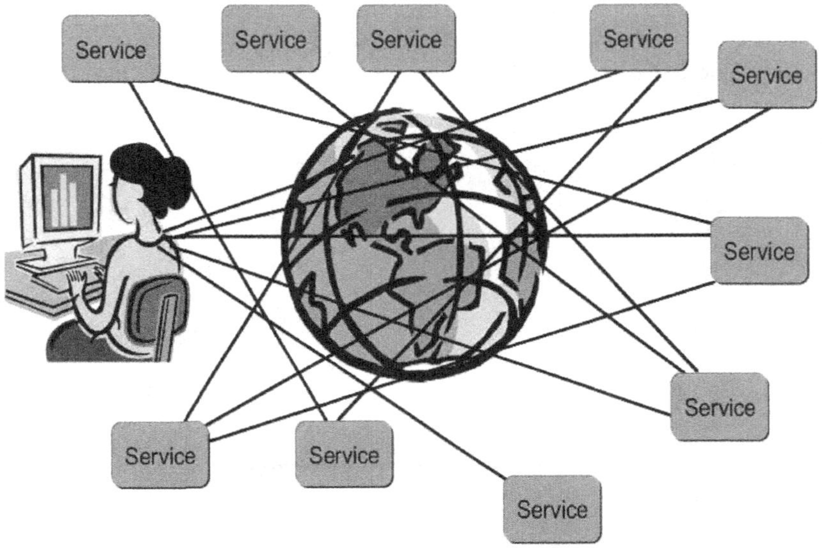


Figure 7.3 Geographically broad interaction
is how business gets done.

One such approach is suggested in 2004 by both the W3C and the OASIS standards bodies. Figure 7.4 shows a service that provides some functionality on behalf of its owner, which is a person or an organization.

The *provider* entity is the person or organization that supplies an appropriate agent to implement a particular service. A *requester* entity is a person or organization that wishes to make use of a provider entity's service. It will use a requester agent to exchange messages with the provider entity's provider agent. The figure illustrates this further. In step 3, the service description and semantics are realized by the requester and provider agents, and in step 4, the requester and provider agents exchange messages, resulting in some task being performed on behalf of the requester by one or more provider entities. This reduces the information and processing overload on human operators. (For more information regarding agent communication and interaction, see Appendices B and C.)

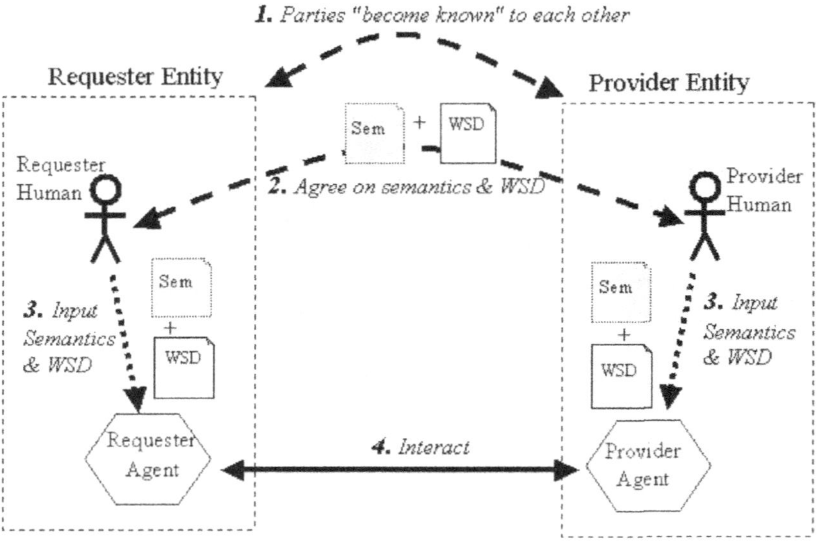


Figure 7.4 Service architectures
enhanced using agents for interaction (from [1]).

When the links between requesters and providers are few and change is not an issue, agents are not needed and conventional IT techniques can be employed. However, when the links require complex, dynamic binding and are subject to rapid change, agent-based approaches should be considered. Prior to the demand for global collaboration, we developed a centralized controller to ensure that all interactions would be appropriately managed. Now, that is no longer possible. The world is too big and so a central bottleneck would paralyze the effort. Furthermore, the access techniques now require a more horizontal style of interaction—rather than one that is centrally administered.

Both collaboration and competition are supported by an agent-based world. For example, auctions can use agents that link a requester's service requirement to a rich world of service providers (e.g., British auction, Dutch auction, eBay auction, or contract net). In the contract net protocol, for example, requester agents send out requests for quotes (RFQs) and award the winning provider(s) with a "contract" to provide a resource. For instance, an energy company like DTE has a finite number of resources (e.g., vehicles and crew members) to handle all the energy related services that are required for a power outage system. Under normal conditions, such planning and scheduling could be handled adequately by human schedulers and dispatchers with automated support. However, an ice storm, knocking out the power at 100,000 locations, will tax even the best human schedulers. Here, agents can be employed to *automate* the process by bidding on behalf of the various resources, including those from power companies in neighboring states and countries.

Cape Canaveral is now installing a similar system for its launch control services and resources using an agent-based approach developed by Intelligent Automation, Inc. [2] NASA is investigating using this technique for planning and scheduling sensor-based services and resources. These systems would use agents to identify, assemble, and execute the services that would form a virtual service for the end consumer. Other agents plan and schedule those resources required.

Managing services and resources in this manner enables and promotes global interaction and collaboration. At the heart of all these systems, agents digitize and decompose the supply chain and move the work around to anywhere in the world. [3]

Agent technology is an appropriate supplement to many technologies. Service Oriented Architecture (SOA) is just one. SOAs have the flexibility and responsiveness to enable organizational priorities to finally drive technology decisions. Many companies are also expanding SOA beyond IT resources to include hardware (such as sensors, electronic equipment, and robotics, as well as human resources). By adding agent-based functionality to the SOA, an even greater flexibility and agility is possible. [4] In particular, agent technology can be used to enable the following features:

- *Resource provision and request* – In both the W3C and OASIS approaches to Web Services Architecture, the actual service requester and provider entities will agree on the service description and semantics that will govern the interaction between the requester and provider agents. The agents will then automate performing services on behalf of the actual requesters and providers. The agents can choose the smartest and most efficient way to accomplish a task by connecting different nodes in a network—whether horizontally or vertically.

- *Processing support* – For complex processes, agents can be used to orchestrate and "team" software processes to solve problems collaboratively or compete intelligently. Services result from self-assembly. The provider agents determine the value proposition for the consumer agents and then identify and assemble the services that will form a virtual service for the end consumer.
- *Resource discovery* – *Dynamic service selection* is increasingly common as organizations recognize the benefits of its flexibility. If an agent has flexibility in picking its business partners, it can select them to optimize any kind of quality-of-service criteria, including performance, availability, reliability, and trustworthiness. A requester agent can be chartered to do this, but specialized *service-discovery agents* are sometimes useful for facilitating this.
- *Middleware support* – Within SOA middleware, agents should be used for functions that require flexibility, autonomy, and robustness. For example, managing application-level fault tolerance, security, performance, and QoS are common uses for agents. In addition, agents can be used as a more "intelligent" way of handling and propagating changes in ontology and dealing with incompatibilities in vocabularies, semantics, and pragmatics among service providers, brokers, and requesters.

Most services adoptions begin with a dozen or so services. Here, discovering, choosing, and binding your services can employ a basic services foundation with human involvement. However, when there are hundreds or thousands of providers offering the same (or similar) services—which can change from moment to moment—the situation becomes more challenging. Furthermore, many services will require the interaction and aggregation of other services. Such a complex and changing world is where agent technology can enhance the services environment most dramatically.

Agents can employ a variety of techniques and roles, because they can mimic the way businesses and people work in the real world. For example, the technique employed at the center of Figure 7.5 is an interaction protocol for making a contract between agents playing the roles of consumer and provider. Here, a consumer agent can broadcast a request for a particular service using a "call for proposal." Those provider agents (on the far right of the figure) that can provide the requested service, respond with their proposal, or "bid." The consumer agent can then choose from among the possible thousands of responses and "award" a chosen provider to supply the service. (Interaction protocols and agent communication languages are discussed in Appendix B and C.)

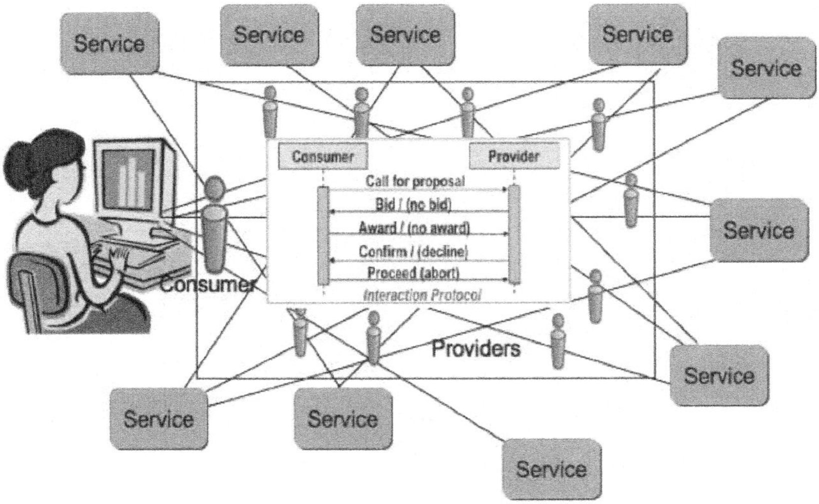


Figure 7.5 Using interaction protocols based on business-based interaction rules.

If there are only a few providers and they are already known, using agents in this manner may not be necessary. However, if many providers are possible (and can change quickly over time), the agent approach for services is highly effective and efficient.

Using agents, then, enables service consumers and providers to link up anywhere in the world. In other words, services can be enabled to be truly collaborative, dynamic, and boundary-less to the degree permitted by the business organizations.

Agents may also act as intelligent brokers and aggregators in both service-oriented and event-driven architectures and applications (Figure 7.6). Here, advanced techniques (such as rules engines, Bayesian processing, and neural networks) can be used by an agent to become a smarter broker for a consumer or provider. Additionally, agents can "organize" themselves into communities (or groups) to aggregate services in an effective and efficient way. Agents can even provide process management and scheduler roles as well as sophisticated process management and service-scheduling support that cannot be accomplished using conventional, centralized approaches.

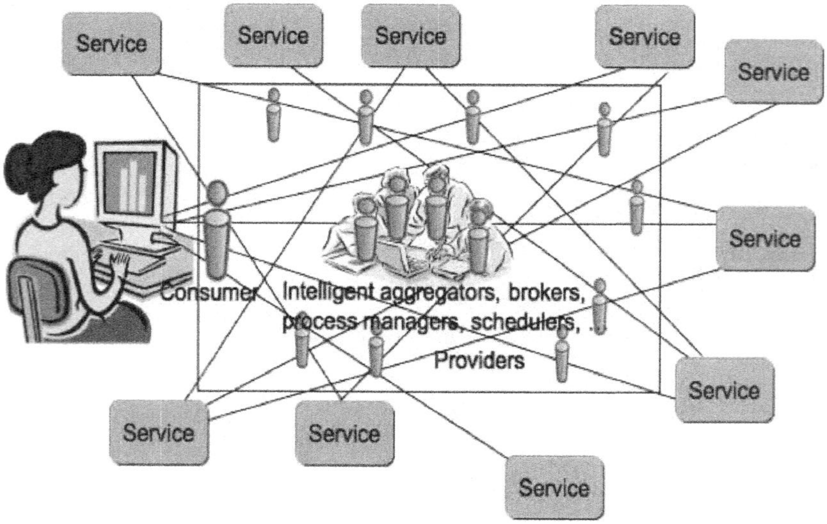


Figure 7.6 Agents can provide sophisticated support, such as brokers, aggregators, process managers, and schedulers.

An *event-driven architecture (EDA)* is an architectural style in which components are driven by events and can also communicate by means of events. In particular, event-driven architecture provides the following functionality (Figure 7.7):

- Monitors and senses for changes and conditions in the system environment/databases.
- Initiates appropriate responses, actions, or processes.
- Modifies processes in real time for optimal response to changing conditions.

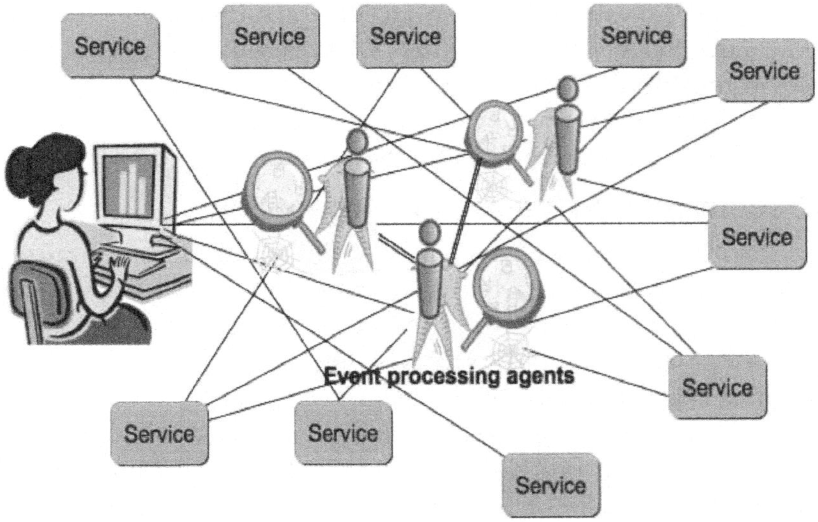


Figure 7.7 Employing agents for complex event processing (CEP) and event-driven architectures (EDA).

Being *event driven*, then, means that process behavior responds to events arriving from external or internal sources. Such processing behavior can be in the form of conventional processing architectures, SOA (Service Oriented Architecture), or BPM (Business Process Management). Many companies use a hybrid approach.

More and more companies are using agents along with software and physical sensors to detect changes in the business environment. (Examples include RFID tags for retail supply-chain optimization, medical monitors, physical sensors that detect changes in air quality, and electronic data-capture tools for patient trials at pharmaceutical companies.) Companies that derive the greatest advantages from agent-based, event-driven architectures have these characteristics: (i) large and heterogeneous environments, (ii) many kinds of changes can occur frequently within the environment, and (iii) the need to deliver and respond appropriately to complex exceptions and state changes in real time.

SOA, BPM, and EDA/CEP are three architectural approaches that can be separately considered for including agent technology. However, agent technology can be used to link business processes and services to facilitate a single architecture that integrates SOA, BPM, and EDA/CEP. Additionally, many other environments and architectures can benefit from employing agent technology. In conclusion, agents can be employed either as a stand-alone technology or with other technologies.

## Decentralization and Self-Organizing

Software agents have their own thread of control, localizing not only code and state but their invocation as well. Such agents can also have individual rules and goals, making them appear like "active objects with initiative." In other words, when and how an agent acts is determined by the agent.

An agent-based approach is employed when a particular situation requires that processing be decentralized and self-organized, instead of centrally organized. While a centrally organized program could have been written to handle the ant simulation (Figure 8.1), the system would have been far too cumbersome. It would have required a single set of top-level rules telling each ant precisely what to do in every conceivable situation. Not only would such an application be touchy and fragile, it would likely end up looking jerky and unnatural—more like an animated cartoon than animated life. [5]

Yet, most developers tend to build centrally organized applications. They are also biased towards object-oriented notions, such as *class, association*, and *message*. While these constructs are useful for a certain category of applications, they do not directly address the requirements of agents. As we have seen above, agents have such characteristics as autonomy, mobility, and adaptability. Furthermore, business users like to express other concepts, such as rules, constraints, goals and objectives, as well as roles and responsibilities. In short, the agent-oriented approach distinguishes between autonomous, interactive, mobile entities (agents), and the passive ones of conventional OO (objects). This does not mean that object orientation is dead or passé. A well-designed, agent-based system uses both objects and agents—just as real-life organizations employ a balance of both active and passive elements. Furthermore, object technology can be used to *enable*, rather than drive, agent-oriented technology.

Agents are similar to object-oriented software (objects) in a number of ways. They can be organized into generalization and specialization hierarchies, to exploit *inheritance* (e.g., a risk assessment agent represents a specialization of a personal assistant agent class). An agent can advertise its services using a variety of means, and how it implements these services should be transparent (i.e., encapsulation of behavior). Different agents can respond to the same service request differently without the requester needing to know about such differences. For example, imagine that a user is supported by a set of E-mail agents (for Internet mail, LAN mail, etc). This user should not have to be concerned with how each agent handles the same request for sending a message (i.e., *polymorphism*). And, intelligent agents communicate asynchronously by message passing, using a variety of rich interaction protocols (e.g., negotiation and conflict resolution protocols).

Intelligent agents differ from software objects in a number of ways. Intelligent agents manipulate objects to perform their tasks. Behavior of intelligent agents (the tasks that they perform and how the tasks are performed) can be modified dynamically, due to learning or influence of other agents. Intelligent agents can be autonomous, can reason about themselves and can be mobile. Intelligent agents can actively and dynamically seek to cooperate to solve problems, using task and domain-level protocols (an important goal is convergence on solutions despite incomplete or inconsistent knowledge or data).

Business objects make a major contribution to modeling *information* in the enterprise while BPM modeling methods are great for modeling work processes in an organization. Using intelligent processing (described in Chapter 4) intelligent business agents extend this capability to provide the breakthrough in modeling knowledge in the enterprise.

A major reason for the apparent failure of object-oriented (OO) and BPM approaches to deliver on reuse is insufficient attention to the issue of domain understanding and the representation of this understanding in an unambiguous and precise way so it can be validated by business people who are domain experts. Arguably, both OO and BPM methods focus too much on notation and not enough on content. OO notions such as class, association, and message are too biased toward the implementation of software systems. Such concepts are not sufficiently expressive of business concepts: rules, constraints, goals and objectives, and roles and responsibilities. Nor are these concepts readily understood by business people, posing a major barrier to the participation of business users in validating OO models. The lack of such validation can have serious consequences for the validity of the software solutions that are later implemented.

The agent-oriented approach provides a more *understandable* paradigm for constructing models of a business domain, as well as offering techniques for creating smart business solutions—all enabled, but not driven, by object technology. The agent-oriented approach to business objects distinguishes between active, goal-seeking objects (agents) and passive objects. Agents are the centerpiece in domain modeling, together with the tasks they perform, how they interact with each other, how their actions generate events, and how they are organized around and manage business processes.

Centralizing a corporation was once considered an efficient way to run an enterprise. Decisions and information processing occurred in an orderly, top-down, hierarchical manner. However, it is now clear that this type of system only works in a reasonably stable market. Globalization and changes in technology are causing today's market to be in a state of constant flux. Companies that cannot adapt fast enough to thrive in new markets will be left behind.

In response, many companies are now building agent-based systems. These systems employ software agents that distribute functionality across vast computing networks. Furthermore, agents not only adapt to their environment but also evolve by learning from the environment and employ a variety of computational approaches, from OO to expert systems, neural networks, genetic algorithms, and so on. Such an approach prepares enterprises for an increasingly complex marketplace and enables them to respond rapidly to change.

As a result, we are moving from a vertical chain of command to a more horizontal chain of collaboration in both commercial and noncommercial activities. However, we need to adjust to make the transition from vertical to horizontal thinking. Vertical thinking typically involves asking who or what commands and controls the system; horizontal involves a more peer-to-peer way of thinking. Agent technology, then, will enable us to create and support a whole class of IT applications and approaches that we previously could not have developed. For this reason, two new SOA standards have emerged: OMG's SoaML [5] and OASIS' Reference Architecture—both explicitly including the use of agent technology for SOA systems.

Agent technology, therefore, is now accepted as a primary enabler to support this new era. In fact, *without* agent technology, our current technology—including SOA, EDA (Event Driven Architecture), and BPM (Business Process Management)—will not scale to support the ever-increasing complexity and global interaction. In response, many companies are now building agent-based systems. These systems employ agents that can distribute functionality across a vast computing network. Furthermore, agents can not only adapt to their environment but also evolve by learning from the environment. In short, they are the ultimate in distributed computing.

As illustrated in Figure 7.8, agents are an *evolution* of existing technologies. What makes it *revolutionary* is the way we think about and use agents to design IT systems. They are being built *from* today's technology and will work together *with* today's technology.

While agents, objects, relational databases, legacy systems, service-oriented architectures, event-driven approaches, and so on each have their own niche, together they can orchestrate rich systems that none of these technologies could provide alone.

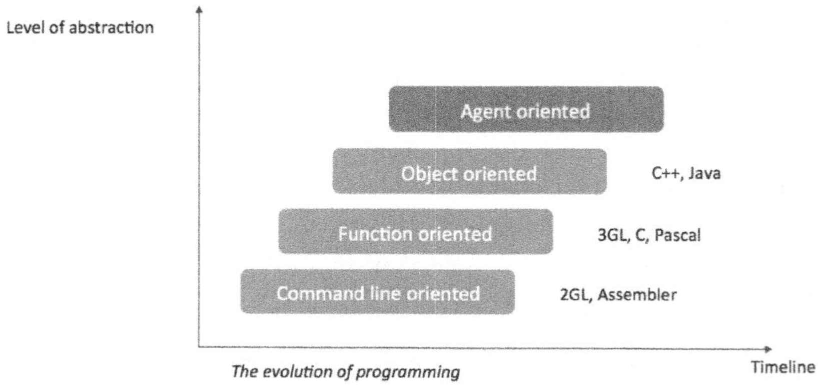


Figure 7.8 Agent technology is an evolutionary approach.

It is advocated that the same perspective and vocabulary be used during analysis, design, and construction of software systems guided by reference architectures. This method of software construction helps reduce cognitive dissonance through the use of constructs in software that can be mapped more naturally and directly to real-world entities than basic objects that underlie process models at the implementation level. In addition, agents can be integrated frameworks that contain, in one package, specific problem-solving functions, data and control. This helps to transform the creation of applications into a high-level task of assembling pre-fabricated frameworks, as opposed to the more complex task of grappling with object libraries or fine-grained components.

## References

[1] W3C, *Web Services Architecture*, W3C Working Group Note, February 11, 2004. http://www.w3.org/TR/2004/NOTE-ws-arch-20040211/
[2] Intelligent Automation, Inc (IAI) – http://www.i-a-i.com/view.asp?tid=21
[3] Cougaar Software, Inc – http://cougaarsoftware.com
[4] Singh, Munindar P. and Michael N. Huhns, *Service-Oriented Computing: Semantics, Processes, Agents*, John Wiley & Sons, Chichester, England, 2005.
[5] OMG, Service Oriented Architecture Modeling Language (SoaML)–Formal Version (of Standard), May 2012, http://www.omg.org/spec/SoaML.

# 8. Agent Technology Uses

Many companies have already tested agent-based applications in their research and development facilities. Successful applications are now used commercially throughout the world. Agents are used for both simulation and real-world execution. They are employed to address a variety of application areas—some of which only agent technology can enable. This chapter discusses some of the ways agent technology has been used to assist organizations in deploying automated solutions that were not otherwise possible.

## Agents in Everyday Life

Biological agents can produce everyday phenomenon such as ant colonies, traffic jams, stock markets, and forest ecosystems. Software agents can enable supply chain systems, planning and scheduling applications, web services, and so on. Software agents need not be complicated. For example, in the ant colony simulation of StarLogo [1][10] or NetLogo [11] illustrated in Figure 8.1, each ant has three simple rules:

- Wander randomly.
- If food is found, take a piece back to the colony and leave a trail of pheromones that evaporates over time; then go back to rule 1.
- If a pheromone trail is found, follow it to the food and then go to rule 2.

In Figure 8.1(a), the ants (grey dots) are just emerging from the anthill (solid black circle in center) to begin their random walks. Eventually, an ant discovers a food source (one of the three solid grey circles around the anthill). The ant then returns its food to the colony, leaving a trail of evaporative pheromones (Figure 8.1(b)). Figure 8.1(c) shows the ant colony well underway in retrieving food. Lastly, Figure 8.1(d) depicts two very depleted food sources and one that has been exhausted altogether.

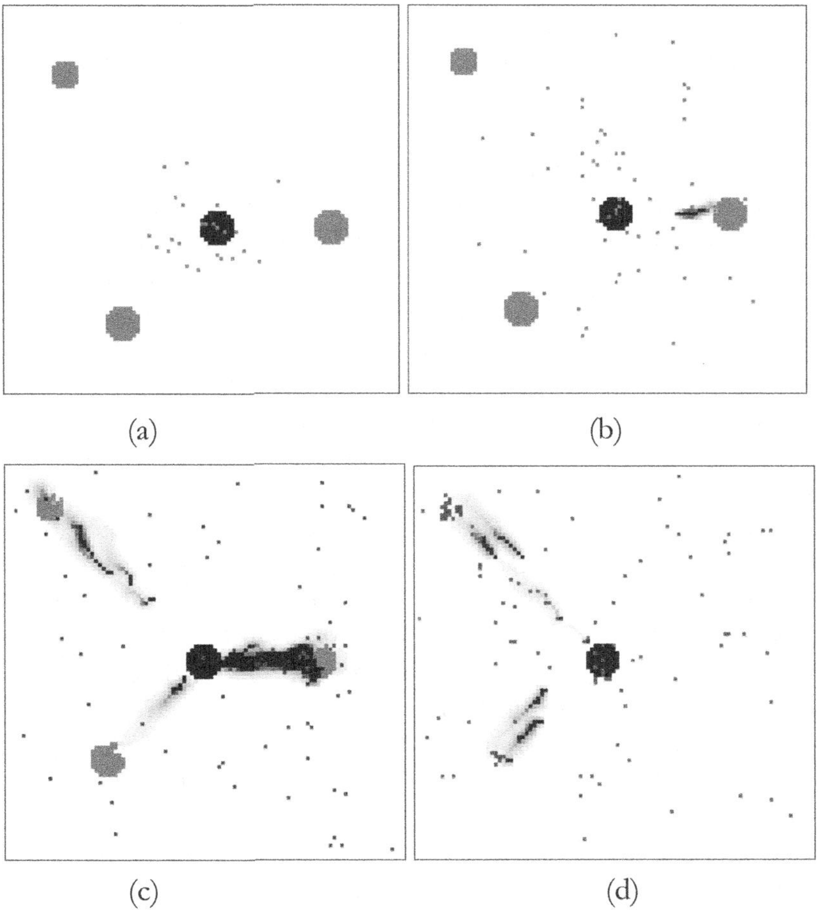


Figure 8.1 Snapshots from an ant colony simulation.

## Ant-like Agents at British Telecom

As it turns out, the foraging technique of the simple ant provides an inspiration to tackling some difficult technological problems. While the insect's totally random approach to locating food appears to be inefficient at best, a new area of research known as *swarm intelligence* [2] has been established.

British Telecom (BT) Future Systems uses swarm intelligence for inspiration to make software systems more intelligent and robust, cheaper, and simpler. The head of BT Future Systems, Chris

Winter, was concerned that the trend of IT systems was toward central control. "Ants walk around at random and there's no intelligent controller telling them what to do," said Winter. "When they find food, they simply run back to the nest laying a little pheromone trail that other ants can smell. The rest of the colony need only follow that path to fetch the remaining food." In other words, the processing is distributed, not centrally controlled

Winter used ants initially to weed out system bugs. In BT's development network, little ant-like programs run around finding problems. They leave pheromone-like timestamps that highlight the fault and draw help from other software. In other words, BT is using the ants as a first step in self-healing systems software. Many software companies are now embedding ant-like agents in systems software and middleware for similar reasons.

In another application, BT and Hewlett-Packard Laboratories created the world's first ant-based systems. [3] Both telephone networks and the Internet typically route connections through a number of intermediate switching stations. When the network is large, many possible routes exist for each connection. However, using a centrally controlled routing approach scales badly and can lead to failure of the entire system. A decentralized mechanism like the ant-based approach above was found both to scale well with the network size and to avoid any possibility of a system-wide failure.

The approach here is to send ant-like agents periodically between nodes. At each node, the agent updates the node's *routing table* with information (pheromones) indicating how long the journey took from its origin and which nodes the agent used along the way. The routing table contains a list of the node's immediate neighbors and probabilities associated with using that neighbor as the next step on the journey towards a target node in the network. The fastest ants will have a positive effect on the probability scores of the nodes they used, while slow ants will have a negative effect.

Network congestion is another problem that was addressed by BT and HP. They considered congestion in a particular section of the network to be analogous to the depletion of a food source near an ant colony. Here, ant-like agents would search for new routes and dynamically update the virtual pheromone trail recorded in routing tables.

## Agent-Based Models (ABM)

In ant-based systems, an ant colony of a finite size searches collectively for a good solution to a given optimization problem. The optimal solution can only be found through the global cooperation of all the colony's ants, where the ants only communicate indirectly by adding evaporative pheromones to the environment. The BT applications above are only two examples of where techniques start with models of ant behavior, then add things that are not present in the real world.

Individual ants are not very sophisticated insects. They have limited memory and a largely random element. Acting as a collective, however, ants can perform complicated tasks with reliability and consistency. Ant colonies, however, are not the only things that work like this. Beehives, flocks of birds, freeway traffic, national and global economies, societies, and immune systems are all examples of patterns that are determined predominantly by local component interaction instead of centralized authority. This broadened approach to agent-based simulation that includes and goes beyond swarm intelligence is called *agent-based modeling*.

An *agent-based model (ABM)* is a class of computational models for *simulating* the actions and interactions of autonomous agents with a view to assessing their effects on the system as a whole. [9]

An agent-based model design is one in which analogs of those real-world entities that are to be modeled are represented as software agents (e.g., ants), or objects (e.g., food) *at a level of detail and resolution necessary to address the questions the model is required to answer*. The agents interact with each other as the model runs, producing dynamic information about the system being simulated. (Figure 8.2)

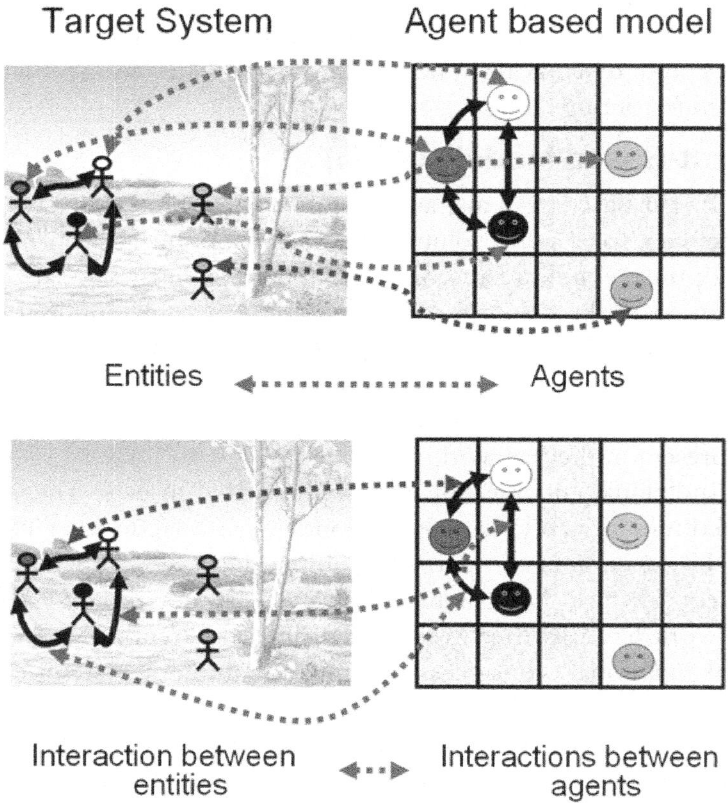


Figure 8.2 The ABM developer maps the target world to an agent-based model of the target world.[12]

Within an ABM, each agent individually assesses its situation and makes decisions on the basis of its set of rules. Agents may execute various roles, such as: producing, consuming, competing, collaborating, or selling. Repetitive competitive interactions among agents are a feature of ABM that enables dynamic exploration that is out of the reach of pure mathematical methods.

At its simplest, an ABM consists of a system of agents and the relationships among them. Even simple agent-based models will demonstrate complex behavior patterns—providing valuable information about the dynamics of the real-world system that it emulates. As mentioned earlier, agents may be capable of evolving, enabling the emergence of unanticipated behavior. More sophisticated ABMs incorporate neural networks, evolutionary algorithms, or other learning techniques that empower learning and adaptation.

ABM is more a mindset than a technology, where this mindset consists of describing a system from the perspective of its constituent units of agents and their interactions. A synonym of ABM would be microscopic modeling, and an alternative would be macroscopic modeling. Many researchers think that the alternative to ABM is traditional differential equation modeling or performing an actual real-world experiment. The ABM approach becomes advantageous when:

- the problem at hand is too difficult to do analytically (e.g., differential equations);
- an approximate theoretical result might not be reliable, and it is necessary to check it with a different method;
- an experiment is expensive or not feasible to perform.

One of the reasons underlying ABM's popularity is its ease of implementation: ABMs are both programmable and a large number of ABM tools exist to build ABM systems.

## Benefits of Agent-Based Modeling

The benefits of ABMs are that they provide a natural description of a system, are flexible, and capture emergent phenomena.

*ABM provides a natural description of a system.* In many cases, ABM is most natural for describing and simulating a system composed of "behavioral" entities. Whether one is attempting to describe a traffic jam, the stock market, voters, or how an organization works, ABM makes the model seem closer to reality. For example, it is more natural to describe how shoppers move in a supermarket than to come up with the equations that govern the dynamics of the density of shoppers. ABM also makes it possible to realize the full potential of the customer data a company may have. Knowing the actual shopping basket of a customer makes it possible to create a virtual agent with that shopping basket rather than a density of people with a synthetic shopping basket computed from equations. Also, ABM looks at the organization from the viewpoint not of business process models but what people inside the organization actually do. One may want to use ABM when:

- Individual behavior is complex. Everything can be done with equations, in principle, but the complexity of differential equations increases exponentially as the complexity of behavior increases. Describing complex individual behavior with equations becomes intractable.
- Activities are a more natural way of describing the system than processes.
- Validation and calibration of the model through expert judgment is crucial. ABM is often the most appropriate way of describing what is actually happening in the real world, and the experts can easily "connect" to the model and have a feeling of "ownership."

*ABM is flexible.* The flexibility of ABM can be observed along multiple dimensions. For example, it is easy to add more agents to an agent-based model. ABM also provides a natural framework for tuning the complexity of the agents: behavior, degree of rationality, ability to learn and evolve, and rules of interactions. Another dimension of flexibility is the ability to change levels of description and aggregation: one can easily play with aggregate agents, subgroups of agents, and single agents, with different levels of description coexisting in a given model. One may want to use ABM when the appropriate level of description or complexity is not known ahead of time and finding it requires some tinkering.

*ABM captures emergent phenomena.* Emergence results from agents and their interactions. By definition, they cannot be reduced to the system's parts because the system's behavior is greater than the sum of its parts' behaviors, because of the interactions between the parts. For example, a traffic jam, which results from the behavior of and interactions between individual vehicle drivers, may be moving in the direction opposite that of the cars that cause it. This characteristic of emergent phenomena makes them difficult to understand and predict. Thus, emergent phenomena can be counterintuitive. Numerous examples of counter-intuitive emergent phenomena will be described in the following sections. ABM is, by its very nature, the canonical approach to modeling emergent phenomena.

Using ABM is appropriate when there is potential for emergent phenomena, i.e., when [13]:

- Individual behavior is nonlinear and can be characterized by thresholds, if-then rules, or nonlinear coupling. Describing discontinuity in individual behavior is difficult with differential equations.
- Individual behavior exhibits memory, path-dependence, and hysteresis, non-Markovian behavior, or temporal correlations, including learning and adaptation.
- Agent interactions are heterogeneous and can generate network effects. Aggregate flow equations usually assume global homogeneous mixing, but the topology of the interaction network can lead to significant deviations from predicted aggregate behavior.
- Averages will not work. Aggregate differential equations tend to smooth out fluctuations, not ABM, which is important because under certain conditions, fluctuations can be amplified: the system is linearly stable but unstable to larger perturbations.

According to Bonabeau [13], "[ABM] may change the way we think about explanation in the social sciences. What constitutes an explanation of an observed social phenomenon? Perhaps one day people will interpret the question, 'Can you explain it?' as asking 'Can you grow it?'"

## Areas of Application

Running an agent-based model in a computer provides a formal proof that a particular micro-specification is *sufficient* to generate the global behavior that is observed during the simulation. Again from Bonabeau, "Agent-based models have been used since the mid-1990s to solve a variety of business and technology problems. Examples of applications include supply-chain optimization and logistics, modeling of consumer behavior, including word of mouth, social network effects, distributed computing, workforce management, and portfolio management. They have also been used to analyze traffic congestion and the traveling-salesman problem. Agent-based modeling tools can be used to test how changes in individual behaviors will affect the system's emerging overall behavior."

"Other models have analyzed the spread of epidemics, the threat of biowarfare, the growth and decline of ancient civilizations, evolution of ethnocentric behavior, forced displacement or migration, language choice dynamics, and biomedical applications including inflammation and the human immune system. Agent-based models have also been used for developing decision support systems such as for breast cancer."

## Beyond ABM: Real-World Execution

Above, we have limited the discussion of agents and agent systems to simulation. Simulation is a process that runs agent systems using non-real-world environments.

However, substituting a real-world environment for a simulated environment, we will be performing computations using actual existing agents. That is, input, processing, and output will occur on data based in real life. In other words, our agent application will go "live." When this occurs in a world with multiple agents interacting among and with other agents; this is called a multiagent system (MAS).

> A *multiagent system (MAS)* is a system composed of multiple interacting intelligent agents. Multiagent systems can be used to solve problems that are difficult or impossible for an individual agent or monolithic system to solve. [7]

For IT applications, this can include order processing, supply chain, shop floor control, inventory management, message routing, and management of multiple databases. In other words, a decentralized approach should be considered where local components also have control, instead of limiting system-design approaches *solely* to the centrally organized one traditionally employed by IT. After all, if New York City can maintain a two-week supply of food with only locally made decisions, why can't a supply chain system perform in a similar fashion.

## Painting Trucks at General Motors

Traditionally, assembly line schedules are centrally developed and controlled. Any change in the schedule must be centrally reconfigured. When the line is small and has few unplanned stoppages, centrally controlled schedules work well. However, scheduling for most real-world assembly lines can be a nightmare: work stations break down, personnel get sick, environmental conditions are not always within acceptable limits, products coming down the line have or acquire unexpected defects, and so on.

Dick Morley, a technology visionary and the father of the programmable controller, swept away old assembly line schedules and developed a better system for painting trucks at GM's trucks in Fort Wayne, Indiana. "How do I schedule the non-schedulable?" Morley wondered. "Trucks do not come down the line in order of their color and frequently no paint booth is available with the correct color." Morley also discovered that many of the paint booths were typically broken down or being repaired.

In his technique, the scheduling program interacts with each paint booth. Instead of assigning unpainted trucks to booths, GM's solution was to have the booths bid on the paint jobs [4]. To accomplish this, each booth was equipped with a simple software agent that was programmed to keep its booth busy and bid on each paint job. The amount of the booth's bid was based on how busy the booth was at the moment of bidding, whether it had to change to a different paint, and whether the booth was functioning properly.

To coordinate the bids for each paint job, a scheduler agent acts as a broker. For example, when a truck arrives to be painted, the scheduler agent tells the booths, "I have a truck that needs to be painted red. A vacant paint booth already loaded with red paint will bid very high. However, a vacant booth with different color would bid lower because of the extra labor and time to clean and reload the paint gun. A booth that has just started to paint a truck, broken down, or otherwise less suited for the job, would bid even lower. Based on the outcome of the bidding activity, the scheduler assigns the truck to the highest-bidding paint booth.

In a top-down planned "push-through" world, if one booth malfunctioned, a centrally controlled system would re-compute its entire remaining schedule. With bottom-up "pull-through" paint booth agents, other booths would be ready to pick up the slack at a moment's notice by bidding for the job. This new design saved a million dollars in nine months and reduced the lines of computer code from hundreds to four.

Dick Morley and GM tackled a problem where centralized scheduling did not work efficiently by adopting an agent-based approach where each booth acts on its own behalf using a market-based bidding system. Even though the scheduler was a centralized element, it deferred to distributed booth agents. Agent-based solutions do not remove centralization; instead, they try to balance it with distributed solutions *wherever it makes sense.* (Note: this approach is now a standard way of handling assembly lines at Daimler Benz and other German automakers.)

## Dynamic Scheduling

Current market trends are driving organizations from mass production (where the supplier tells the customer what to buy) to mass customization (where the customer tells the supplier what to provide). For small supplier organizations where resources and requirements are reasonably stable, this does not present a problem. The larger and more complex the organization, however, the more difficult it is to support centrally managed operations—particularly, large suppliers with volatile and demanding conditions that include unscheduled resource failures, periodic surges in new orders, and changes in requirements and priorities. Here, using agents can change the perspective to a more *distributed* approach, making the solution more scalable, adaptable, and robust. In fact, many organizations have already realized their limit and can no longer scale using a centralized approach. Organizations like DHL and Credit Suisse have found that an agent-based approach is their *only* option for successfully managing the previously unmanageable size and complexity within their businesses.

At the heart of the solution, two primary forms of agents were used to gain distributed control:

- *Process-based agents* – have the knowledge of how to combine resources and create products as part of a workflow in a supply chain.
- *Resource-based agents* – manage the capacity-constrained resources of the systems, such as people, machines, materials, and facilities.

Several other types of agents were used, as well (e.g., order agents, dispatch agents, and supervisor agents). However, process and resource agents are key to understanding the approach.

## Business Processes and Resources Using Agents

Figure 8.3 contains an example of a workflow diagram for a process that installs utility poles for an electric company. The round-cornered rectangles represent processes and the square-cornered rectangles are those resources required by the processes.

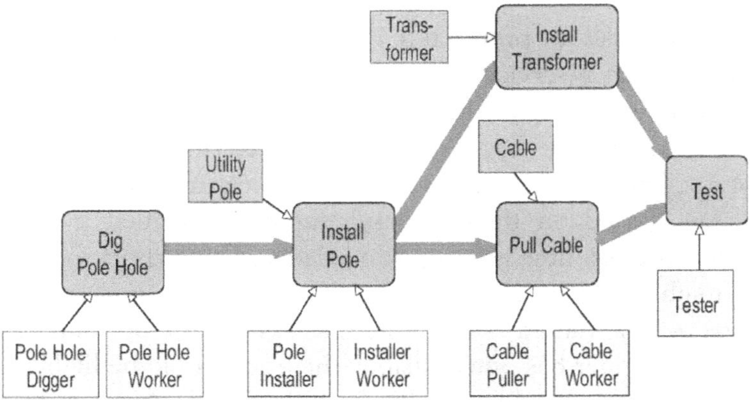


Figure 8.3 Example of a business process where processes and resources are managed using agents.

In business process management (BPM) systems, such activities are usually centrally managed. Using agents, however, the process and resources can be managed in a distributed manner. For example, an Install Pole agent is a specialized entity that knows its Install Pole process needs a utility pole, pole-installer equipment, a person to operate the pole installer, and the prior completion of a Dig Pole Hole process.

Such knowledge can be used in several ways. For instance, in Figure 8.4, a requester might be interested in an Install Pole service but would like to know its cost before the service is invoked.

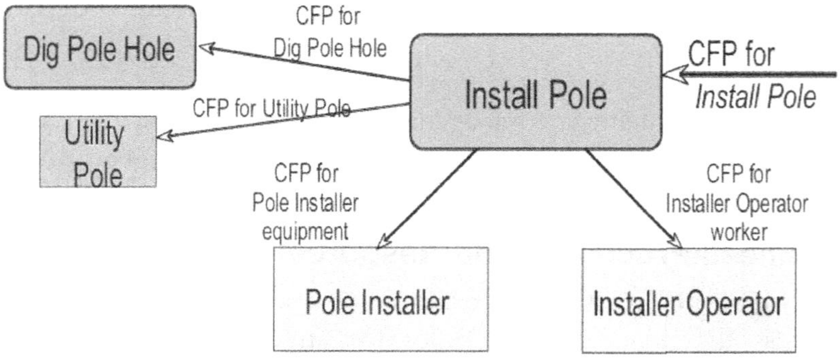


Figure 8.4 Call for proposal (CFP) to the Install Pole agent results in a CFP to all of its resources and preceding operations.

Here, a call for proposal (CFP) would be sent to an agent that provides such a service embodied in a service-oriented architecture. The agent would then send a CFP to those resources and preceding services that would be required for the Install Pole process. Each resource agent would then calculate the charge for its usage based on the time and duration specified by the requester. If a resource is urgently needed and is in short supply, the cost might be high; if not, the price would be low. For example, if the requestor wanted a Utility Pole in two hours, but only an expensive provider has one available, the price would be higher than if the requester could wait for two days and obtain it from a cheaper supplier. In contrast, the agent representing pole installers might be able to provide a person immediately. In two days, however, they all might be busy on other assignments—but would do the requested job at double-time rates.

Once the resources had responded to the CFP with a bid, the Install Pole agent would tally up the cost for the service as a whole and send a consolidated bid to the requestor for the Install Pole service. In other words, the Install Pole agent acts like a broker on behalf of the process. If the requestor accepts the bid, the broker is notified of the award and will confirm (or decline) the award.

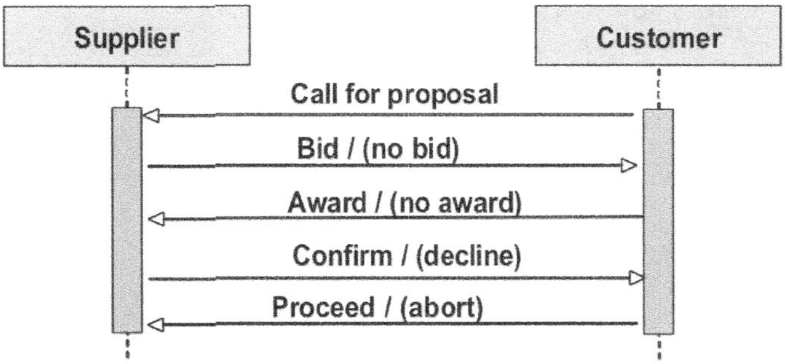


Figure 8.5 An interaction protocol for making a contract.

## Agent negotiation

This interaction protocol just described is expressed using the sequence diagram depicted in Figure 8.5. The requester is playing the role of Customer and the provider is playing the role of Supplier. Interaction protocols are useful because they define the expected behavior between interacting agents—whether either can be a resource agent or a process agent.

## Agent Renegotiation

In the real world, suppliers can over commit, have resource failures, and experience process delays. Using a top-down, centralized approach, the schedule changes tend to be re-optimized from a global level. Such a technique would work in a small operation but would not scale to a large one. However, using an agent-based approach—which is distributed by nature—enables more dynamic scheduling by adapting to these unexpected situations on an individual and local basis rather than a massive and global one.

For example, an important job request is received for Resource A, which is *already* allocated to Job 1 and Job 2. The agent representing Resource A needs to interact with the process agents for each job to determine whether the extra work can be accommodated. In Figure 8.6, the agent for Resource A asks the agent for the first step in Job 1 about any extra, or *slack*, time.

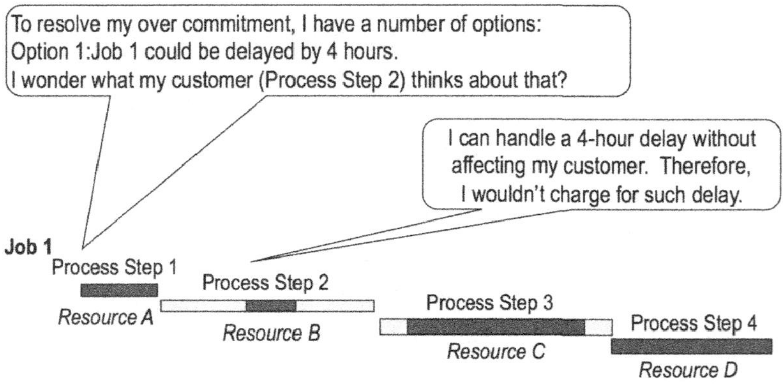


Figure 8.6 Renegotiation example for Job 1 by process and resource agents. (based on [5])

It turns out that if Resource A takes on the new job, it will delay Step 1 by four hours. Now, Step 1's agent can ask Step 2 if a four-hour delay would affect its processing. Since Step 2 has lots of slack time, it can absorb the delay without affecting the overall schedule. (Note: the bar represents the total time allocated to perform the process; the dark segment within the bar indicates the *actual* amount of time needed by the process.)

Resource A's agent must now examine the remaining option of changing Job 2 (see Figure 8.7). Step 1 would be delayed by three hours. Step 1's agent then asks Step 2 if a three-hour delay would impact its processing. Step 2's agent indicates that such a slippage would also cause a three-hour delay for it. Step 3 has a similar result and, therefore, its agent must ask the end customer if this slippage presents a problem. In this example, the customer has a large penalty clause built into the contract for late shipments. In summary, Job 2 would result in a penalty if modified to handle the extra requirement for Resource A.

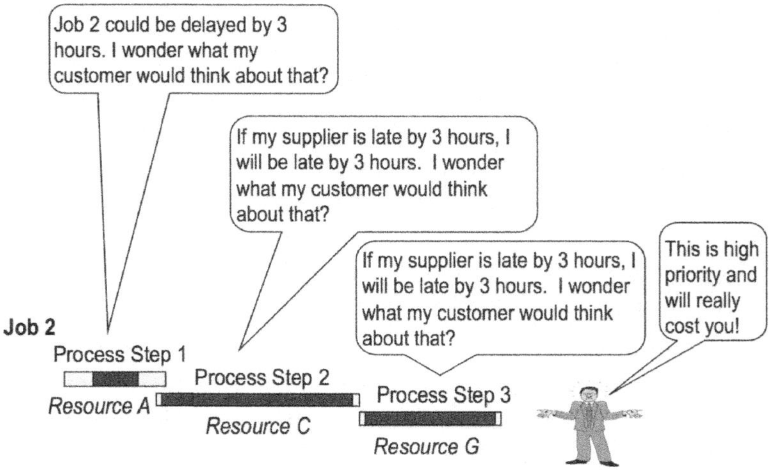


Figure 8.7 Renegotiation example for Job 2 by process and resource agents. (based on [5])

However, adapting Job 1 would enable Resource A to be assigned to a new job without affecting the overall schedule. All decisions in this example were based on a local optimization rather than a global one—enabling decisions to be made in seconds instead of hours or days and reducing costs as well as time-to-market.

## Agents and Dynamic Scheduling

The agent-based approach described above was developed with support from Rock Island Arsenal (RIA) as part of a DARPA contract to build an agent-based factory-scheduling prototype, named AARIA. In one benchmark test using these techniques, inventory costs were cut by 47 percent, lead times were cut 59 percent, and schedule reducible costs (such as overtime and inventory holding charges) were cut by 93 percent. [4]

Since that time, agent-based schedulers have been designed for suppliers in many industry sectors: manufacturing, finance, energy, and transportation. Magenta Technology (www.magenta-technology.com), Cougaar Software (www.cougaarsoftware.com), and Intelligent Automation, Inc. (www.i-a-i.com) have been active in this area.

Magenta Technology has developed an agent-based system that dynamically schedules the deployment of ships and cargo. Intelligent Automation is developing a "generic" scheduler that rapidly generates tailored and optimized scheduling engines. Using their software, an end user who has only domain expertise can define the:

- Components (e.g., resources, work center, parts, tasks, operations, and jobs) required for the scheduling application, using the component libraries
- Protocols (interactions and constraints between components) using a standardized representation language called an Agent Interaction Protocol (AIP)
- Rules and Policies that define the order of interactions and the content of an interaction based on a user-defined scheduling algorithm

## Other Agent-Based Uses

### Some Common Applications

Many companies have already tested agent-based applications in their research and development facilities. Successful applications are now used commercially throughout the world. A brief overview of some of them include the following:

- *Logistics, Material Management and Transportation:* High fuel costs, increasing competition, and rising customer demands for flexibility and visibility has created challenges for the existing IT infrastructure of transportation companies. Costs must be managed with the best possible routing, taking into account environmental, traffic, fuel price, and other issues on each possible route and that planning must be dynamic and re-planning must be continuous even during execution. Less than full loads must be optimized. And all of this must be done without scrapping your existing IT investments. What is needed is a layer of intelligence to put you in control of your organization.

  An agent-oriented layer atop existing IT systems helps provide more visibility with integrated, comprehensive and local dynamic views of the distribution network. It also enables more effective management of local distribution operations, and provides robust and secure collaboration and execution. With situational awareness and representation, an agent-oriented extension to existing systems gives companies the ability to collaborate and partner effectively with supporting distribution partners. The user can create an accurate, global, and understandable operational picture of the current transportation situation as well as provide advanced event management, execution monitoring, and collaborative decision support. Users can monitor activities during execution and dynamically re-plan in the face of external changes or modified operational requirements.

- *Smart and Green Buildings:* With rising energy costs and the desire to support environmental concerns, businesses and building managers need to find every possible way to improve the efficiency of their facilities. However this cannot be done at the expense of employees' comfort or productivity. How to manage this trade-off space between efficiency and employee choice is key. Similarly within the efficiency trade-off space, there are trade-offs within every decision – such as between artificial light that uses energy and natural light that might add heat when the air conditioning is on – that must be managed in real-time as conditions change. Finally, security is becoming more complicated with too much data from sensors and cameras being delivered for human processing. Security systems must take the load off of humans so they can focus where human decision-making is best used. To be as green, efficient and safe as possible, buildings must be as smart as possible.

  Agent-oriented technology can provide this intelligence by adding a thin layer of intelligence to integrate and enhance existing building systems. This lets you harness your existing investments to support new intelligent capabilities without disruption. Intelligent agents are distributed to the places in the building where they can do the most good from sensor to mainframe, providing a virtual nervous system. Using an agent-oriented cognitive model also provides the "brain" as well. This creates a common operating picture to integrate all building operations from lights, to networks to security. This gives building managers the ability to monitor and control all aspects of building operation so as to optimize its operation while maintaining worker control. It can automate certain decisions while watching for an unexpected event to bring to the attention of decision makers. It can also negotiate with suppliers such as telecommunications and electricity suppliers for the best pricing based on parameters you set. (Cougaar Software)

- *Smart Manufacturing: Autonomic Manufacturing Solutions* – Manufacturers today face competition from globalization as well as opportunity. But the benefits of globalization can only be met if the value global supply chains can be maximized. Central to success is processing the vast amount of information to create situational awareness and common operating picture of the supply chain. Companies must move beyond the obsolete and risk fraught Just-in-Time Paradigm to the dynamic, agile, and less fragile Sense-and-Respond Paradigm that is replacing it. Managing uncertainty and risk and balancing those against efficiency is the key. Within the factory, whether it is an assembly line or a traffic management system, adaptive capabilities are key to handling the demands of networked manufacturing equipment. Self-management of the system is key, while at the same time using complex event processing to alert managers when unexpected events occur.

Solutions built with agent technology can manage, track and audit supplier relationships, while maintaining accurate, appropriate, and minimal inventories to ensure production processes have the right material at the right time and avoid interruptions, delays, and errors in production processes. This will allow you to gain competitive advantage while increasing customer loyalty and retention by increasing supply chain velocity, reducing time to market, decreasing costs of materials, managing operating processes, and managing complex intelligent machines—and the data they generate for prognostics.

(Cougaar Software)

- *Energy, Oil, Gas and Refining:* Energy businesses are perhaps the most global companies in the world – and they are also in the most harsh and demanding locations. Mistakes can cause huge losses and even cost lives. Managing these far flung operations is a logistical and operational challenge second only to the military. Add to these issues of deregulation, M&A, global compliance, safety and security and there is a need for distributed intelligent solutions that tie all aspects of operations to one common operating picture. Such a solution would provide global or localized visibility of assets, supply chain, and operations both throughout the company and to partners, as well as process automation and decision support.

  Solutions built with agent technology puts intelligence where it is most needed whether it is in your organization, your partners or suppliers, with highly distributed architecture. Most importantly, agent environments act as a fabric of intelligence between your existing systems, so your current IT investment is not only re-used but enhanced.
- *Just-in-time delivery:* When operating in a highly competitive market, delivering just-in-time products and services is vital. SCA Packaging turned to an agent-based modeling solution that explored different strategies for reducing inventory levels without compromising its delivery commitments. An agent-based simulation developed by Eurobios (www.eurobios.com) enabled the company to reduce inventory levels by 35% while maintaining its delivery commitments. [7]
- *Adaptive Logistics (AL)* have been developed to prototype and demonstrate different disciplines of Logistics, Distribution, Maintenance, and Supply. In particular, the Army's Adaptive Logistics (AL) project now integrates the use of intelligent agent technology and cognitive decision support tools as key drivers of Sense and Respond Logistics (S&RL). The intelligent agents monitor and synthesize large volumes of data from disparate sources to improve situational understanding and rapidly provide COAs to facilitate decision-making. The Army's AL

project demonstrates how the net-centric decision support capabilities and intelligent agent technologies can be extended to the strategic level. (Cougaar Software, cougaarsoftware.com)

- *Production Planning:* Production planning is a logistics approach that provides intelligent maintenance estimation and recommendations on optimal allocations, capabilities, performance analyses, "What if" simulations, and dynamic monitoring and alerting. Cougaar Software developed the MyProductionPlanner (MPP) tool has been developed by LOGSA for Army Sustainment Command (ASC), Distribution Management Center (DMC). Figure 8.8 illustrates the MPP process flow.
- *Distribution optimization:* Delivery of goods and services between site and customer is a problem for many industries. Companies such as British Telecom, DHL, and Air Liquide require transportation networks that can flexibly adapt in real time to changing and unforeseen run-time conditions, fluctuations, and requirements. Not surprisingly, at least three companies provide agent-based solutions to this area: Eurobios, Whitestein Technologies (www.whitestein.com), and Cougaar Software.
- *Collaborative decision making and distributed control:* As systems become increasingly decentralized and autonomous, technology needs to support collaborative, team-based decision making and control. Agents can work individually and socially in teams to aid and accomplish this. In particular, Intelligent Automation has developed applications for team formation, cooperative sensing, tracking, monitoring, and traffic management.

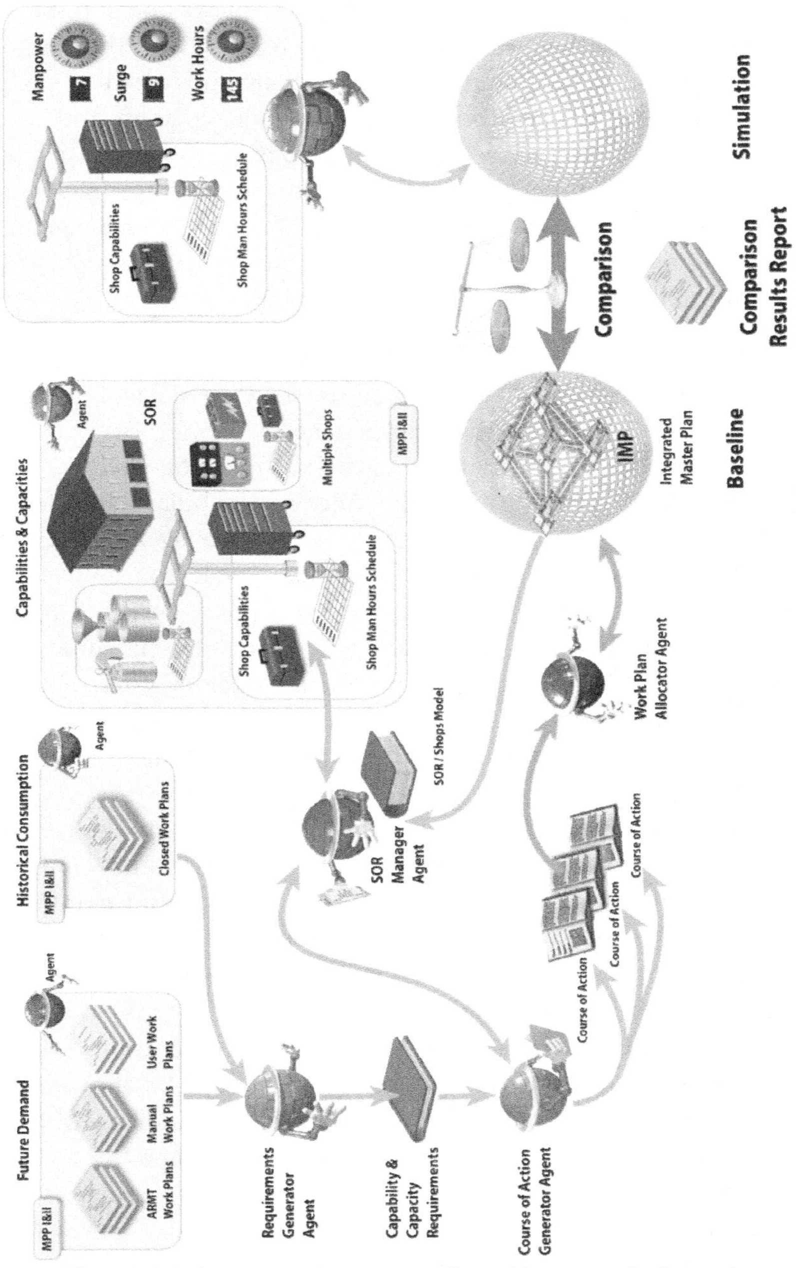


Figure 8.8 Army MPP process flow (Cougaar Software)

- *Supply chains and logistics:* Today's supply networks need to be flexible, responsive, adaptive, and able to cope with the variability of demand. Traditional supply chain and logistics optimization systems are not designed to handle volatility and complexity or to function in a real-time environment. Using an agent-based approach is now a common solution for many companies. Software vendors include Magenta (www.magenta-technology.com), Cougaar Software (cougaarsoftware.com), and Intelligent Automation (www.i-a-i.com).

## Architectures, Ontologies, and Agents

In addition to specific applications, software developers must address current architectural approaches. A brief overview of those particularly appropriate for agents are described below.

*Ontologies:* Agents require a common vocabulary and set of concepts to communicate effectively with other agents (See Appendix B for more information regarding agent communication languages). Cybele (www.cybelepro.com) and Cougaar (www.cougaar.org) have been adapted to use the semantic web language (OWL), the semantic web rule language (SWRL), and the services ontology (OWL-S) for the specification of agent systems. In addition, agents can be used to manage and maintain large distributed ontologies.

*Peer-to-peer (P2P)* – P2P applications display agent-like characteristics that include both applying self-organization techniques that ensure continuous operation of the network, and employing interaction protocol designs to enforce correct behavior among interacting nodes. For example, commercial e-marketplace systems like eBay include simple credit-reputation systems to reward socially beneficial behavior. As P2P systems become more complex, increasing the use of agent technologies will be appropriate. For example, the auction-based mechanisms and negotiation techniques used by agents could be used to enhance the level of automation of peers in popular applications. Since complex P2P applications are "social" in nature, they will require increasingly sophisticated approaches both to trust and reputation and to the application of social norms, rules, and structures. Social simulation would be particularly appropriate here to better understand the population dynamics of independent agents. [7]

*Web Services (WS) and Service Oriented Architectures (SOA):* Agents can be used to support WS and SOA in many places. For example, Verizon chose a decentralized agent-based approach to SOA, rather than a centralized approach where all services are handled by a server or a central set of servers. Additionally, they employ agents to support the subscription, management, and dashboard layers of their SOA, using their IT Workbench software. By the end of 2004, Verizon was handling nearly three million service transactions per day.

Another goal of companies like Verizon is not only to reduce redundancies by building reusable services, but to put the services together to create more sophisticated and valuable services. *Service composition* aggregates services to create new functionality. Often, the composed functionality would itself be exposed as a new service with a standard interface. If this happens, a new service could be composed that would intelligently guide the service requester throughout the lifetime of a particular business process. Such an intelligent service could be implemented as an agent. The W3C Web Services Architecture study [6] recommends an agent-based approach to using service-oriented architectures—both on the service-requestor side and the service-provider side. Such an approach is not necessary or useful for simple services. However, an agent-based approach is useful when the services and their interactions require an active computational entity that: (i) has a persistent identity, (ii) can perceive, reason about, and initiate in its environment, and (iii) can communicate with other agents, including humans.

Agents act with varying levels of autonomy, depending on environmental constraints and their ongoing interactions. Because services are often best modeled as autonomous and heterogeneous, they can naturally be associated with agents. Agents make it possible to capture the interactions among services and the creation of new services as subtle compositions of others. Agents are not a panacea. However, applying agents in the appropriate places within applications and systems enables us quite naturally to (i) capture deeper constraints on what services are willing to offer, thereby capturing richer requirements for service composition, (ii) discover trustworthy services, (iii) negotiate with external service providers, and evaluate the compliance of service providers within their contracts. They can also provide a more natural, human-like way of interacting with service requesters, as well as ensuring the entire process is carried out effectively and efficiently. [8]

*Business Process Management (BPM)* – BPM has come to mean an integrated collection of critical process technology necessary to support the business process life cycle. (Also called the BPM suite.) The actual business process logic can be centralized in one location, as opposed to being distributed across and embedded within multiple services. However, as illustrated in Figure 8.9, multiple business processes can be used to satisfy the service. For example, to request a product's price, the computation could vary depending on the location of order, time and date ordered, quantity, customer, and other items in the same order. To enable this, BPM agents contain the rules that determine which process should be invoked and under which condition.

Figure 8.9 Services can be carried out by many different business processes depending on business conditions and rules.

The DHL pricing system had nearly 500 different processes for pricing an order because of the number and combination of variables. To handle this, DHL used agents to choose the appropriate process. In other words, each agent contained a process-execution engine that would select and execute the appropriate process for each pricing-query service request. Furthermore, if a problem arose in the middle of a process, the agent would select an alternate process. DHL found that using an agent-based approach not only executed the process faster, but the process was easier to change. Changes to a process or process rule (such as adding a fuel surcharge) would take hours rather than weeks. The software they used employed a graphic editor based on UML activity diagrams, so that even a user could change the process. Again, agents are not always appropriate for controlling business process logic. If the process is simple, straightforward, and does not require frequent changes and processing robustness, a simple rules-based language could be used. However, for complex processes that involve various operating conditions and require frequent and timely changes, agents should be used.

*Event-driven architectures (EDA):* Real-time response is often critical to customer satisfaction. Abnormal events or a combination of events can have a significant impact on an organization. More and more companies (such as Cougaar Software and Tibco) are using agents along with software and physical sensors to detect changes in the business environment. (Examples include RFID tags for retail supply-chain optimization, medical monitors, physical sensors that detect changes in air quality, and electronic data-capture tools for patient trials at pharmaceutical companies.) Companies that derive the greatest advantages from agent-based, event-driven architectures have these characteristics: (i) large and heterogeneous environments, (ii) information that changes constantly in a variety of ways, (iii) complex exceptions and state changes in real-time, and (iv) the need to deliver and respond appropriately to that information.

Business communications are numerous and often complex. One communication could be monitored by thousands, and then filtered, analyzed, and aggregated with other communications – which in turn can become noteworthy events for others, and so on. As this continues to grow in size and complexity, our ability to understand, analyze, and control can quickly go beyond the abilities of conventional technology. Here is where agents can step in.

For example, Figure 8.10 from Roy Schulte (Gartner) is a token representation of a complex event processing (CEP) environment. On the left, you can see an event processing agent (EPA) receiving two events. As a result of these two events, the EPA may determine that another event should (or should not) occur. For instance, a Buy and Sell event for a particular customer's stock might have occurred. If the Sell event occurred prior to the Buy, a trading-error event could be generated. This event might be one of three events that another EPA was monitoring, resulting in another event. Which, in turn, are monitored by another EPA, resulting in one of perhaps two events, depending on results of its analysis.

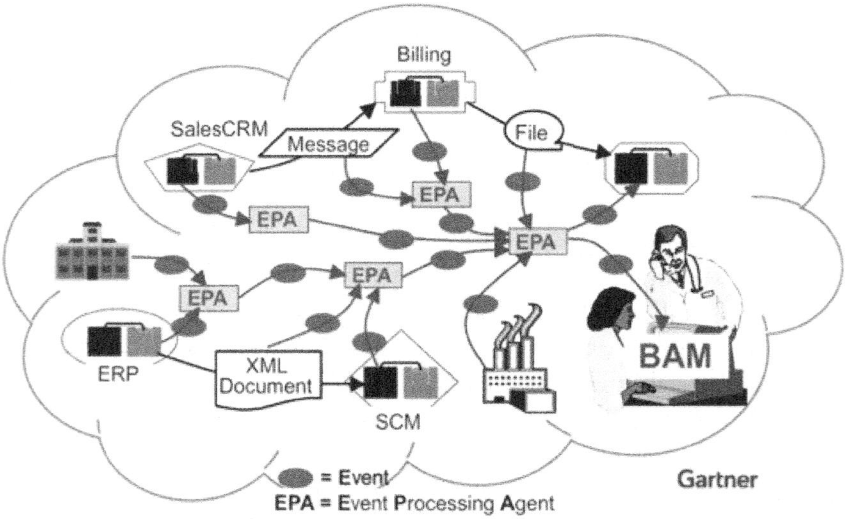


Figure 8.10 Complex Event Processing (CEP) using event-based producers, processing agents, and consumers (based on [15])

## So, Why Use Agents?

Why not use a large brain-like approach that would solve the event processing centrally, such as using an expert system or neural network? You could — up to a point. However, when your

CEP starts requiring thousands of rules to be processed, maintaining a single expert system would quickly become unwieldy to maintain and test. So, another approach is to divide the expert systems into smaller, manageable—yet federated—expert systems. This would be tangible for up to a dozen or so expert systems, but what happens then? Would you understand and manage them? If your expert systems each had a particular business-based theme, you might be able to manage them because there would be some rhyme or reason for the rule grouping. The result, then, is a set of smaller, yet federated, set of event-processing business-organized "brains." But again, as each expert system becomes too large, it too must be partitioned into multiple, business-based, smaller ones.

So, where does this all stop? As an organization expands or changes, this constant divide-and-conquer approach will not stop. The agent approach, then, offers a more sane alternative. Start with small business-based units to begin with and then you may continue to add and expand as the need arises. Agent-oriented extensions to BPM systems have the inherent ability to grow.

Agents are autonomous and interactive entities that are defined on the basis of a specific need. They can play multiple roles, can learn, and evolve if need be. They behave socially and can self-organize. In other words, they are adaptable so that they can service specialized needs and communicate with others. Just like social beings, each has the ability to understand, analyze, and control its specific niche.

Agents, then, are a way to divide and conquer the problem, much as humans (and other organisms) do. It's still software, but it's modularized based on a business-based need and can be thought of as small-grained "intelligent objects." They can mimic social configurations and interactions and can scale and perform as an organization. Leveraging agents in this manner, then, enables event processing that is concurrent and distributed. Does this sound like the living, breathing world around us? It should. This is why agent-based applications are able to better manage complex systems and be adaptable.

So, what is the relationship between agents and events? Agents enable event-processing networks to scale in size and complexity—and be designed in a more human-understandable manner. Agents can be used for monitoring, filtering, analyzing, and aggregating events and notifying other agents. As Paul Vincent indicated in his blog, agents can also be used within CEP middleware.

## SOA, BPM, and EDA

These last three architectural approaches can be considered separately for including agent technology. Additionally, agent technology can be used to link business processes and services to facilitate a single architecture that integrates SOA, BPM, and EDA, as illustrated in Figure 8.11.

Figure 8.11 Agents can be used to integrate SOA, BPM, and EDA.

## The Bottom Line

The list above provides a sampling of uses for agent-based systems happening now within the business community. The underlying question, though, is why did these companies decide to use agent technology? Adopting any new technology is disruptive. As stated in the previous chapter, the reasons that agents were chosen by these early-adopter companies include one or more of the following benefits:

- Faster return on investment (ROI)

- Lower maintenance
- Higher productivity
- Leverage of existing infrastructure
- Reuse of processes and services
- Provides foundation for future projects
- Reduces time to market
- Increased agility to respond to business needs
- Enabled an organization to use and provide services and resources in ways that were not previously possible

In the coming chapters, this book will provide more insight into what agents are and how they can be used. It is one thing to say that agents can provide a helpful, distributive approach to software and hardware applications; it is another to understand what that means and entails.

## References

[1] Resnick, Mitchell, Turtles, Termites, and Traffic Jams: Explorations in Massively Parallel Microworlds, MIT Press, Cambridge, MA, 1994

[2] Bonabeau, Eric, Marco Dorigo and Guy Theraulaz, *Swarm Intelligence: From Natural to Artificial Systems*, Oxford University Press, New York, 1999. (StarLogo software available from http://education.mit.edu/starlogo/)

[3] Schoonderwoerd, R., Holland, O., Bruten, J. and Rothkrantz, L., 1996: "Ant-based Load Balancing in Telecommunications Networks," *Adaptive Behavior*, vol.5, No.2, .

[4] Christopher Meyer (ed.). *Embracing Complexity: Exploring the Application of Complex Adaptive Systems to Business,* 1996 Colloquium on the Business Application of Complexity Science, Ernest & Young Center for Business Innovation, July 17-19, 1996.

[5] Baker, Albert, Parunak, H. Van Dyke, and Erol, Kutluhan, "Agents and the Internet: Infrastructure for Mass Customization," *IEEE Internet Computing*, Vol. 3, No. 5, September, 1999.

[6] W3C, "Web Services Architecture," W3C Working Group

Note, 11 February, 2004. (Downloadable from W3C at http://www.w3.org/TR/2004/NOTE-ws-arch-20040211/)

[7] Luck, Michael, Peter McBurney, Onn Shehory and Steve Willmott, *Agent Technology Roadmap: A Roadmap for Agent-Based Computing*, report for AgentLink III, September, 2005.

[8] Singh, Munindar P. and Michael N. Huhns, *Service-Oriented Computing: Semantics, Processes, Agents*, John Wiley, Chichester, UK, 2005.

[9] Wikipedia page on Agent-Based Model. http://en.wikipedia.org/wiki/Agent-based_model

[10] StarLogo: a programmable modeling environment for exploring the workings of decentralized systems—systems that are organized without an organizer, coordinated without a coordinator. With StarLogo, you can model (and gain insights into) many real-life phenomena, such as bird flocks, traffic jams, ant colonies, and market economies. education.mit.edu/starlogo/

[11] NetLogo: - a multiagent programmable modeling environment. It is used by tens of thousands of students, teachers and researchers worldwide. You can download it free of charge. ccl.northwestern.edu/netlogo/

[12] Galán, José Manuel, Luis R. Izquierdo, Segismundo S. Izquierdo, José Ignacio Santos, Ricardo del Olmo, Adolfo López-Paredes and Bruce Edmonds, "Errors and Artefacts in Agent-Based Modelling," *Journal of Artificial Societies and Social Simulation* vol. 12, no. 1 1, 2009. jasss.soc.surrey.ac.uk/12/1/1.html

[13] Bonabeau, Eric, "Agent-based modeling: Methods and techniques for simulating human systems," PNAS May 14, 2002 vol. 99 no. Suppl 3, 7280-7287, 2002. www.pnas.org/content/99/suppl.3/7280.full

[14] Wooldridge, Michael, *An Introduction to MultiAgent Systems*, John Wiley & Sons Ltd, 2002.

[15] Roy Schulte, Event-Driven Architecture: The Next Big Thing, Gartner, paper presented to Application Integration & Web Services Summit 2004, Los Angeles, CA 17-19 May 2004.

# 9. Organization and Coordination of Work

Human organizations exist primarily to coordinate the actions of many individuals for some purpose. That purpose could be to create such structures as profitable business units, charitable organizations, ballet companies, or Little Leagues. Using human organizations as an analogy, we will now explore systems involving many agents whose coordination benefits from the same human patterns.

## Coordination

*Coordination* – the combination of agents or functions to act together harmoniously. [OED]

Common agent applications that involve coordination include supply chains, scheduling, vehicle planning, problem solving, contract negotiation, and product design. Without some degree of coordination, such systems could not be possible—in either human-based or agent-based systems.

Furthermore, the analogy requires that we consider a heterogeneous population of agents. Human organizations are not constructed with a population of identical individuals doing the same thing. Instead, we diversify, delegate, negotiate, manage, cooperate, compete, and so on. The same approach needs to be employed in agent-based systems. Careful consideration in the design and structure of these systems will increase the likelihood that agents will be coherent in their behavior. While this limits and controls agent spontaneity, it still preserves agent-level flexibility.

## Agent Communities

One of the most difficult challenges for automated systems is designing and constructing large-scale systems. Here, life-as-an-analogy brings with it many useful concepts, including some excellent examples on how to scale up. In the physical systems leading up to life, for example, subatomic particles form atoms, and atoms cluster to become molecules in solid, liquid, and gaseous form. Continuing up this hierarchy, molecules can be organized to form organelles and cells, cells can aggregate to form organisms, and so on. In other words, living systems and their components emerge in a hierarchy of interlocking mechanisms.

If such an emergent approach works in nature, it can also provide a good model for developing agents and agent-based systems. For example, Figure 9.1 depicts the classical biologic cell structure known as a *eukaryote*. Notice that the eukaryotic cell consists of many interacting components. The mitochondria, for example, is a cell in its own right. It is also an important energy source for the cell that contains it. Mitochondria, then, provide a good example of an agent inside of an agent, where the whole depends upon the parts for its functioning.

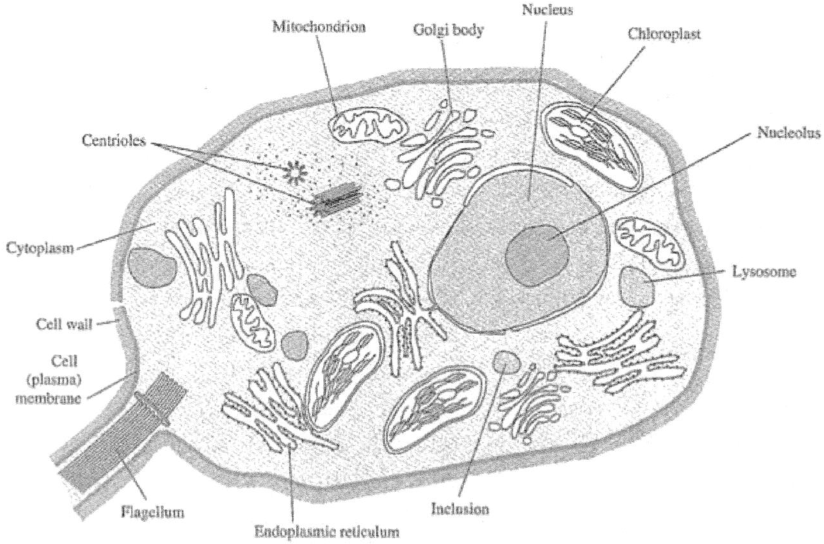


Figure 9.1 Eukaryotic cells provide a good example of composite agents and forming a community group.

To live and maintain life, eukaryotic cells do not consist of just any matter inside its membrane. To function properly, the eukaryote needs certain roles to be played by the internal components. For example, every eukaryote needs a component that provides energy. Mitochondria play that role. Maintaining the cell's shape and size is enabled by the cytoskeleton, and protein transport is provided by the endoplasmic reticulum.

Furthermore depending on the kind of eukaryote, chloroplast can play the role that converts solar energy to organic compounds and oxygen, flagella and cilia provide a means of locomotion; multi-role heliozoans with their many stiff, microtubule-supported projections are used for capturing food, sensation, movement, and attachment. In short, eukaryotes contain a number of components—all which play important roles in defining the cell's organization and existence. Some roles can be played by multiple components; some components can play multiple roles.

In reality, Nature has no construct called *role*—it is a human concept. We use the notion because it is useful to group certain capabilities that can be thought of as a unit, independently of any entity that actually ends up playing the role. For example, the roles of customer or supplier exist independently of any entity filling them, because the set of behavior involved in being a customer or a supplier is important to the success of a business. Roles, then, provide an intuitive mechanism for modularity, flexibility, reusability, modifiability, and extensibility.

Agents not only play roles, they can be grouped to form variable structures. These communities can be colonial in nature (such as sponges and coral reefs) or multi-cellular animals (such as dinosaurs and humans). Agents that adhere to one another can behave in a unified manner and still maintain their own autonomy. Automated agents might choose to group for various reasons, such as protection, resources, or improvement. In other words, the agents might decide that they are better off together than apart. Furthermore, the agents may adapt to serve the community as a whole.

## Roles

Agents in a multiagent system may have been designed and implemented by different parties, each with different assumptions and goals. Although these agents may not share the same goals, they may need to interact to achieve the preferred results. In more constrained applications, all decisions can be hardwired into the agent at design time. However, the more adaptive a system is, the more its agents must be capable of coordinating dynamically at runtime. This latter aspect is what makes the agent approach more effective and efficient than conventional software development.

## Using Roles

In the ant colony example, all the agents were of the same type. They were uniform because each had the same goals and the same programming. Even the ant-swarming example was constructed with uniform agents. So, building an effective agent-based system is possible using a uniform agent architecture (Figure 9.2).

Figure 9.2 Uniform agent architecture

However, one agent *could* be constructed that does everything (as mentioned earlier). Unfortunately, these "fat" agents represent a bottleneck for speed, reliability, maintenance, and so on. Dividing functionality among many agents provides modularity, flexibility, reusability, modifiability, and extensibility. Furthermore, specialized knowledge is not often available from a single agent. Knowledge that is spread over various agents can be integrated for a more complete view when needed (as we will see in the coming sections titled Task Sharing and Result Sharing). In other words, a multiagent system is typically designed using various roles.

> A *role* is a defined set of behavioral capabilities and other features that an entity can possess.

## Facilitator Roles

One of the most common roles used in agent systems is the

*facilitator* role. A facilitator functions as a middleman, by distributing and coordinating resources among a number of client agents (Figure 9.3).

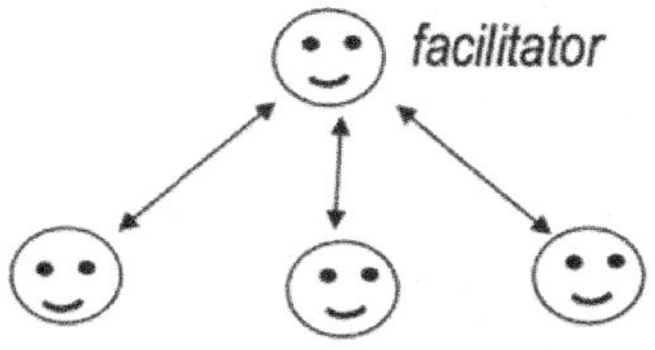


Figure 9.3 Facilitated architecture

The facilitator can be used for most applications and possesses a number of services and domain-independent strategies for coordinating resources. Figure 9.4 depicts five facilitator-related roles commonly used along with their interaction protocols: the subscriber, broker, recruiter, matchmaker, and broadcaster roles.

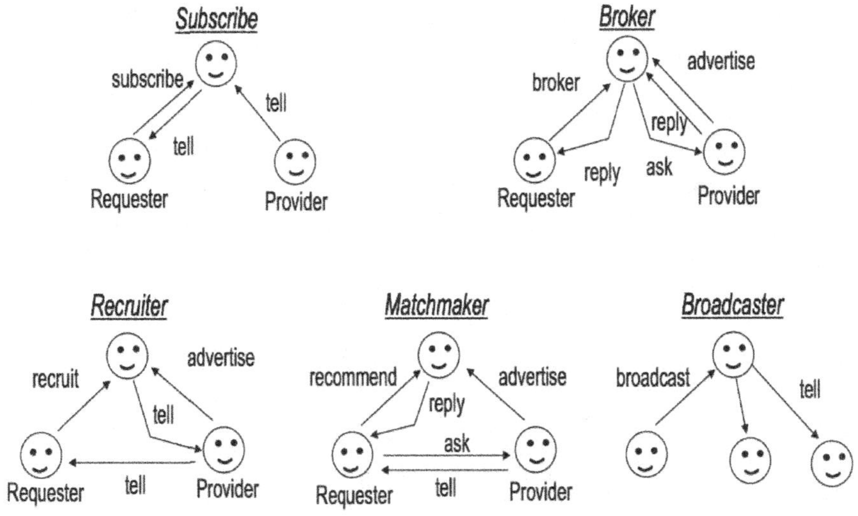


Figure 9.4 Facilitation roles and their interaction protocols.

A *subscribe* agent receives a SUBSCRIBE request communication from a requestor who wishes to receive messages on a particular topic. Anytime a provider agent sends ("tells") a communication to the facilitator that fits the subscriber's topic, the subscribe facilitator passes on the communication to the requester.

A *broker* agent receives both broker communications from requesters and advertise communications from providers. When the facilitator finds a match, it notifies the requestor directly. The *recruiter* is similar to the broker, except that it notifies the provider who contacts the requestor directly.

The *matchmaker* works in much the same way as the broker and recruiter by putting together, or matching, agents that can work together. Once this match is made, the requester and provider agents can communicate with each other directly without depending on the matchmaker.

In the *broadcaster* protocol in Figure 9.4, an agent requests the facilitator to broadcast a message to a number of agents.

Facilitator agents can apply whatever "intelligence" they possess (e.g., neural networks, learning, planning, rules) to help them make key decisions. Their source of provider agents can come from their direct knowledge or via agent directories that use extended forms of UDDI.

## Roles, in General

Roles identify activities and services necessary to achieve objectives that enable the coordination of an agent-based system. Just as roles appear in nature—particularly in human-based organizations (Figure 9.5)—employing roles for the "society" of agents is also useful.

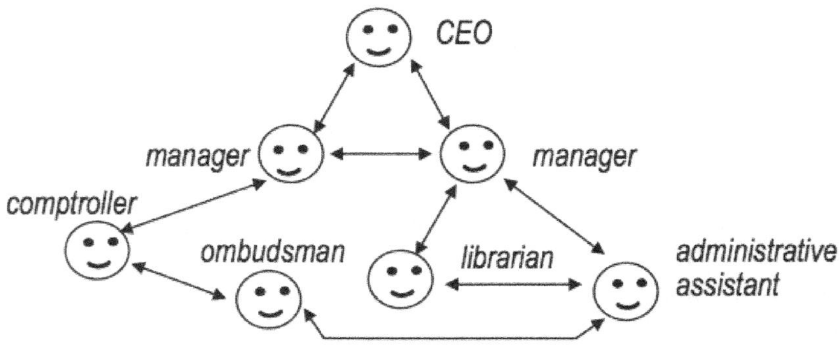


Figure 9.5 Specialized architecture

For example, a *manager* agent could coordinate a series of activities in a complex business process management (BPM) system. The manager agents could themselves take their strategic directions and goals from a "higher" agent—with a hierarchy all the way up to a conceptual top-level agent, much like a CEO. *Librarian* agents could both maintain "libraries" of information and provide a facilitation role for agents requesting information.

Specialized roles can be used for two different purposes. First, agents can be defined that correspond to actual roles in a human organization. Here, the agent enables the various role-based services that are permitted and required for a given organizational role. When such role-based interfaces need to be adaptive and autonomous, agents provide a good implementation mechanism.

The second usage is to provide a technique for defining, organizing, and reusing common groups of structure behavior. In object orientation, the *class* provided this function. Since agents are perceived more dynamically—even to the point of developing agent social systems *within* traditional business systems—the notion of *role* is more familiar to the humans who analyze and design such systems. In other words, roles are a familiar metaphor for humans to organize the active entities in their world. Roles and classes can be used for agents—where the agents can be software, hardware, or human.

For an in-depth explanation of role activity theory and role activity diagramming, especially as they relate to process management, see Figure 9.6.

and

Figure 9.6 Role Activity Theory and Diagramming

## Communities as Social Structures

Imagine unleashing thousands or millions of agents in a system. Would it be reasonable to expect all these individuals to coordinate in some manner? In ant colonies and bird flocks, this seems to work very effectively. For building cities, transportation infrastructures, and large companies, this will not work. Instead, agents and roles need to be grouped in some manner. From organization theory, we know that *community* structures [2] can be defined that organize employees and employee roles in ways that can maximize cohesion and minimize coupling. (Also mentioned in the Community-based Interface section of Chapter 5.) Communities can be seen as active components or modules that have their own internal processing and can interact with other communities. In human society communities can be defined for alliances, teams, coalitions, conventions, markets, and organization units.

Furthermore, each community *itself* can become an agent. For example, IBM, HP, the United Nations, the Yankees baseball team, and the US Supreme Court are all communities that are recognized agents in their own right—which also consist of agents that are communities, and so on down to "atomic" level agents. In this way, the Requester or Provider (in Figure 9.4, above) could be an atomic agent or a legally recognized organization like Daimler-Chrysler that is requesting bids from Provider companies. Yes, a person in each of these organizations might actually process the bid, but such knowledge is unnecessary. In this way, communities as social structures reduce the danger of combinatorial explosion of agent interaction. Instead, they provide a structured scheme for focusing and enhancing the coordination of agent activities, making richer, more complex structures possible—while hiding unnecessary details. In short, they enable a scalability technique for large populations to produce significant deliverables. The case study in Chapter 10 describes how this technique can be used in a large manufacturer—that literally is designed using structures called *manufacturing cells.*

Figure 9.7 depicts several grouping options. The first option, of course, is that there is no community. The second option is that two or more agents can group as a single unit community. The containment boundary indicates that the entire construct can be treated as an agent in its own right. In option 1, the agent and the boundary are the same. In option 2, the boundary can be treated as an agent separate from the two agents it contains. The term *boundary* is chosen because it also provides an interface barrier much like that of a cell membrane. Agents *on* the membrane (as in option 2) are still accessible from the outside as individuals while benefiting from the proximity to chosen neighbors. In contrast, agents that are contained completely *within* the boundary, as illustrated in option 3, are encapsulated. Only those agents on or immediately within a boundary may communicate with encapsulated agents. In a complex community configuration (option 4), the nesting continues.

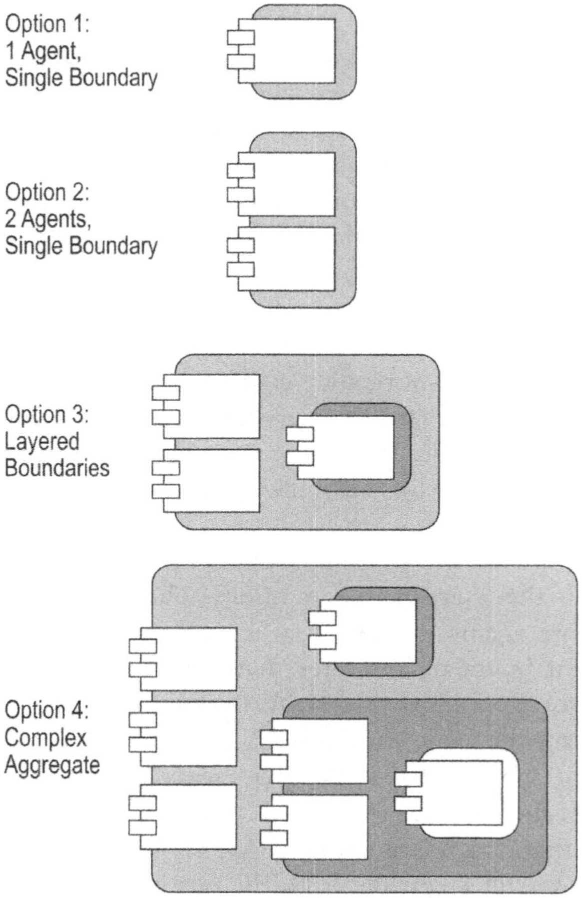


Figure 9.7 Agent grouping approaches that form communities [1]

## Agreement

### Reaching Agreements

In human society, individuals and organizations often have differing viewpoints and interests, and we use various techniques for reaching agreements. If we use software agents to represent us in marketplaces, web services, and other automated situations, some of these same techniques can be used. For example, a manufacturer may be running low on a particular part and sends out a notification to its suppliers. The suppliers send in their bids, and the manufacturer can then choose among the suppliers. With an agent-based software system in place, this kind of activity can occur among software agents, instead of human ones.

Software and hardware agents do not need to represent individuals or organizations to use this approach, they can represent themselves or other entities, as well. The Painting Trucks at General Motors' example in Chapter 8 or the manufacturing cells described in the case study of Chapter 10 are both examples of this. Service-oriented architectures could include software agents that select service providers based on auction-related techniques. Techniques such as auction, negotiation, and deliberation are the most commonly employed by agent-based systems.

**Auctions**

Prior to the Internet and the Web, auctions were relatively rare in everyday life. Now, individuals and businesses can participate in auctions at a very low cost with one of the best examples being eBay. Besides being inexpensive, auctions are popular because they have simple and well-defined interaction protocols. This also means that auctions are easy to automate, making them a good technique for automated agents.

Auctions take place between an *auctioneer* agent and a group of *bidder* agents. The auctioneer's purpose is to allocate an auctioned item to one of the bidders. The auctioneer tries to maximize the price, while the bidder tries to minimize it. The actual auction process can have several variations.

- *English auction:* This is the most common form where the auctioneer might start out with a minimum price. Bids are then invited from agents, where each must offer a higher bid than the previous bidder. Eventually, the auction item is awarded to the agent with the highest bid.
- *Dutch auction:* The Dutch flower auction was the inspiration for this form. Here, the auctioneer starts with a high price and then lowers it until a bidder accepts the price. The auction item is awarded to the agent with the first bid.

- *Single-round auction:* Each agent bids only once in this sealed-bid auction. The agent with the highest bid is the winner. This option has two variations: one where the winner pays the amount they bid, and the Vickrey variation where the highest bidder actually pays the second-highest bid amount for the auctioned item. The Vickrey auction is unusual and unintuitive but is found to encourage bidding the true valuation.

Other auctions exist, as well. For example, the reputation-based single-round auction may not award the auctioned item to the highest bidder, if the second- or third-highest bidder has a close bid on a better reputation. Another variant is the eBay auction that uses an English auction but can offer an additional approach that bypasses further bidding to the first bidder that offers to pay a predetermined "buy it now" price.

### Negotiation

*Negotiation* is a process by which two or more parties can reach an agreement, each attempting to achieve different goals. A common example is the simplified contract negotiation, illustrated in Figure 9.8, where a requester agent sends out invitations to bid on a job contract. If a provider agent wishes to participate in the negotiation, it can respond with a bid.

Because many provider agents might respond, the requester agent has to decide which provider should be awarded the contract. Once the contract has been sent to the provider, the provider can choose to confirm. If the provider declines, the requester must choose another provider. This pattern could support various negotiation scenarios, such as ordering supplies, requesting equipment, or obtaining human resources.

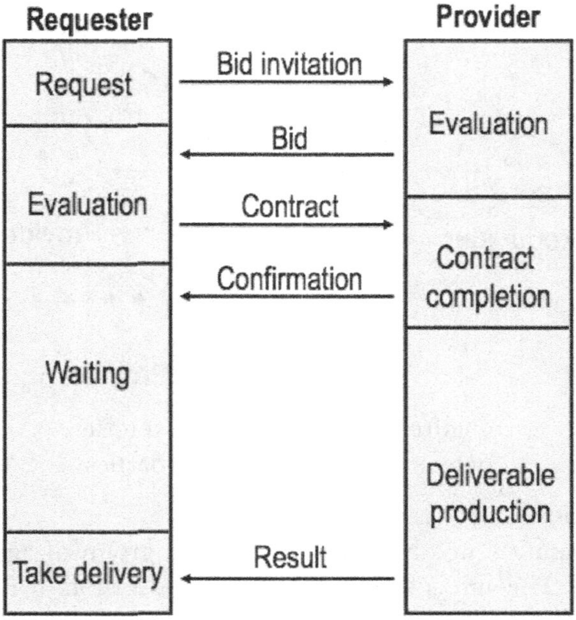


Figure 9.8 Agent interaction protocol for contract negotiation.

Common variants to the contract interaction protocol can include:

- Bidding can invite a single bid or multiple bids. Awarding a bidder in multiple bidding negotiations brings in one of those auction variations mentioned above.
- Contracts can be awarded to zero, one, or many providers.
- Bidding processes can be interactive, open, secretive, etc.
- The contract process can have its own sub-negotiation and counter offers.
- Contracts can specify penalties—and either party in the contract may choose to violate their contracts by weighing costs and benefits.
- Intermediate negotiation brokers can be used, as illustrated in Figure 9.9. This offers centralization of a specialized agent, when there is a way or need to do so.

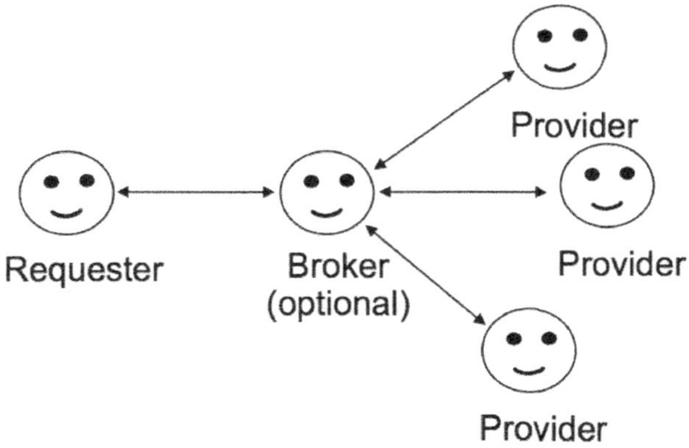


Figure 9.9 A negotiation exercise between two equal sets of parties.

**Deliberation**

Deliberation involves deciding what a group of agents wants to achieve. The aim is to jointly arrive at a decision or form a plan of action that may or may not be initiated from a conflict. Decisions could be made by a "judge" agent that takes into account arguments presented by various agents. This could be performed by software mechanisms such as rules engines and neural networks.

Democratic means is another technique, where a simple or some form of "super" majority vote determines the outcome. Majority can also be determined by other factors that include weighting of a vote. For example, the votes of some agents might have a higher valuation than others, due to a number of factors such as importance, credibility, and so on. An automated delivery system could determine the next location in a delivery through agent voting, or though some sort of auction.

**Others Ways of Reaching Agreement**

Auction, negotiation, and deliberation are the primary techniques currently employed for software agents to reach agreement. Researchers are working on others that are inspired by nature such as argumentation, intimidation, bribing, and brute force. While these approaches may not enter into commercial systems in the near future, agent system designers need to consider both existing and novel techniques.

## Beyond Coordination

This chapter has discussed coordination as a property of agent systems performing activities in a shared environment. As designers of agent-based systems, we want the combination of agents or functions to act together harmoniously. The degree of coordination, then, is the extent to which the agents: avoid extraneous activity, reduce contention, avoid deadlocks and livelocks, maintain applicable security, and maintain quality of service.

To further aid in accomplishing this, extended forms of coordination are possible [2]:

- *Cooperation:* the process whereby agents coordinate their actions to achieve a common purpose. For example, most organizations are cooperative, because each organization defines its particular goals. This suggests: non-antagonistic agents, sociability, and goal sharing. Cooperation is coordination, but not necessarily the other way around.
- *Competition/contention:* The act of agents that coordinates their actions where the success of one agent implies the failure of others. For example, agents that participate in negotiations or auctions are competitive. Such agents can be antagonistic agents, yet still perform activities in a shared environment.
- *Coherence:* The behavior of agents that align with system-level goals.

## Policies

In our every day lives, our actions are subject to norms and social laws that provide a means for regulating social behavior. A *policy* is a constraint on the behavior of agents as they perform actions or access resources. In short, they are "business rules" for agents.

Various kinds of policies exist. Some relate to accessing resources in particular ways, others relate more generally to the allowable actions agents may perform, both as provider agents and as requester agents. For IT, they are particularly important for security and quality of service. Security is fundamentally about constraints on the behavior of an action and on accessing resources. Similarly, quality of service is also about constraints on service.

Two of the kinds of policies that are commonly employed include: permissions and obligations.

- A *permission* is a kind of policy that defines the allowed actions and states of an agent and/or resource. An example of a permission policy would be: every Order must have at least one line item and may not have a negative total charge. Such a rule is common in database systems. It also applies to agents because it constrains how an order-placing service must behave.

  Related to permissions are prohibitions. A prohibition is a policy that can be thought of as the opposite of a permission. It specifies what may not be done.
- An *obligation* requires an agent to perform particular actions or be in particular states. That is, when an agent has an obligation to perform some action, it is required to do so. For instance, when a customer agent and a supplier agent have made a contract, they have mutual obligations. The supplier has an obligation to deliver a specific commodity on an agreed-upon date; the customer has an obligation to pay for the commodity if delivered as agreed. Not all obligations relate to actions. For example, an agent providing a service may have an obligation to maintain a certain state of readiness. Quality-of-service policies are often expressed in terms of obligations.

Closely associated with policies are the mechanisms for establishing policies and enforcing them. Permission-related polices can be enforced proactively. Obligations, by their nature, cannot be proactively enforced though they can be monitored. Agents that violate their obligations can be subject to retribution mechanisms.

## Problem Solving and Distributed Problem Solving

As seen above, roles and interaction protocols provide basic building blocks that enable agents to coordinate. By themselves, they can be used to solve simple problems. When an application becomes more complex, however, other techniques can be employed on top of these basic building blocks. For example, one Order Processing agent can be built to handle an entire order-processing activity by itself. In a more effective approach for complex orders, the Order Processing agents would delegate some of the Order Processing activity to other roles. Or in another example, one agent could be designed to handle a massive database search or solve a large problem. A more efficient approach might decompose the problem into smaller parts and to have multiple agents find solutions concurrently.

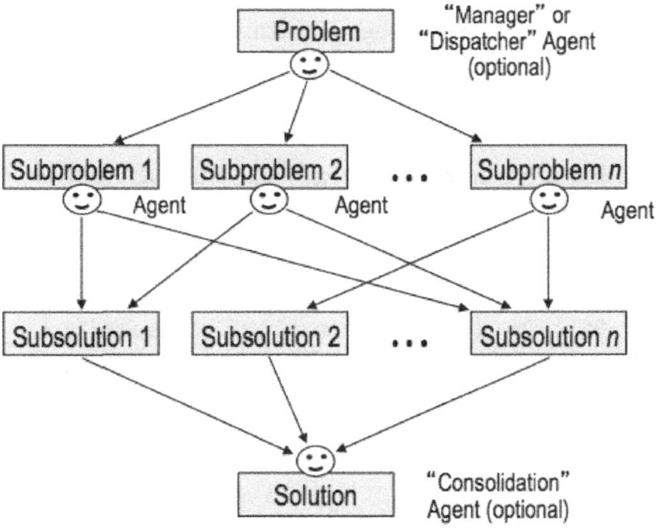


Figure 9.10 Solving problems using multiple agents.

When using agents, this divide-and-conquer approach to solving difficult problems is often appropriate (Figure 9.10). Conceptually, problem solving can be viewed as a three-stage activity:

1. Division of a problem into subproblems – In this step, a problem is decomposed into smaller subproblems. Determination and assignment of subproblems can be done by a manager agent or by each agent individually.
2. Solution of the subproblems – Here, each subproblem is individually solved. One or more agents can produce solutions to

the same (and multiple) problem—which can conflict. The agents might communicate to solve problems or resolve solutions.

3. Combination of the subsolutions – Solutions to the individual subproblems are integrated into an overall solution. This integration can be performed by each agent or by a consolidation agent.

Grid applications or large database searches are obvious applications for such a problem-solving approach. Business process management (BPM) is another application for this approach. The order processing activity in Figure 9.11 provides a good example of this. One activity (or component) could be constructed to implement all actions within this process. However, other receivables and payables services might already exist in different locations—and most probably different organizations.

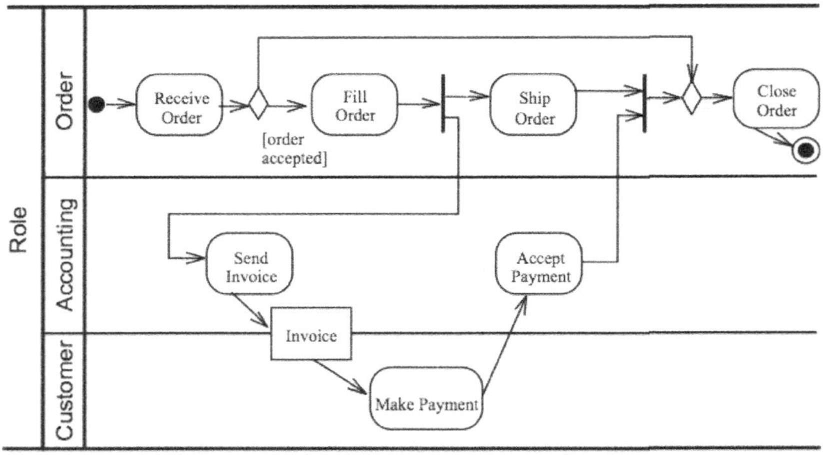


Figure 9.11 Activities as task sharing among roles.

In reality, an Order agent would instead delegate some or all of the actions to other agents playing other roles. This "delegation" could be hard wired or requested at runtime using a *service-oriented* approach. When this approach is used, the Order agent would become the service requester and the supporting agents would become the service providers. Finding appropriate service providers could be accomplished by using directory services, service broker agents, auction interaction protocols, and so on. If the service providers are few and well known (or even hard wired), an agent-based approach may not be necessary. However, for a complex environment requiring adaptive solutions, the agent-based approach is the only viable solution.

## Conclusion

Imagine unleashing thousands or millions of agents in a system. Would it be reasonable to expect all these individuals to coordinate in some manner? In ant colonies and bird flocks, this seems to work very effectively. For building cities, transportation infrastructures, and large companies, this will not work. Instead, agents and roles need to be organized into communities in some manner. From organization theory, we know that organizational structures can be defined to include roles that have processing capabilities that can—to put it in IT terms—maximize cohesion and minimize coupling. Communities can be seen as active components or modules that have their own internal processing and can interact with other communities. In human society, communities can be defined for alliances, teams, coalitions, conventions, markets, and organizational units.

Furthermore, these communities *themselves* can become agents. For example, IBM, HP, the United Nations, the Yankees baseball team, and the US Supreme Court are all communities that are recognized agents in their own right—which also consist of agents that are communities, and so on down to "atomic" level agents. In this way, a Consumer or Provider could be an atomic agent or a legally recognized organization like DaimlerChrysler that is requesting bids from Provider companies. A person in each of these organizations might actually process the bid, but such knowledge is unnecessary. In this way, communities as social structures reduce the danger of combinatorial explosion of agent interaction. Instead, they provide a structured scheme for focusing and enhancing the coordination of agent activities, making richer, more complex structures possible—while hiding unnecessary details. In short, they enable scalability technique for large populations to produce significant deliverables.

## References

[1] Coveney, Peter, and Roger Highfield, *Frontiers of Complexity: The Search for Order in a Chaotic World*, Fawcett Columbine, New York, 1995.

[2] Parunak, H. Van Dyke, Sven Brueckner, Mitchell Fleischer, and James Odell, "A Design Taxonomy of Multi-Agent Interactions," *Agent-Oriented Software Engineering (AOSE) IV*, Paolo Giorgini *et al.* ed., Springer-Verlag, Berlin, 2004, pp. 123.

[3] OMG, Agent Metamodel and Profile (AMP) – Initial Submission, 2009, OMG document ad/2009–08–04, http://tinyurl.com/k6t69nb.

# 10. Agent-based Manufacturing, a Case Study

This case study describes how agent-based technology can be applied in business applications. While the example is for an automotive company, the general concepts are applicable to many other industries.

## Introduction

In traditional manufacturing, information systems mimic organizational structures, utilizing a top-down, command-and-control structure. Communicating decisions and information down through the organization is time consuming—making it impossible to respond and adapt quickly to external forces.

Furthermore, traditional manufacturing relies on schedules as a means of forecasting what needs to be produced. Schedulers sequence jobs based on the assumption that the environment will not significantly change during the schedule's time span. This approach works adequately in a predictable market. However, in a turbulent marketplace a schedule is impractical. Any small, unanticipated change in demand or factory floor conditions can substantially affect the schedule, rendering it obsolete.

Another problem with traditional schedulers is that they try to anticipate and plan for every possible change that may occur. Unfortunately, the range of scenarios and the possible combinations of parameters are infinite, because manufacturing is so complex. Even if it were possible to pre-code all possible scenarios, the cost of considering and programming all possible combinations is prohibitive. An unanticipated or unknown scenario could cause the system to fail.

In short, traditional manufacturing facilities have shortcomings that affect their ability to compete in today's constantly changing marketplace:

- They do not have mechanisms in place to accommodate rapid

changes in business conditions caused by global competition and changing market demands.
- They do not have mechanisms in place to modify systems while they are executing.
- They are rigid and slow to make significant organizational or functional changes.
- They do not have a mechanism to recover gracefully from partial failures on the factory floor.
- They are unable to form or participate in virtual enterprises.
- They are not scalable for changes in the market.
- The business model and the operational philosophy are not customer driven.

These shortcomings cause problems such as reduced productivity, increased costs, and missed market opportunities. To remain competitive in today's marketplace, manufacturing must change its approach. In response, a major automotive company is building an agent-based manufacturing system under the direction of Dr. David Greenstein. [1] Here, the agents not only adapt to their environment but can also evolve by learning *from* the environment. Such an approach prepares manufacturing enterprises for the increasingly complex marketplace and enables them to respond rapidly to change.

## An Agent-Based Solution

The Agile Manufacturing Information System (AMIS) is a new approach and operational model that addresses the problems of traditional manufacturing practices. Because today's dynamic marketplace is similar to ecosystems, AMIS is modeled after the behavior of the natural world, an approach that is agile, adaptive, and dynamic. It can adjust to changes in the marketplace and in technology—making it effective and competitive.

Traditional manufacturing systems rely on a rather rigid, top-down structure to represent a manufacturing enterprise. AMIS uses a loose aggregation of software agents to represent a manufacturing entity. For example, *resource agents* represent the capabilities and capacity of the various resources available, such as machines, tools, people, and computers. The work performed within a facility is represented by *job agents*. In a small system, the interaction of the resource agents with job agents manages the manufacturing process.

However, in systems involving many jobs and resources, the interaction could tax even modern information systems. Here, resource agents can be grouped into *cells*. Since cells are agents in their own right, they can form virtual organizations—able to adapt constantly to the changing global marketplace. This dynamic structure enables each cell to remain agile. Rather than being constrained by a fixed hierarchy, the cells and, therefore, the overall business, can thrive in a continuously changing and unpredictable environment.

Each cell can be treated as a manufacturing business unit. Since it is responsible for its own bottom line, each cell must be profitable over time. When a cell is consistently unprofitable, it is dissolved and other cells absorb its resources. Similarly, each resource in a cell is responsible for maintaining a positive bottom line and contributing to the cell's overall profit. This distributed profit responsibility allows the cell to maintain a suitable size and the right mix of resources for the current workload, while maintaining the flexibility to address future needs.

As David Greenstein states, "For a manufacturer to succeed in today's competitive world, it must have the optimal mix of people, equipment, and knowledge to make the product. The AMIS architecture provides the flexibility and agility in a software system, which enables a manufacturer to monitor, evaluate, and adjust the mix of resources, people, and tools required as market demands change." [1]

## The AMIS Agents in more Detail

### Cell Agents

In living systems, a cell is a self-contained unit that has its own structure and behavior. It consists of other self-contained structures that interact to support the cell. How well the cell and its components work together determines whether the cell lives or dies. In a manufacturing system, each cell agent is a business unit representing a collection of physical resources, including machines, tools, and people. The cell operates as a self-contained business unit and only continues to exist if it meets its profit and production goals and its responsibilities. The cell also controls its own size—it changes the mix and number of resources over time to maintain its profitability and competitiveness in the marketplace. The architecture of a cell is summarized in Figure 10.1.

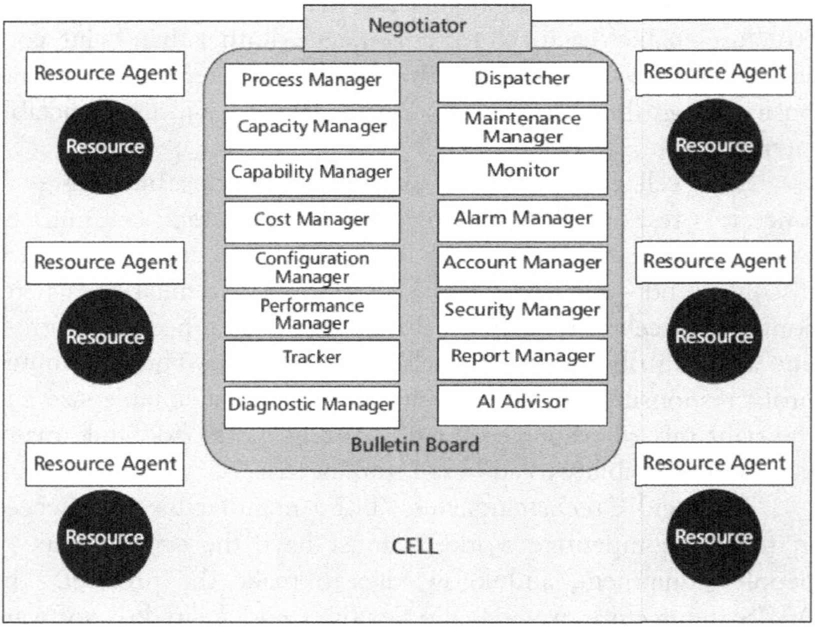


Figure 10.1 – Typical cell agent architecture for a manufacturing system.

## Common Function Agents

The *common function agents* interact with each other and with the resource agents. They provide the complete set of business functionality required to operate the cell as an independent business unit. Each common function agent is responsible for a different business or manufacturing function within the cell. Some of these agents contain information about the resources within the cell, such as the capabilities of the resources. Other agents provide interfaces to the people working in the cell, such as process planners and machine operators.

For example, the maintenance manager schedules and directs maintenance activities whether they are scheduled, opportunistic, or reactive. It also keeps track of the maintenance history.

The *process planner* determines whether the cell will bid on RFQs (Requests for Quote) received by the cell. A broad analysis is made of the cell to judge the cell's ability and desire to produce a quote for this RFQ. The analysis uses criteria associated with the type of product being requested (automotive, pharmaceuticals, electronics, etc.); the processes needed (welding, casting, packing, etc.); and the resources needed (five-axis CNC, drill, sheet metal press, etc.). If it is determined that the cell either lacks the appropriate abilities or cannot subcontract them, then the cell will not bid on the RFQ. If the cell does bid on the RFQ, the process planner generates the process workflow (e.g., a UML Activity Diagram) that will be used to execute the quote, if selected.

The *capability manager* uses the process workflow to verify that the cell has the resources needed to carry out the job. It verifies each step in the process (job agent) with the available resources in the cell. The verification of the capability is based on the information contained in the workflow (time, quality, special characteristics, and cost criteria). If the capability is not present in the cell, the capability manager initiates the subcontracting process through the process planner.

Similarly, the *capacity manager* uses the information from the workflow to provide capacity to the job agents. The jobs currently accepted by the cell are taken into consideration when deciding if the cell has the capacity to take on this new job. If sufficient capacity is not present in the cell, the capacity manager initiates the subcontracting process through the process planner.

## Negotiator Agents

*Negotiator agents* (at the top of the cell architecture diagram in Figure 10.1) communicate with the outside world on behalf of the cell. The negotiator provides an interface between the cell and the outside world. It routes messages received from the outside world to the appropriate common function agent. When preparing quotes for new jobs, the negotiator assembles the quote information provided by the other agents and summarizes the final quote information for the customer. Similarly, when the cell receives quotes from subcontractors, the negotiator works with other agents to select the winning quote.

## Resource Agent

Each *resource agent* represents a physical resource within the cell: a machine, tool, computer or person. Each physical resource provides a specialized utility or function to add value to the order completion process. The resource agent captures the attributes of the physical resource, allowing the agent to represent it in the cell and to coordinate the cell's use of the resource.

Each resource agent lists the capabilities that define those processes that the physical resource can perform. For example, a resource might be able to perform several types of milling operations. The capability list allows the resource agent to determine whether to bid on the various jobs in the cell.

Resources keep track of their assigned jobs by maintaining a prioritized list of jobs that the resource wins. Each job defines its job type, the earliest start time for the job, the expected job duration, the latest finish time, and the estimated cost.

The resource agent also maintains profit and loss figures for the resource. The best interest of a resource is to maximize profit by working on as many jobs as possible. If the resource does not maintain a profit over time, the cell may sell the resource to another cell. The resource agent is responsible both for ensuring the resource is optimally utilized and for representing the resource when bidding for new jobs.

## Job Agent

The *job agent* represents the customer through the order placed into the system. The *job agent* defines the processes needed to complete the final product specified in a customer order. Each node in the process workflow is a subjob and is handled by an agent. Each subjob agent contains information about that specific process, including the type of process, set-up time, run time, and cost.

The job agent is responsible for monitoring its current status and due dates. As due dates approach for the overall job or for individual subjobs, the subjob agent will raise alarms to initiate corrective action. The subjob also communicates with its neighboring subjobs, passing state information and alarms to allow the previous and following subjobs to monitor more accurately their status and take appropriate action. The job and subjob agents are active agents responsible for making sure that they are completed by the expected due dates and at the lowest cost.

## Broker Agent

The *broker agent* helps customers find providers of services and products. In the AMIS environment, each provider is a cell that registers with the broker, specifying the types of products and services it provides. For example, car buyers do not have to contact each automobile manufacturer. Instead, they send the attributes of the desired model (including such criteria as price, delivery date, color, and accessories) to the broker. The broker forwards the request to each automobile-producing cell that has registered with the broker.

The customer specifies the date by which all cells must provide quotes. The broker waits until this date and then collects all the cell bids and returns them to the customer. When the customer selects a winning quote, the broker forwards the customer award notification to the winning cell. Losing cells can view the attributes of the winning bid and compare it to their bid, in order to improve their bids in the future.

AMIS organizes brokers in a hierarchy based on geographical regions. First, the local broker forwards the customer request to its local cells that have registered. If no local cell can meet the customer request, the broker forwards the request to the regional broker. The regional broker forwards the request to each local broker within that region. In turn, these local brokers forward the request to every cell within their local area that manufactures the requested product.

The bids from each cell pass back through this hierarchy, going from the local information brokers to the regional broker. The regional broker returns the bids to the customer via the local information broker that originally received the customer request.

If no cells within the region can meet the customer requirements, the regional broker forwards the request to the global broker. The process is repeated with the global broker forwarding the request to each regional broker, down through the local information brokers, and to each cell worldwide that produces that product.

In some cases, the customer may wish to solicit quotes from cells worldwide without initially limiting the scope to cells registered with the local broker. In this case, the customer sends the requirements directly to the global broker, bypassing the local and regional brokers.

## Adaptation in Natural Systems

Adaptation is no stranger to manufacturing operations. Manufacturers that fail to adapt rapidly to the ever-changing world become extinct. They go out of business. Adaptation enables the system to react to changes in the market or in the manufacturing environment. When designed properly, the individual parts of the system can be empowered to change based on their environment and market conditions.

An adaptive agent is one that responds to its environment. The simplest form of adaptation is *reaction*, that is, a direct, predetermined response to a particular event or environmental signal usually expressed by an IF-THEN form. From atoms to ants, the reactive mode is quite evident. A carbon atom would have a rule that states in effect, "If I am alone, I will only bond with oxygen atoms." An ant would have a rule that if it finds food, it should return the food to its colony, while leaving a trail of pheromones. Reaction rules do not change in and of themselves, but change can come through other mechanisms such as learning and evolution. Without learning and evolution, ants and atoms are still quite able to support complex "societies." *With* learning and evolution, however, the rules can be changed based on experience—resulting in new and perhaps improved results.

## Learning

Learning is change that occurs during the lifetime of an agent and can take many forms. The most common techniques enable rules and decisions to be weighted based on positive (or negative) reinforcement. For example, in a basic bidding system, a bid could be selected simply on the basis of bid price. However, other considerations might also be appropriate, such as the bidder's ability to deliver its goods in the quantity, quality, and time frame requested. Over time, a *purchasing agent* can learn to choose from reliable *vendor agents* instead of just choosing the lowest bid. If a vendor's performance improves (or declines), the purchaser's decisions are modified accordingly. In other words, the agent *continues* to learn. Popular learning techniques that employ reinforcement learning include credit assignment, Bayesian and classifier rules, and neural networks.

## Evolution

Evolution is change that occurs over successive generations of agents. For example, cell agents in AMIS continually evolve to address changing market and business needs. Here, the mix of resources within a cell dynamically evolves and changes so the cell can produce the products demanded in the market place. Each resource agent in a cell must continue to win jobs and maintain a positive bottom line, thereby contributing to the overall profitability of the cell.

A resource that consistently fails to win jobs will eventually have a negative cash balance. If a resource maintains a negative cash balance long enough, the cell may decide to replace that resource. The nonproductive resource can either "die" due to malnutrition of cash or be sold to another cell. The original cell can then buy a replacement resource possessing different capabilities—ones that are better suited to the products made by the cell. In other words, there is a "survival of the fittest" quality to the mechanism, where each internal change represents a new generation of cell. By evolving in this way, the cell maintains a set of resources that allows it to remain profitable and survive in a dynamic marketplace.

### Best Interest

Whether adaptation is by learning or evolution, each agent is responsible for acting in its own best interests to ensure that its goals are met. The cell agent's best interest is to win as many jobs as possible and keep the cell busy fulfilling customer orders. The cell also generates as much profit as possible, ensuring its continued viability as a virtual business enterprise.

The resource agent's best interest is to win as many jobs as possible and keep busy processing jobs. The resource also generates as much profit as possible, guaranteeing that it remains a viable member of the cell.

The job agent's best interest is to complete the job quickly, to make certain that it is finished by the customer's due date. The job agent also looks for the cell and resource that can complete the job at the lowest possible cost.

The best interest concept embodies the metaphor of free market behavior, as the cell, resource, and job interact and compromise to reach a solution that balances each agent's best interests. This balancing of best interests between these three entities and their dynamic interaction allows a dynamic, adaptive, and productive structure to emerge in agent-based manufacturing systems.

## Seven-Step Negotiation Process

When you decide to purchase a product, your decision is influenced by certain requirements. For instance, the cost of the product must be within your budget. Another requirement might be how long it takes to perform the work. Once all the elements of your decision criteria are met, you award the work to the manufacturer that best fits your needs.

AMIS uses a standard seven-step bidding interaction protocol to form an agreement to provide a product. This bidding process allows customers to obtain products through a common market process, ensuring that all purchases are at fair market prices. All seven steps of the negotiation bidding interaction protocol must be completed successfully in order to complete the transaction.

- *Request for quote:* The Request for Quote (RFQ) is the first step in the AMIS bidding process. A customer (or *customer agent*) creates an RFQ that specifies the desired products or services—along with a response date—and sends it to a broker agent. The broker acts as a liaison, forwarding the RFQ to each cell that has "subscribed" to provide the requested product.
- *Receive quotes:* Each cell agent determines its ability to complete the job according to the customer's RFQ specifications. If a cell is able to meet the customer's requirements, it creates a quote for the job. Quotes contain estimated information on the delivery date, price, quality, and special characteristics related to completing the job. Cells return their quotes to the broker, which holds the quotes until the RFQ response date has been reached and then returns all the quotes to the customer.
- *Select winner:* When time has expired for the cells to submit quotes, the customer (or customer agent) begins the selection process. The customer selects the winner from the submitted quotes by finding the most desirable mix of cost, time, quality, and special characteristics, based on its requirements for the job. The customer sends an award notification to the cell with the best quote.
- *Winner confirms:* The winning cell accepts or rejects the job depending on whether it still has the capacity to do the job. The cell might reject the job if it has accepted other jobs between the time it prepared the quote and received the award. If the winner rejects the job, the customer offers it to the cell with the next best quote. This continues until a cell accepts the job. After the winner accepts the job, the other cells that submitted quotes are informed of the decision. At that time, losing cells are able to access data on the quotes, which helps them evaluate why they lost the job—and perhaps learn and modify their behavior for future quotes.

- *Issue purchase order:* After a cell has confirmed the customer order, the customer authorizes the cell to begin production by issuing a purchase order to the cell.
- *Generate product:* The cell completes the work on the product, delivers the product to the customer, and sends an invoice to the customer.
- *Make payment:* The customer ends the process by paying the cell for the work done.

The seven-step process establishes a common approach for business interaction between cells. The same process is followed when a cell wants to subcontract part of a job to another cell.

## Summary for Agent-Based Manufacturing Case Study

### Distributed Organizational Control

To be agile, large centralized manufacturing organizations must be decomposed into simpler, smaller business units that are responsible for their own business, financial, and production success. This distributed organizational control allows these smaller units to reorganize and react quickly to changing market conditions. These smaller units—cells—can easily be reconfigured to maximize efficiency or respond to market changes. Distributed organizational control enables the system to respond locally to unexpected failures or shutdowns by quickly reallocating the necessary resources.

Furthermore, distributed organizational control can be based on the concept of survival of the fittest. Therefore, if a cell within an organization consistently fails to contribute to the greater well-being of that organization, that cell ceases to exist. On the other hand, if every cell is successful, the entire operation is successful. Distributed organizational control allows a successful manufacturing operation to emerge from the interaction of smaller units.

Another benefit of a distributed organization is the ability to quickly form *ad hoc* formations of business units that achieve common business goals. Here, individual cells cooperate as a unit for a common benefit—and then dissolve when no longer needed.

The components of such a virtual organization do not have to be aligned with a physical organization, adding another degree of flexibility not found in traditional systems.

**Capacity Management**

The more unpredictable the manufacturing environment, the more significant the problems associated with advanced scheduling. For that reason, AMIS does not use the concept of scheduling. Instead, it manages the *capacity* of the resources.

As a business entity, each cell has limited resources that have limited capacity. All jobs in a cell are temporarily put into the holding capacity queue of that cell. Then, just before a job starts, each resource in a cell bids on the job in the queue. Because the bidding is done right before the job starts, the chance of an unexpected event affecting the completion of the job is significantly reduced.

However, if a problem occurs during the production process, the system is not disabled. This is an important benefit of capacity management. Because the resources in the cell are self-loading and balance the load among themselves, a job that cannot be completed by a resource is returned to the cell's queue for re-bidding and re-allocation. This dynamic allocation of jobs to resources greatly reduces the effects of the unpredictable nature of the shop floor. While this is not the only technique for capacity management, it works well in the automotive industry.

**Market-Driven Economy**

In a market-driven economy, manufacturers build products in response to market demand, rather than in anticipation of demand. Businesses compete for limited resources and customers, but cooperate when it is beneficial. Change is constant as new products emerge and customer demands evolve.

AMIS relies heavily on the economic laws of supply and demand. Rather than try to forecast market demand and schedule production based on rigid plans, AMIS provides an architecture that adapts to the dynamic marketplace. Both inside and outside the cell, agents operate in a profit-driven economy. The competition between cells or resources will drive the market to an equilibrium or a market-clearing price. The producer's need for higher profit and faster production times interact with the customer's need for lower prices and higher quality. These opposing forces result in the best prices and products for everyone involved.

## Conclusion

As designed by David Greenstein, AMIS provides a means for a manufacturer to be more productive and adaptive in responding to changing market demand. Specifically, it will allow a manufacturer to:

- Increase machine (resource) utilization by better matching capacity to workload.
- Increase throughput by making the right products at the right time.
- Reduce the number of late jobs by better capacity planning and monitoring.
- Utilize and tune the correct resource types and mix by monitoring resource efficiency.
- Create a flexible and dynamic architecture that responds rapidly to a continuously changing market.
- Enable an Activity Based Costing (ABC) approach to collect and calculate actual production costs.
- Reduce "single points of failure" in production systems.

Agent-based manufacturing is a new way of thinking about and applying information. The primary benefits of the agent-based approach are that they provide dynamic, reliable, and agile systems. As such, it will enable organizations of the future to accommodate rapidly changing business conditions, increase market responsiveness, lower cycle times, increase productivity, and better utilize resources—and most importantly, it will benefit the bottom line. In other words, the agent-based approach will be the way modern manufacturers develop their systems to compete in the twenty-first century.

## Acknowledgments

The authors would like to acknowledge Dr. David Greenstein (dgreenst@tir.com) for providing a comprehensive description of his agent-based AMIS case study.

## References

[1] Greenstein, David, and Kelly Thomas, "Intelligent Agents for an Emergent Industrial Ecology," *Intelligent Manufacturing Systems*, Proceedings of IJCAI, 1995.

# 11. aoBPM: Getting There

In this key chapter we explore how to apply the agent paradigm to business, explore architectures and standards, and explain the relationship with object and BPM technology. An in-depth exploration of this topic could fill a few books. This chapter aims to describe the terrain and to provide a road map of the territory.

So far in this book we concluded that information systems based on intelligent agent technology are inevitable, even though the tasks of conceiving, designing, and building them are not trivial. As we turn our attention to these tasks, we will benefit from keeping the fundamental question in mind, "How can we conceive, design, and build adaptive, multi-enterprise-scale information systems and business processes?" Intelligent agent technology is an enabler of such systems, but is not an end unto itself. When combined with the maturing disciplines of object technology and BPM methods, their synergy, embodied in *agent-oriented BPM* (aoBPM), can take us to a new level in the search for the prize of managing complex business ecosystems and multi-company business networks.

Our approach to building agent-based systems can be characterized in terms of three distinct, but related, topics:

- *A full-lifecycle solution development process* that explicitly addresses domain modeling—the effort spent in domain and problem understanding can be leveraged to guide and accelerate information systems development.
- *Ontology-based domain models* are needed as fully understanding the domain is essential to understanding the problems in the domain. The richness of domain models determines reuse and flexibility.
- *Architecture.* Agents must follow a consistent architectural approach so they can interoperate with each other.

After a brief introduction to the agent-oriented lifecycle, we focus our attention on the heart of the matter, domain modeling and architecture.

## A Full-Lifecycle Solution Development Process

The agent-oriented lifecycle model should be iterative and incremental. Over a decade of experience has taught us that agent orientation will enrich contemporary OO and BPM approaches by providing an *active* modeling paradigm and better analysis models that enable reuse.

As shown in Figure 11.1, our agent-oriented domain modeling and architectural frameworks can be integrated with best practice software engineering lifecycles, leveraging the contributions of agent technology and object-oriented software engineering.

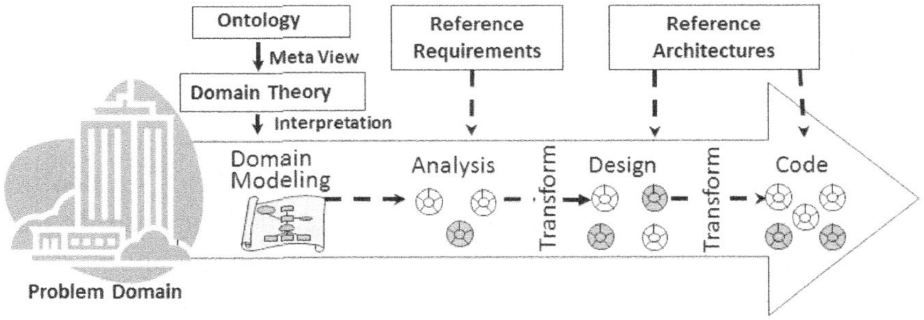


Figure 11.1 Agent-oriented Lifecycle

We thus preserve considerable intellectual capital while taking the next step in development methods for truly intelligent and adaptive information systems. Radical new methods will not be accepted, as corporations are not in this to advance computer science; they are in business.

## Ontology-Based Domain Models

Our approach to building agent-based solutions emphasizes the importance of domain modeling as a critical initial step in producing business technology solutions. There are at least three distinct approaches to domain modeling: business process management (BPM), object-oriented (OO), and artificial intelligence (AI) which is an underpinning of intelligent agent (IA) technology. All three approaches are model-based and offer techniques for describing problem domains.

As shown in Figure 11.2, the three approaches offer differing perspectives of the problem domain.

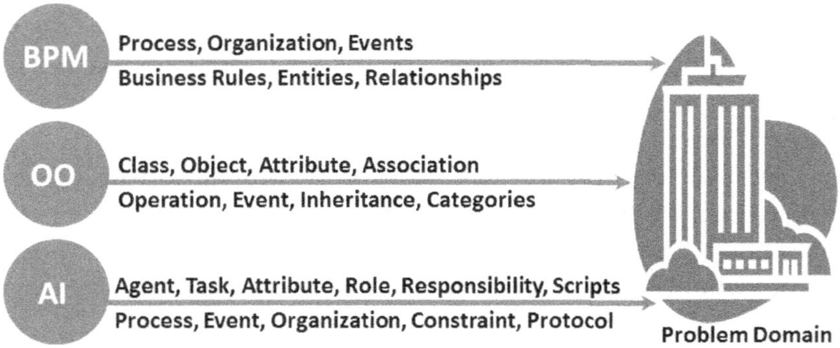


Figure 11.2 BPM, OO and IA
Perspectives on Business Domain Modeling

The convergence of OO, BPM, and AI methods results in a significant breakthrough in building models of the enterprise that are capable of end-to-end integration of business analysis and software systems. Although the fusion of these disciplines is not yet complete to the point of standardization, pioneering companies have recognized the competitive advantage and launched major agent-oriented development initiatives.

Traditional BPM methods are expressive and easily (often, naively) understood for describing business processes and organizations. But traditional BPM produces separate models of data, processes and organization that soon become unmanageable. The models are difficult to integrate, validate, or leverage for the development of software systems. Information is captured using informal techniques even though more formal notations such as BPMN are deployed, and incomplete lifecycle models lack a clear implementation path.

Underlying high-level process models, object-oriented methods are well suited to software engineering and have potential for reuse. They are, however, not inherently business oriented, not sufficiently expressive of most problem domains, and often foster premature commitments to design and implementation strategies. Consequently, they do not capture a sufficiently rich domain model for significant reuse. In practice, most OO methods are informal and not repeatable. Traceability is questionable and robust design heuristics are hard to find.

Business models must make a distinction between passive objects and *active, goal-seeking* agents if we are to close the gap between model and reality. Business object and process models need to contain behavioral declarations, role definitions, ontological awareness and constraint axioms.

Intelligent agent technology can be leveraged to enhance enterprise modeling as well as offer new techniques for developing intelligent applications and smart technical infrastructure services. An agent-oriented perspective allows us to develop rich and expressive models of the enterprise as the foundation for adaptive, reusable business software.

An agent-oriented approach such as the Knowledge Analysis and Documentation System (KADS) supports richer representation of the problem domain and tends to be more rigorous and mature compared to BPM and OO. A method like KADS entails little commitment to design in early modeling phases and allows alternative implementation paths. On the downside, methods like KADS are not widely known outside the artificial intelligence community. They tend to be weaker on infrastructure issues and lack the diversity of commercial tools found in the mainstream technology world. Traditional artificial intelligence is knowledge-base centric and can result in monolithic design.

What's new under the sun? Object-orientation and artificial intelligence have been around for decades. And, many informally describe "BPM" as new clothes on industrial systems engineering. It is the melding of these disciplines into a unified approach to enterprise modeling that represents the breakthrough. Blending the strengths and sifting out the weakness of each discipline, agent-oriented BPM can take us one great step forward. aoBPM is a full life-cycle proposition, not just a programming or implementation issue.

The secret to aoBPM's success is to apply agent technology up front as a *domain modeling metaphor* while using the maturity of object-oriented methods to provide the infrastructure lacking in the artificial intelligence world. Figure 11.3 shows that agent-based domain modeling produces the business object model in terms of ontologies, and uses ideas and techniques from traditional business analysis (Process Modeling/BPMN), OO (UML), and AI (Agents and Rules). While devoid of implementation details, the business object model is agent-based and is used to support user task analysis, requirements modeling, and the specification and design of the software object model. The flow of activities in the figure would be somewhat different if we were working in a green field. In the real world of business, green fields are rare, and the figure reflects the use of preexisting BPM and OO business analysis models.

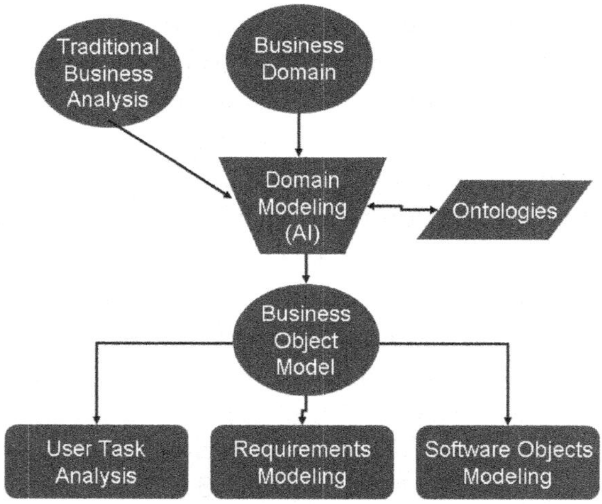


Figure 11.3 Combined BPM, OO, and Agent Domain Modeling Process

A domain model is commonly defined as a representation of entities, their attributes, their behaviors, and the processes that bind them together within a domain—nothing new to the experienced business analyst. What is new and highly beneficial is to define the information in a domain model in terms of ontologies and then to use these to construct business object models.

What is an *ontology?* Tom Gruber of Stanford University provides the short answer, "An ontology is an explicit specification of a conceptualization."

He explains, "A body of formally represented knowledge is based on *conceptualization:* the objects, concepts, and other entities that are assumed to exist in some area of interest and the relationships that hold among them." An ontology defines the basic terms and relations comprising the vocabulary of a topic area, as well as the rules for combining terms and relations to define extensions to the vocabulary. All domain models embody an ontology—albeit mostly implicitly. Our agent-oriented approach to defining business objects emphasizes the use of explicit ontologies as implementation-neutral representations of knowledge that can then be mechanically translated into different target modeling tools.

Thus an ontology is a formal, explicit specification of a shared conceptualization. An ontology renders shared vocabulary and taxonomy that models a domain with the definition of objects and concepts, as well as their properties and relations.

An ontology can be expressed in a variety of ways, for example: informally (Natural Language, Graphical Notations), semi-formally (Ontolingua), and formally (first order logic languages such as Knowledge Interchange Format [KIF]). Today, most ontologists use OWL (Web Ontology Language from the W3C), because OWL provides for the representation of knowledge about the representation of knowledge. Storing business knowledge in OWL opens up many opportunities for delivering reuse and validation at the knowledge level. In other words, OWL enables an ontology to be both machine readable and machine understandable.

## Architecture is the Key to Agent-Oriented Development

In their book, *Business Architecture: The Art and Practice of Business Transformation*, William Ulrich and Neil McWhorter write,

"Visualizing a business through architectural disciplines is not entirely new. Creating a business-friendly framework that allows business professionals to visualize and transform organizations, however, is a groundbreaking achievement!"

"Business architecture is a blueprint of the enterprise that provides a common understanding of the organization and is used to align strategic objectives and tactical demands."

"The most important aspect of business architecture is enabling business executives, managers and professionals to take ownership and drive enterprise transformation, a role that has oftentimes been delegated by default to IT. Historically, the term 'enterprise architecture' has a tendency to turn off business professionals because they immediately assume that the concept is an IT focused creation. This is not an indictment of IT but rather a call to action for business executives to take ownership of business architecture and related business transformation strategies. The decisions that are made today can make or break organizations going forward into a complex, uncertain future."

Ulrich and McWhorter make a good point about "enterprise architecture" turning off business professionals as they assume it's about IT architecture. If we look back at the roots of enterprise architecture we'll discover the reason, for what is widely known today as enterprise architecture came from IBM's Business Systems Planning (BSP), a method for analyzing, defining and designing an information architecture of organizations. It was first issued by IBM in 1981, though the initial work on BSP began in the early 1970s. At first, it was for IBM internal use only. Later it was made available to customers and this method became an important tool for many organizations. It is a very complex method dealing with data, processes, strategies, and organizational departments that are interconnected. John Zachman is one of the founding developers of IBM's Business Systems Planning (BSP), and worked on IBM's executive team planning techniques. In 1987 he originated the Zachman Framework a standard for classifying the descriptive representations (models) that comprise enterprise architecture.

| | DATA *What* | FUNCTION *How* | NETWORK *Where* | PEOPLE *Who* | TIME *When* | MOTIVATION *Why* |
|---|---|---|---|---|---|---|
| Objective/Scope (contextual) *Role: Planner* | List of things important in the business | List of Business Processes | List of Business Locations | List of important Organizations | List of Events | List of Business Goal & Strategies |
| Enterprise Model (conceptual) *Role: Owner* | Conceptual Data/ Object Model | Business Process Model | Business Logistics System | Work Flow Model | Master Schedule | Business Plan |
| System Model (logical) *Role:Designer* | Logical Data Model | System Architecture Model | Distributed Systems Architecture | Human Interface Architecture | Processing Structure | Business Rule Model |
| Technology Model (physical) *Role:Builder* | Physical Data/Class Model | Technology Design Model | Technology Architecture | Presentation Architecture | Control Structure | Rule Design |
| Detailed Reprentation (out of context) *Role: Programmer* | Data Definition | Program | Network Architecture | Security Architecture | Timing Definition | Rule Speculation |
| Functioning Enterprise *Role: User* | Usable Data | Working Function | Usable Network | Functioning Organization | Implemented Schedule | Working Strategy |

Figure 11.4 The Zachman Framework

Zachman, pictured below with Peter Fingar at the October 2012 BBC Conference is still going strong at 78 years of age. He is all about business, but the roots of enterprise architecture in IBM's BSP programs still keep a lot of business people shied away as the term is still associated with IT.

Peter Fingar and John Zachman, 2012

Agent technology does not provide immunity to bad software engineering. Building enterprise-scale agent-oriented systems requires an architectural approach with a strong emphasis on software engineering processes and methods. Our approach to architecture for multiagent systems is based on a consideration of fundamental design variables that can be instantiated in different ways to accommodate the creation of agents with reactive, deliberative, or hybrid behaviors. Our approach to architecting distributed, multiagent systems can be summarized as follows:

*Given:* A set of goals, objectives and tasks to be achieved or performed by a community of agents and a set of design variables,

*Find:* Appropriate instantiations for each design variable, based on available options, subject to applicable hard and soft constraints. High-level design variables include:

- *Internal architecture of agents*—how each agent is constructed internally
- *Control and Coordination approach*—how intra- and inter-agent activities and processes are managed
- *Cooperation style*—whether and how agents work together to succeed in common goals
- Communication, interaction and knowledge sharing approach—how agents exchange and share information
- *Granularity of agents*—covering both process granularity and task granularity

- *Depth of adoption of agency*—starting from the user-interface, through application services and infrastructure services, determine to what extent should agents be used
- *Distribution model*—the method of distributing application functionality among agents which run across multiple processors.

The following constraints are typical in enterprise systems: information bandwidths, limits of agent processing, resource availability, need for varied but guaranteed response times, reliability, security, distributability, scalability, and portability.

By examining the characteristics and capabilities of intelligent agents, we can identify many of the architectural components that are needed to support an agent-oriented environment. For handy reference, Figure 11.5 repeats the illustration of a commonly employed anatomy of an intelligent agent to center our discussion of architectural requirements (See more in Appendix A).

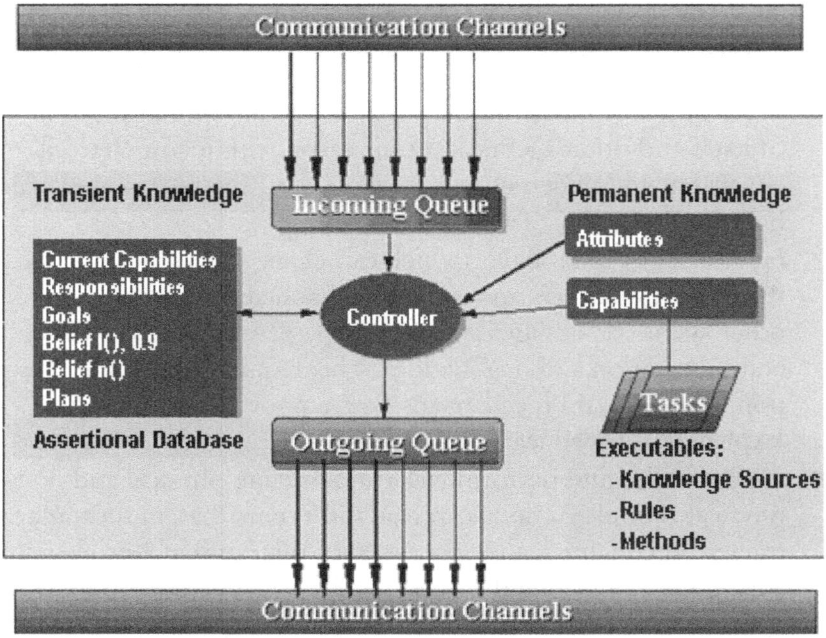


Figure 11.5 A Common Anatomy of an Intelligent Agent

As mentioned earlier in Chapter Four, intelligent agents are agents that employ degrees of raw intelligence, social intelligence, agility, autonomy, and visualization. The level of each of these dimensions determines the degree and type of agent's intelligence.

An intelligent agent can:

- Send and receive information to and from other agents using appropriate protocols (sensing and communication). This requires communication services that support message queue management, asynchronous messaging and content-based routing of messages.
- Generate multiple objectives, goals, and process flows (referred to as *plans* in Figure 11.5) for itself and other agents, process information received and perform reasoning (e.g., inferencing, synthesis and analysis). These require services that support rich knowledge representation schemes (e.g., for Rules and Objects), alternative logics (e.g., fuzzy logic, temporal logic, Bayesian logic), alternative inferencing strategies (forward, backward, opportunistic), planning (plan generation, plan execution, plan repair), and concurrent operations.
- Maintain explicit data models (referred to as *beliefs* in Fig.10.5) of itself and other agents and can reason with incomplete, inconsistent and uncertain information. This requires support for belief revision (e.g., Truth Maintenance).
- Have a set of capabilities (which can change dynamically)—i.e., the tasks it can perform—and can reason about its own and other agents capabilities and skills (e.g., planning, inferencing, communication and negotiation). This requires a task specification language, and mechanisms that support "learning" (e.g., Explanation-based learning, Induction).
- Assume roles and perform tasks and execute physical and nonphysical actions. Actions can result in events that, in turn, may trigger other actions and processes (in this context a process is analogous to a plan and consists of a pre-defined, temporally ordered, set of activities that are designed to achieve a given goal). This requires task selection and execution mechanisms.
- Engage in complex interactions with each other, such as nego-

tiation and task delegation. This requires support for interaction protocols (e.g., Contracting, Conflict Resolution, Resource Allocation, Basic Communication). The Agent Communication Language (ACL) [2, 3] from FIPA is the *de jure* standard for designing inter-agent interaction protocols.

- Dynamically join or leave groupings or organizations. Organization may be functional or social. This requires support for specification of organizational structure, organizational procedures and rules, and roles and responsibilities.
- Have its own internal architecture (e.g., Blackboard, Actor or Stimulus/Response). This requires different architectural specifications and alternative control algorithms.
- Explain its reasoning in terms of 'how' and 'why.' This requires explanation mechanisms.

The kinds of agents in multiagent systems strongly influence architecture. Four major types of agents are central to large-scale enterprise systems:

- *System agents:* These agents are responsible for providing infrastructure-level services to problem-solving and application agents (e.g., access to operating system services, access to data repositories, communications management, and security monitoring).
- *Communities:* Communities are conceptual agents that represent a group or collection of agents. They define a number of global characteristics for a grouping of cooperating agents (e.g., common goals and objectives; organizational procedures and roles and responsibilities). Important benefits include structuring communication while reducing uncertainty, and increasing system coherence. Figure 11.6 illustrates the relationships between communities, agents, roles, and services. [1]

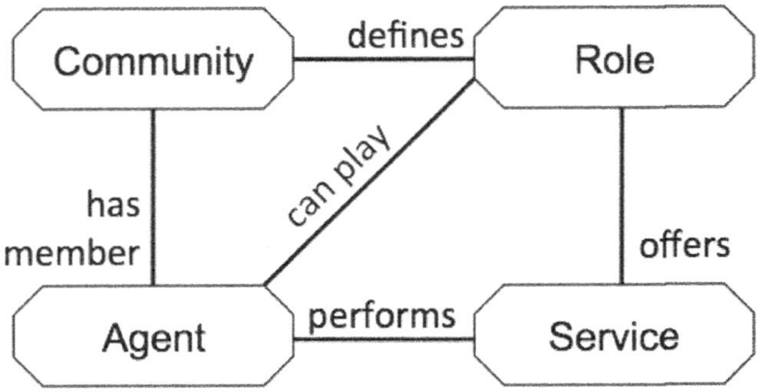


Figure 11.6 Relationships between communities, agents, roles and services.

- *Application agents:* These agents embody functionality or application logic within a domain (e.g., risk management). An application can be viewed as a group consisting of a cohesive set of agents which share information and cooperate to provide services to their clients.
- *Interface agents:* These mediate between application agents and external users of their services. Two sub-types of Interface Agents are: User Interface Agents and Wrapper Agents. Human users interact with the system via User Interface Agents that orchestrate other agents and groups to deliver user-level services. External computer systems are linked-in via wrapper agents that encapsulate their APIs behind standard protocols.

Agents are constructed from classes within three distinct hierarchies: *Controller Class Hierarchy*–contains prototype architectural behaviors (for example, Blackboard, Actor, Stimulus/Response); *Agent Class Hierarchy*–contains prototype agent behaviors, multiple inheritance being supported (for example, epistemic agent, mobile agent, social agent); and *Task Class Hierarchy*–contains default task definitions (for example, interaction management, problem-solving tasks). An agent represents a logical entity that physically comprises a cluster of components (each component type can be implemented as a separate Class of object). Such agents can be implemented in a variety of ways. For example an agent may be implemented using two frames (an Object-based AI data structure: a base frame and a meta-frame). The controller can be placed in the meta-frame and the attributes and the assertional database can be placed or be referenced in the base-frame. Alternatively, an object-oriented approach may be used where each component is defined in its own class. The process that loads agents assembles their components and creates instances at run-time.

Agents communicate with other agents through one or more communications channels that are linked to mailboxes or message queues. Figure 11.7 shows a logical view of a system architecture that allows agents to interoperate.

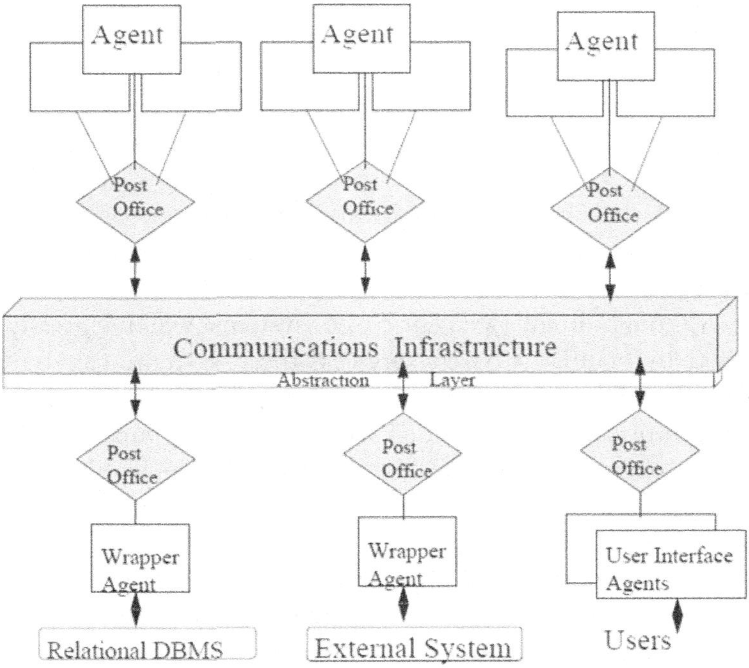


Figure 11.7 Logical View of the System-Wide Architecture

The post offices in the figure provide delivery services for the mailboxes. This abstraction of communication services allows alternative standards and delivery technologies to be deployed. Each agent has a knowledge-base consisting of non-executable (attributes and own capabilities) and executable (how to perform tasks) knowledge. In addition, each agent has an internal assertional database for storing dynamic information, such as its beliefs about other agents. Local services support internal operations of agents (e.g., Message-Queue Management, Query Management, and Belief Management). The architecture can be physically distributed across many threads, processes, or processors, depending on requirements.

The figure highlights the way individual agents connect to communication services and the underlying technical infrastructure. The figure also shows how "external" applications or legacy systems such as data repositories can be wrapped to appear as agents—agent wrappers are more sophisticated than object wrappers. They maintain rich semantic models of the application, database, or systems they represent. Abstraction layers insulate the agents from needing to know specific operating system or middleware APIs. The infrastructure should provide a common set of interfaces through which agents may plug into operating system services.

Although building agent-based systems will be greatly enhanced by standards-based services, these systems can be built today if a solid systems architecture is defined. Components of the architecture can be superseded with standards-compliant components as they become available. Corporations in highly competitive industries cannot wait for full standardization because their competitors are not waiting.

This discussion has described an approach to developing complex agent-based software systems. A holistic, *agent-oriented* view of design was advocated, and an appropriate lifecycle model was introduced. The discussion of implementation strategies identified a number of technical issues. Currently, a mix and match software strategy has to be adopted, resulting in the need for well defined systems architecture to maintain coherence.

Corporations will not take the step to agent-oriented BPM because they can, but they will do so because they must.

Now is the time to move from the current methods and tools that deliver excellent results for expert programmers, to the ubiquity of business process management where processes are developed by unsophisticated programmers and business people using visual modeling and development tools.

While this vision of simplicity is appealing, the underlying enterprise framework is extremely complex and simply needs intelligent agent technology to manage and hide the complexity. With careful planning, sound software engineering, and solid systems architecture, an intelligent greenhouse can be architected to grow the software of the future—today.

## Fractal Enterprise Architecture

Euclidean geometry is modeled by our notion of a "flat plane." Other geometries have been introduced to go beyond a flat plane, e.g., Elliptic and Hyperbolic geometry. To illustrate, on a sphere, the sum of the angles of a triangle is not equal to 180°.

The physics of traditional business processes might be ripe for change for the complex global enterprise goes well beyond a flat plane, and fractal geometry principles just may provide a fresh foundation for business modeling and Enterprise Architecture.

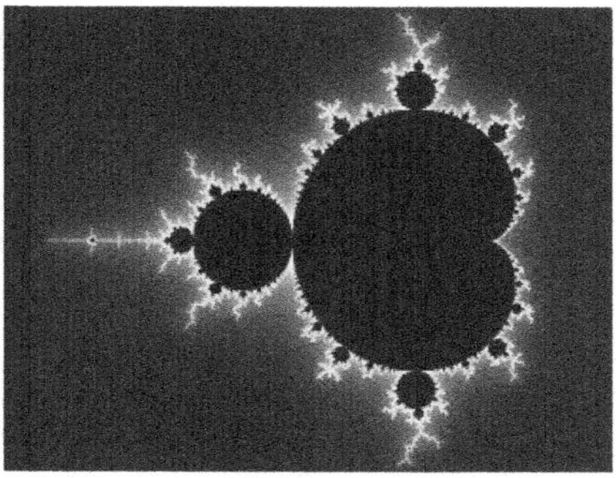

The main characteristic of fractals is *self-similarity*, implying *recursion*, pattern-inside-of-pattern. The term fractal was coined by Benoit Mandelbrot in 1975 and was derived from the Latin fractus meaning *broken* or *fractured*. A mathematical fractal is based on an equation that undergoes iteration, a form of feedback based on *recursion.* Mandelbrot sets display self-similarity, because they not only produce detail at finer scales, but also produce details with certain constant proportions or ratios, though they are not identical. Because they appear similar at all levels of magnification, fractals are often considered to be infinitely complex. Natural objects that are approximated by fractals to a degree include clouds, mountain ranges, lightning bolts, coastlines, snowflakes and thunderstorms. In nature, small parts resemble the whole: The veins in leaves look like branches; branches look like miniature trees; rocks look like miniature mountains. That's kind of like a company's real business processes distributed throughout today's complex, global ecosystem comprised of ever growing numbers of business partners and social networks—fractals. Hmmm? Can complex, global 21st century enterprises be adequately described without embracing the concept of fractals?

The fractal factory, the fractal company, the fractal business process? Not isolated to academia, Mandelbrot demonstrated the practical application of fractal geometry to financial markets in his 2006 book, *The (Mis)behavior of Markets: A Fractal View of Financial Turbulence. ( http://goo.gl/897SG)*

Other practical sightings of fractals in business can be found in the emerging world of Agile Manufacturing, which is seen as the next step after LEAN in the evolution of production methodology. Let's turn to *A Comparison of Emerging Manufacturing Concepts* by Tharumarajah, Wells and Nemes, "The concept of fractal factories proposes a manufacturing company to be composed of small components, or fractal entities. These entities can be described by specific internal features of the fractals. The first feature is self-organization that implies freedom for the fractals in organizing and executing tasks. They may choose their own methods of problem solving including self-optimization that takes care of process improvements. The second feature is dynamics where the fractals can adapt to influences from the environment without any formal hindrance of organization structure. The third feature is self-similarity interpreted as similarity of goals among the fractals to conform to the objectives in each unit. In addition to the above characteristics, there is a need for the factory fractals to function as a coherent whole. This is achieved through a process of participation and coordination among the fractals, supported by an inheritance mechanism to ensure consistency of the goals. Fractals are structured bottom-up, building fractals of a higher order. Units at a higher level assume only those responsibilities in the process which cannot be fulfilled in the lower order fractals. This principle guarantees teamwork among the fractals and also forces distribution of power and ability in order to coordinate the actions of the individual fractals and put in place mechanisms that permit self-organization and dynamic restructuring."

(goo.gl/h0Rds)

Hmm? Is Enterprise Architecture and BPM, as practiced today, ready to take on the fundamentals of the fractal factory?

Much progress has been accomplished in the field of agent technology. Here are some annotated references as the technology relates to BPM: Fractal Enterprise Architecture and Agent-Oriented BPM: goo.gl/Dz3qG

## The Role of Choreography in the Great Dance of Business

As globalization continues its march to becoming the greatest reorganization of the world since the Industrial Revolution, companies in a variety of industries are increasingly adopting a *choreography* role. They are building complex business ecosystems comprised of ever-growing numbers of highly specialized business partners and *prosumers* that place the consumer directly in the heart of business processes that produce value. *Back office* systems of record and transaction processing have been mastered, but *front office* systems for actually *conducting* business with disparate systems of systems that interact across the ecosystem are today's game.

A company is a complex social system, a system that must be treated as such, a complex organism of many dimensions and components—customers, employees, and suppliers (and their information systems) fused together as one entity to create Value Networks. The days of the vertically-integrated, one-dimensional company are over. Linear Porter value chains have morphed into complex, multidimensional business ecosystems that have a lifecycle that goes from birth, to optimization, and on to a state of entropy as do all systems in the universe. Yet we still attempt to model our enterprises and processes on a *flat plane* as rather static entities. Worse, Enterprise Architecture is often separate from BPM in the minds of many practitioners in today's companies.

Consider a snippet from the manuscript of Wolf Rivkin's forthcoming book, *The Eloquent Enterprise*, "*Enterprise Growth Dialectics*: An Enterprise changes according to the same laws of change that govern any structure: the negation of the negation and the transformation of quantitative changes into qualitative ones according to the pattern of thesis-antithesis-synthesis. Therefore, any prospective framework describing this new qualitative state of an enterprise must offer a new, qualitatively different set of artifacts to describe the highest level of abstraction of the previous state. Only internal dialectic factors push an Enterprise from one Architectural State to another."

Thus an Enterprise Architecture is a living, changing thing. "Enterprise Architecture is not a theoretical discipline that provides a nice-to-have variably detailed description of a static Enterprise or of one that is moving forward without deep structural changes and can therefore be described by a static, rigid framework. It is rather, a must-have practical guide for Enterprise Transformation, providing a dynamic description of the profound but smooth structural change of an Enterprise that seeks effectiveness, efficiency and the resulting competitive edge."

With the emergence of Cloud-based, long-lived, loosely-coupled, stateless architectures, the existing Enterprise Architecture approaches and today's BPM systems will quickly demonstrate their lack of flexibility and inability to choreograph participants in complex business ecosystems made up of large numbers of actors spread across the globe.

To elaborate, let's turn to social visionary, Dee Hock, the founder and former CEO of VISA International, an organization that he says was founded on *chaordic* principles, from a blending of chaos and order. VISA now connects over 20,000 financial institutions, 14 million merchants, and 600 million consumers in 220 countries. Hock explains that "By chaord, I mean any self-organizing, self governing, adaptive, nonlinear, complex organism, organization, community or system, whether physical, biological or social, the behavior of which harmoniously blends characteristics of both chaos and order." In his view, today's current forms of organization are almost universally based on compelled behavior, or tyranny. The chaordic organizations of the future will embody community, based on shared purpose. A chaordic organization harmoniously blends characteristics of competition and cooperation [coopetition]. Hock's book, *Birth of the Chaordic Age,* is a broadside against the dominance of today's command-and-control institutions.

There's a much deeper, scientific treatment of the notion of chaords. This is from Michael Schillo and Klaus Fischer's short article, "Holonic Multiagent Systems": "The term 'holon' was originally coined by Arthur Koestler, basing it on the Greek word 'holos' for 'whole' and the suffix '-on' that denotes 'part.' According to Koestler a holon is a self-similar or fractal structure that is stable, coherent and that consists of several holons as substructures and is itself a part of a greater whole. As biological examples he names a human being, which consists of organs which in turn consist of cells that can be further decomposed and so on. Furthermore, the human being is part of a family and a society. None of these components can be understood completely without their sub-components or without the supercomponent they are part of. The concepts of fractal and holonic system design in manufacturing were proposed to combine top-down hierarchical organizational structure with decentralized control, which takes the bottom-up perspective. While earlier approaches in this area restricted self-similarity and did not employ the recursive power."

Complex adaptive systems are indeed holonic and fractal and thus require multiagent systems to power them.

Is the current state of the BPM lifecycle based on "command-and-control"? Are current BPM modeling techniques able to model a "self-organizing, self governing, adaptive, nonlinear, complex organism, organization, community or system, whether physical or social, the behavior of which harmoniously blends characteristics of both chaos and order"? Is it time to question the first principles of Enterprise Architecture in light of global Chaords that are neither centralized nor anarchical business networks?

If we consider intelligent agents as fractals in a multidimensional business ecosystem, some of the key components of *multi-agent problem-solving* are essential. To achieve common goals, agents need coordination. Effective coordination requires cooperation, which in turn can be achieved through communication and organization.

The difference is between active, central control and adaptive coordination—Orchestra versus Ballet.

- In *orchestration*, the conductor tells everybody in the orchestra what to do in real time and makes sure they all play in synchronization. The conductor is an active leader, corrects for anomalies in real-time, and can introduce new information only he or she has. Orchestration in formation systems also has an equivalent: the orchestration engine.
- In *choreography*, the choreographer coordinates the *plan* but is not part of execution. Each participant is responsible for its own adaptive behavior. Orchestration defines a procedure and Choreography defines a protocol.

Military style "command and control" management is giving way to "connect and collaborate," and the reason is clear. In today's world of total global competition, no one company is in control. Thus orchestration of the entire business ecosystem by a single conductor is of days gone by.

Choreography via the foundation of peer-to-peer multiagent systems, with autonomous mobile agents sharing common goals is the future. Of course, no sane person would hand over control of enterprise transactions to an unsupervised network of software agents. To investigate, negotiate, design, implement, monitor and maintain complex, long-running enterprise partnerships you need a system that not only supports cross-boundary processes natively but has the right model. Such a model isn't based on the flow of work through a diagram, but on a framework including object types and distributed policy management (Role, Person, Interaction, Entity, Activity, Rule, and so on).

Just consider human interaction management as a peer-to-peer multiagent system. While Web 2.0 usage of the Internet has opened up new frontiers of possible human communication, it has also opened Pandora's box of noise, chaos and distraction. If we turn to human interaction management systems we find that an agent-based platform can bring management control to all the noise, and the goal-oriented organizational design (GOOD) method can bring about chaordic collaboration within the onslaught of Web 2.0 communication. (see humanedj.com).

To continue this investigation of Fractal Enterprise Architecture and agent-oriented BPM, what would your answers be for the following questions?

Can Enterprise Architecture be modeled with fractal geometry, such as complex, nonlinear systems are modeled in nature?

Can such Enterprise Architecture become *executable,* at least as a simulation of the real business?

Because what an enterprise "does" is far more important than "what it is," can BPM be fused with Enterprise Architecture and both be executed in real-time?

When a part of a complex business system "dies" (entropy) is that the end, or does extropy extend the march to order? How does this apply to a business or its parts located in the midst of a global business ecosystem?

We are sure if JFK was asked such questions when considering putting man on the moon in the 1960s, much skepticism would have been shouted out: "Impossible. Far too complex. Get real." But the times were ripe. And, just perhaps, the time is ripe for Fractal Enterprise Architecture and Agent-Oriented BPM.

With the current reality of total global competition and world-wide operation of companies, this shift will require polymorphism, not just at the software object level, but also in our enterprise architecture: "Fractal Enterprise Architecture."

The *goal-oriented* BPM system (goBPMS) with *choreography* (not just old-fashioned process orchestration) will be at the heart of multiagent systems that seek the common goals set by the goBPMS. An informative goal-oriented method is described in the BPTrends Column, Goal-Oriented Organization Design(GOOD). http://tinyurl.com/cehhc5g

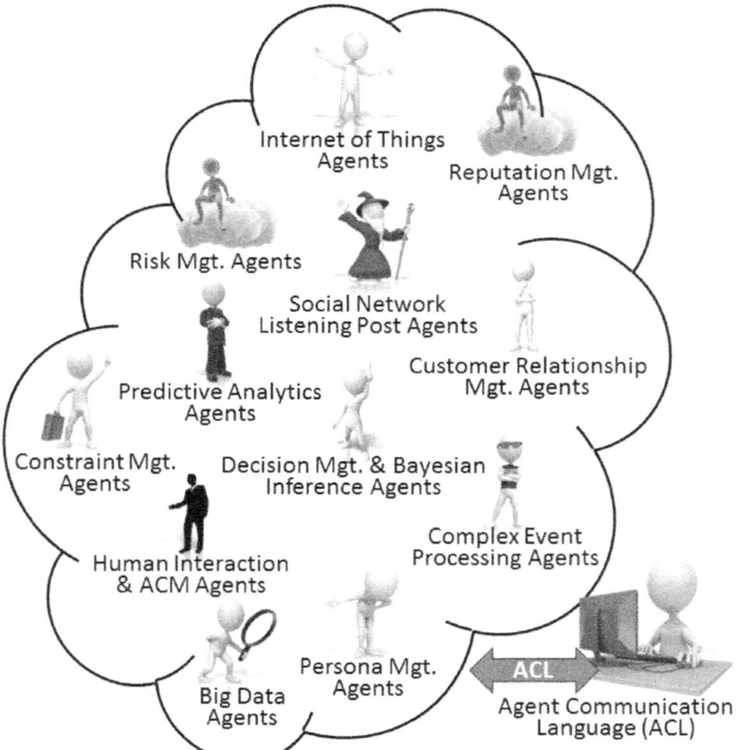


Figure 11.8 Goal-Oriented BPMS with Agent Choreography

## Start Small: Mount Sinai Hospital Case Study

In 2009, one of the authors of this book spoke at GE Global Research's Whitney Symposium in Niskayuna, New York, a 600 acre research campus on the Mohawk river, the legacy of one

Thomas Edison. (View the PDF of the presentation, *Business Process Management and Systems Thinking*, here: http://goo.gl/t8gmp.)

It was a huge honor and an eye-opening experience (1,000 PhDs representing 22 disciplines in one building!). The Theme for the Symposium was "The Engineering of Customer Services." Sound boring? Not so, when you consider that 80% of the U.S. GDP is not about Agriculture, not about Manufacturing, but about Services! Like IBM before it, GE had been pushing hard to become a services-driven company versus just a product company, and the Symposium brought together thought leaders on services sciences, engineering, and management, including speakers from IBM's legendary Thomas Watson's Research Lab, MIT, Columbia University, and think tanks from Europe.

That was 2009.

Here's a 2012 update on GE from the *New York Times*, "G.E. is America's largest industrial company, a producer of aircraft engines, power plant turbines, rail locomotives and medical imaging equipment. It makes the heavy-duty machinery that transports people, heats homes and powers factories, and lets doctors diagnose life-threatening diseases. GE resides in a different world from the consumer Internet. But the major technologies that animate Google and Facebook are also vital ingredients in the industrial Internet—tools from artificial intelligence, like machine-learning software, and vast streams of new data. In industry, the data flood comes mainly from smaller, more powerful and cheaper sensors on the equipment.

"Smarter machines, for example, can alert their human handlers when they will need maintenance, before a breakdown. It is the equivalent of preventive and personalized care for equipment, with less downtime and more output. 'These technologies are really there now, in a way that is practical and economic,' said Mark M. Little, GE's senior vice president for global research. 'GE's embrace of the *Industrial Internet* is a long-term strategy. But if its optimism proves justified, the impact could be felt across the economy." On a related note, a hot 2012 startup, SmartThings in the UK, is bringing the capabilities of the industrial Internet of

Things to the consumer market (http://smartthings.com)

Now, GE has opened a whole new research center in "Silicone Valley. More from the *New York Times* (November 23, 2012): "When Sharoda Paul finished a postdoctoral fellowship last year at the Palo Alto Research Center, she did what most of her peers do—considered a job at a big Silicon Valley company, in her case, Google. But instead, Ms. Paul, a 31-year-old expert in social computing, went to work for General Electric. Ms. Paul is one of more than 250 engineers recruited in the last year and a half to GE's new software center here, in the East Bay of San Francisco. The company plans to increase that work force of computer scientists and software developers to 400, and to invest $1 billion in the center by 2015. The buildup is part of GE's big bet on what it calls the 'Industrial Internet,' bringing digital intelligence to the physical world of industry as never before. The concept of Internet-connected machines that collect data and communicate, often called the 'Internet of Things,' has been around for years. Information technology companies, too, are pursuing this emerging field. IBM has its 'Smarter Planet' projects, while Cisco champions the 'Internet of Everything.' But GE's effort, analysts say, shows that Internet-era technology is ready to sweep through the industrial economy in much the same way as the consumer Internet has transformed media, communications and advertising over the last decade."

"At Mount Sinai, GE has worked on optimization and modeling software that enables admitting officers to see beds and patient movements throughout the hospital, to help them more efficiently match patients and beds. Beyond that, modeling software is beginning to make predictions about likely patient admission and discharge numbers over the next several hours, based on historical patterns at the hospital and other circumstances —say, in flu season. The software, which Mount Sinai has been trying out in recent months, acts as an intelligent assistant to admitting officers. 'It essentially says, 'Hold off, your instinct is to give this bed to that guy, but there might be a better choice,' Mr. Keathley explained. At a hospital like Mount Sinai, GE estimates that the optimization and modeling technologies can translate into roughly 10,000 more patients treated a year, and $120 million in savings and additional revenue over several years." See: goo.gl/ZbNZn

We chose this kind of simple case study from GE and Mount Sinai to illustrate that the move to agent-oriented BPM isn't a future big bang, ERP conversion, or Orwellian event. This isn't Star Wars stuff and in no way implies complicated systems or some esoteric stuff from some research lab. We are talking about practical technology that has been working for many years. It works.

Don't let the bad-news stories of seemingly exotic agent technology providers, past and present, create fear. Perhaps you've read about HP going after its recently acquired Autonomy Corp. for financial shenanigans, a UK firm that grew out of Cambridge University in 1995. Despite all of the rancor, Autonomy pioneered the use of Bayesian inference in the intelligent agent world. It works. Autonomy counts the U.S. Department of Homeland Security, the U.S. Department of Defense, the U.S. Securities and Exchange Commission, the Olympic Games Security Committee, the UK Houses of Parliament, General Motors, Ford, GlaxoSmithKline, Philips, BMW, Nestle and Ericsson among its forward-thinking 65,000 customers: http://goo.gl/k3RRc.

So, don't panic when you hear the term aoBPM. Don't take on all the rules nor all the possible types of analytics, or try to build an all-encompassing agent infrastructure. Focus on a given process where multiagent systems agents can make a difference, as did Mount Sinai when choosing to take on just its admission process. Such beginnings can grow into a bright future in today's world of unexpected change and total global competition—and can launch your journey to mastering aoBPM.

## Mastering aoBPM

Although implementing aoBPM can deliver immediate value, BPM technology alone is not enough. Implementing aoBPM technology will not make a business "competent" any more than the act of buying a car means a person knows how to drive. Experience with prior technology acquisitions, such as ERP, shows that businesses that adopted the same technologies—and even used the same implementation consultants—achieved very different business results as a consequence of how they actually learned to exploit the strengths, and avoid the weaknesses, of the technologies. Thus, to use aoBPM effectively companies must develop and acquire process management competencies.

Before considering how to develop the needed competencies, here's a warning!

In Switzerland, the famous Matterhorn casts a shadow over the cemetery at its feet in the town of Zermatt. The cemetery is a warning to those who would proceed up the steep slopes. Early pioneers who had neither maps nor guides are buried there, along with the primitive tools they thought were up to the task. Today, Swiss law prohibits the inexperienced from climbing the steep slopes without a guide.

Today's business and technology professionals tasked with adopting Internet generation computing, new knowledge management systems, customer relationship management and digital marketplaces should heed the message sent down from the Matterhorn, "Don't go it alone." Because the trek is through territory unfamiliar to the inexperienced, even years of knowledge and skill in somewhat related domains do not directly apply. Too much is at stake to go it alone without an experienced guide to point out opportunities as well as pitfalls. The guide's map shows many alternative paths, and the guide charts the paths based on current circumstances and the goals of the climber.

Who are you going to call on as aoBPM guides?

*Agent software used in very large systems:*

- ActiveEdge - www.cougaarsoftware.com/
- CybelePro and CybelePro Enterprise from Intelligent Automation, Inc. - www.i-a-i.com/cybelepro (Note: IAI also has advanced proprietary agent software that is available when IAI assists.)

*Other agent software (partial list):*

- Agent Factory - www.agentfactory.com
- JACK and CoJACK - aosgrp.com/products/jack
- JADE (Java Agent DEvelopment Framework) jade.tilab.com
- WADE (Workflow and Agents Development Environment jade.tilab.com/wade/
- Agent-based modeling software (i.e., agent simulation) (See Excel spreadsheet) - http://tinyurl.com/kqaa76y

*BPM vendors that already employ an agent-rich architecture:*

- Living Systems Process Suite (LSPS) www.whitestein.com/products/process-suite/

*BPM vendors expected to aim for intelligent agents over time:*

- IBM, Metasonic, Pegasystems, TIBCO, Bosch Software Innovations

*Other vendors expected to aim for intelligent agents over time:*

- EnterpriseWeb, Modus21 (BPM service provider)

Building an aoBPM competency requires three components: a sound understanding by senior managers of aoBPM's strategic importance to the business; the setting of clear targets by strategists, defining precisely how aoBPM is going to be used; and the possession of appropriate skills by implementers so that they can do their work effectively and efficiently. Because these three competencies reinforce one another, they must be developed together.

When an organization adopts a new tool, a common assumption is that training is a binary proposition, i.e., that people are either trained, or they are not. Experience indicates that this assumption is flawed. Meilir Page-Jones, industry luminary and president of Wayland Systems, developed a seven-stage model of expertise that describes what people actually go through as they learn and develop skills associated with a new paradigm. Developing an environment and a process for moving people through these seven stages should be high on the CEO's and CIO's priority lists. The following discussion outlines how Page-Jones' stages may be applied to aoBPM.

*Stage 1: Innocent—Never heard of aoBPM.* Some have never heard of aoBPM. Others have already seen references to business intelligent agent technologies in trade publications. They may be vaguely aware of the existence of agent technology, but may not see the possible relevance to their situations. Someone may be considered innocent if that person has not learned enough about agent technology to be aware of some of the tradeoffs associated with it: some of its costs, some of its benefits, or where and when it might be appropriately applied.

Business processes have become insidiously more and more complex, yet there was no sharp transition. The earth was not hit by a complexity asteroid that suddenly made business processes three orders of magnitude more complex and cast our reptilian process techniques into extinction. Page-Jones calls the way in which process complexity actually increased as the "Frog in the Pan." This is because although a frog will jump out of a pan of hot water, a frog that is placed in a pan of cold water and slowly heated will fail to leap forth and will actually boil to death. The temperature gradient is so gradual that there will never be a point at which the frog declares, "Boy, it's suddenly gotten hot in here! I think I should hop out." Many Innocents are experiencing "Frog in the Pan" and are trying to tackle problems of the 21st century with approaches of the past, without realizing that the problems they're facing are the very ones that aoBPM can alleviate.

Moving someone from the innocent stage to the next stage is a process of providing gentle introductions to the technology through articles, presentations, seminars, and participation in related associations. The goal is to inform and educate. Management-level introductory presentations can place the more global issues of aoBPM into perspective.

*Stage 2: Aware—Has read something about aoBPM.* Stage 2 people have noticed that the water is getting decidedly warm, if not downright hot. So, they are actively seeking advanced BPM methods and techniques that will get them out of the pan or at least reduce the heat. Their interest level is high but their knowledge level is low, being limited to a few terms and definitions and not based on any practical experience.

A person at this stage has not yet achieved the paradigm shift. The Aware's intellectual framework for aoBPM is still based upon drawing analogies to the old ways of doing things, and the person probably still draws upon erroneous assumptions when thinking or making decisions about aoBPM. Moving a person from this stage to the next involves establishing and executing an initial training program of readings, seminars and workshops in the working fundamentals of aoBPM.

*Stage 3: Apprentice—Has studied aoBPM.* At this stage, the person is well aware of the high level concepts of aoBPM; however the Apprentice may or may not have experienced the paradigm shift. This person cannot effectively apply the technology on his or her own, but can begin to contribute to the use of the methods and techniques. It could be said that most Stage 3 people know just enough to be dangerous! Moving the person from this stage to the next involves establishing and executing a training program that focuses on the details of aoBPM.

*Stage 4: Practitioner—Ready to use aoBPM.* The rite of passage to Stage 4 is the use of aoBPM methods and techniques on at least one significant project. Achieving "Stage 4-hood" is for many people the most difficult transition of the six transitions between stages. The fledgling Stage 4 is asked to take newly learned techniques and apply them to a corporate project with the usual demonic cocktail of politics, deadlines, changing requirements and distractions. At the same time, the Practitioner is attempting to recall what he or she learned in class and scale up the examples 10- or 100-fold. At this stage, the Practitioner is ready to make process-engineering decisions on his or her own. Movement to the next stage is a function of time, practice, an increasing knowledge base, and specific mentoring.

*Stage 5: Journeyman—Uses aoBPM naturally and automatically.* At this stage, participants are able to apply the technology in normal situations and do not require the presence of a mentor to accomplish quality work. This stage also requires a self-managed learning program to increase understanding. The Journeyman still calls upon the mentor when new or especially complex problems appear. Movement to the next stage is a function of experience, increasing depth of knowledge, and the evolution of the generic, problem-solving framework. This problem-solving framework is developed through interacting with a Master-level person on new or complex situations. In this stage, the solution process is more important than the solution details.

*Stage 6: Master—Has internalized aoBPM and knows when to break the rules.* The Master is not only adept with aoBPM techniques and technologies, but also possesses a profound methodological foundation. Beyond the "whats" and "hows," the Stage 6 knows the "whys" of aoBPM. This depth allows the Master to sometimes break a surface rule, while adhering to a more fundamental methodological principle.

For the Master, continued learning is a matter of keeping up with progress being made with aoBPM methods and technologies. Every organization needs access to Masters, either on staff or on retainer. The Master can handle new or complex applications of aoBPM, review Journeyman level work, show alternative or creative solutions to problems, point out subtleties in process engineering decisions, and help keep the organization up to date.

Movement to the next stage is strictly up to the individual. It is based on the individual's thought processes and experiences. Moving up to the Expert stage generally requires the individual to be actively engaged in a broad range of applications of aoBPM in new or unusual situations.

Stage 7: Expert—at the pinnacle of aoBPM methods and technologies. The Expert writes about aoBPM modeling and methodology, publishes learned articles, gives lectures, and develops ways to push the envelope and extend aoBPM methods and technologies. The Expert is generally recognized for his or her contributions to the industry, and is often asked to lecture or give presentations at national meetings for peers.

In short, *knowledge transfer* is the key to success in implementing aoBPM. aoBPM is not a big-bang conversion. The seed must be planted, initial aoBPM infrastructure(s) put in place, and pilot projects undertaken to establish aoBPM competency. Having established such a greenhouse for nurturing competencies based on the seven-stage process of aoBPM mastery, a company can grow into a mighty process-managed enterprise.

At some time during the journey from *innocent* to *master* an epiphany will occur. It will be something like, "This is as it should always have been." However, no methodology and no technology is a silver bullet—including BPM. BPM will advance in step with the growing communal knowledge of those who master it.

To kick off your aoBPM mastery journey, a little *prodding* may be in order. C-level execs, consider prodding your Chief Information Officer (CIO) or your Chief Digital Officer (CDO) to research and fill you in on what aoBPM portends for competitive advantage. CIOs and CDOs, prod your current BPM and other technology providers to investigate and start proof of concept projects. Join standards bodies such as the OMG and FIPA. Reach out to universities such as Oxford's Department of Computer Science (www.cs.ox.ac.uk) where the likes of Michael Wooldridge hangs his hat, or the University of Southampton where Sir Tim Berners-Lee (the WWW guy) and N. R. Jennings keep pushing the agent technology envelope (read or skim Jennings' "Implementing a Business Process Management System Using ADEPT: A Real-World Case Study"

eprints.soton.ac.uk/253740/1/aaij2000a.pdf

## Conclusion and Next Steps

BPM has successfully delivered benefits over a long period of time and continues to do so, but as process scopes expand, BPM needs to morph and change because of how businesses want to use their processes as they incrementally transform into digital enterprises. The idea of having all the intelligence centrally managed and delivered is a challenging, if not impossible outcome. Thus agent-oriented BPM (aoBPM) is what will allow BPM to take on all of what is expected of it as organizations accelerate growth and connect better with their customers, while providing greater agility and near real-time responses. As the Internet of Things, social, mobile and Cloud are baked into more and more business processes, they will rapidly reshape how business gets done today and tomorrow. Business and IT executives should be investigating and performing process projects that leverage the distributed intelligence that will enable all kinds of agents, human or otherwise. This book portends the beginning of aoBPM and the digitally savvy organization's journey with what BPM has grown up to be for the future—and the future is now; it's just not evenly distributed! As exclaimed in the book, *Business Innovation in the Cloud*, "Innovate or Die."

> *We thought that we had the answers, it was the questions we had wrong.*
> —Bono
> *My greatest strength as a consultant is to be ignorant and ask a few questions.*
> —Peter Drucker

If you came to these pages looking for pat answers and how-to solutions for the challenges we all face, then all we can say is, "Don't look elsewhere for *cookie-cutter answers* because you won't find such." Only *you* can invent your future, and we hope we have provided the information for you to *ask the right questions.*

We will let Albert provide the closing statement for this book.

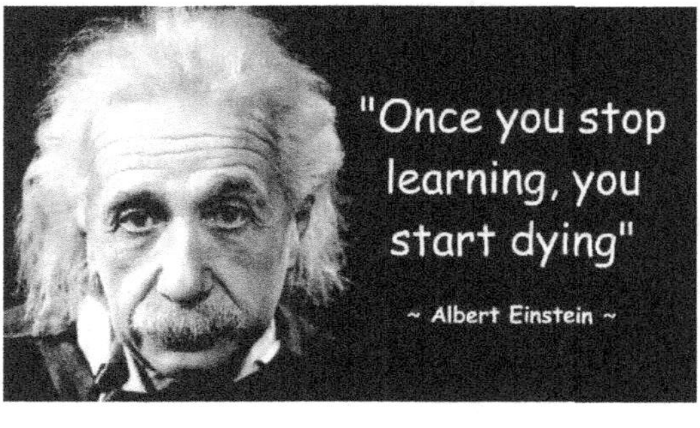

## References

[1] OMG, Agent Metamodel and Profile (AMP) – Initial Submission, 2009, OMG document ad/2009-08-04, http://tinyurl.com/k6t69nb.

[2] Foundation for Intelligent Physical Agents (FIPA), FIPA ACL Message Structure Specification, http://www.fipa.org/specs/fipa00061, 2000.

[3] Foundation for Intelligent Physical Agents (FIPA), FIPA Communication Act Library Specification, http://www.fipa.org/specs/fipa00037, 2000.

# Technical Appendices

The Appendices section of this book contains additional content regarding agents and their usage for BPM. This material has been placed here because it is of a more technical nature than the main body of the book. It is, therefore, supplemental reading that is useful for readers who would appreciate a more technical grounding in aoBPM. The appendices are as follows:

*Appendix A* - A Deeper Look at the Anatomy of an Agent

*Appendix B* - Agent Communication

*Appendix C* - Agent Interaction

*Appendix D* - Security and Architecture

*Appendix E* - Agent Standards

# Appendix A. A Deeper Look at the Anatomy of an Agent

## Introduction

As we discussed in the main body of the book, agents are autonomous entities that can adapt to and interact with their environment. To accomplish this, agents must have some means by which they can perceive their environment and act upon those perceptions.

## Agent as a Black Box

At its simplest, each agent can be thought of as an interactive black-box, where no indication of an agent's internal structure and behavior is given other than that which is visible from outside the agent. Figure A.1 depicts this by illustrating that agents have input from, and output to, the environment – i.e., it receives and emits events. An agent's environment can be thought of as everything outside of the agent. For robotic agents, the environment would consist of the terrain, the constraints of motion and control, and other agents. For software agents, the environment would consist of the hosting platform, its operating systems and supporting middleware, and other agents.

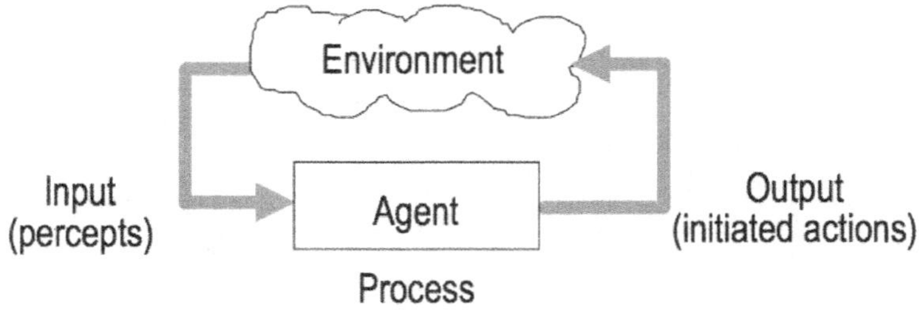


Figure A.1 – An agent and its environment.

Input can be whatever the agent "perceives," such as messages, requests, commands, and other events. Based on such input, the agent can decide how to act, which typically results in some output from the agent, such as communicating with, or making a change to, its environment. For instance, our Robotic agent could receive a move command, and then change its state through movement (events). An Inventory agent could receive a request for the quantity-on-hand for a given commodity, causing it to determine the requested quantity and send a response event to the requestor. The Inventory agent would also receive notification events regarding inventory being removed and sent to a customer. The agent process would then recompute the quantity-on-hand and decide if a reorder point has been reached, and if so, would send out requests-for-bid to appropriate suppliers.

## Agent Processing Overview

For an agent to interact with its environment, it must not only detect and effect its environment but also understand what it is detecting, determine an appropriate response, and act on it. In other words, for the agent to be an interactive entity, it also requires some degree of autonomy and adaptivity. The internal structure of an agent can be visualized as illustrated in Figure A.2.

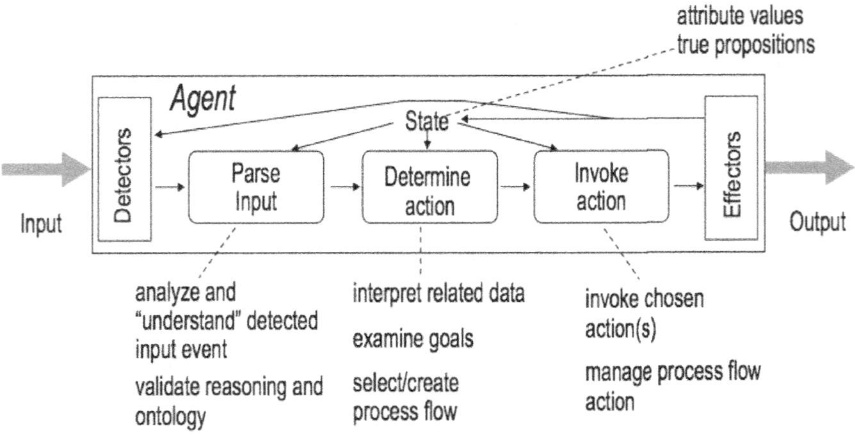


Figure A.2– The basic internal architecture of an agent.

## State

Just like objects, agents can have a form of memory, referred to here simply as *state*. State includes the data that it needs to operate and is maintained or is accessible in some manner (such as via a database or automated blackboard) by the agent. For example, the Inventory agent would need to maintain information such as the reorder point for a particular product or the algorithm needed to compute the reorder point. The agent might also maintain the list of valid product vendors that it can contact for reordering—or at least know where the information might be found, or which other agent it can delegate that request to. The agent could even make inferences about its own state or the state of other entities in its environment. State, then, can be metaphorically interpreted as anything that the agent can "know" or "believe" about itself or its environment.

## Detectors

*Detectors* provide the agent's interface to the environment. They receive input events that are of interest to the agent. Detectors can both receive input sent to them ("push" model) or actively scan the environment for it ("pull" model). Detectors can receive simple messages and event notifications, or they can scan message logs or monitor event occurrences. In particular, event-monitoring agents (in *event-driven architectures*) may be specialized to recognize particular kinds of state changes in the environment. For example, master data agents could watch for certain kinds of changes in a database such as metamodel modifications, customer-address changes, or even the database going offline. If any of these events were detected, the agent could notify other agents that can react appropriately, such as the system monitor agent that notifies the DBA. In event-driven architectures (EDA), this is particularly useful. Robotic agents may employ such sensors as cameras, global positioning hardware, or infrared devices for detectors, and directly process and interpret the associated images and event streams.

## Parse Input

Once the detector receives input, the agent needs to analyze and "understand" the input. This action typically involves recognition, normalization, and exception handling. For conventional object-oriented software, there is virtually no parsing: the OO "signature's" first parameter identifies the object, its second specifies the requested operations, and its remaining input contains the data required for the operation execution. Because the signature syntax is already defined in this manner, the message does not need to go through any "determine action" step. Instead, it goes immediately to invoke its specified method.

In a system with a more complex style of input, the OO approach cannot provide a satisfactory solution. For example, some IT agents need to process complex syntax and receive input in one or more languages, such as SQL, Prolog, BPEL4WS, BPML, or ebXML. They may need to understand complex ontologies expressed in OWL before any further action can be determined against some RDF data. For complex event processing (CEP) agents, this parsing involves condition checking and decision determination for events handled by a given type or agent. Such event pattern recognition is important for agents because they apply to processing of input and out artifacts, preconditions and conditional effect—especially those that need to recognize many potential new state situations (e.g., self-healing systems).

Granted, activities like parsing require greater complexity than a traditional object. In fact, not all agents will require such sophisticated behaviors. Yet, when system requirements demand richer behavioral control at execution time, agents need to be able to accomplish what traditional objects cannot. Activities such as parsing or accepting rule updates extend the notion of the semantic net to enable the semantic approach to system interaction.

## Determine Action

As suggested earlier in the book, traditional OO recommends that the method requested of an object is determined *before* a message is sent to the object. This is because each object class defines separate methods, one for each kind of message "signature." If the number of possible methods is tangible, this is not a problem; for those situations requiring hundreds or thousands of possibilities, such an approach is impractical. For example, insurance companies have hundreds of ways of rating a policy; retailers and shipping companies have an equally large number of rules and procedures for pricing a product or service. To support this need in an agile and adaptive manner, the agent approach also needs the ability to determine the appropriate method *after* it receives a request for service. In this way, a Policy agent can decide on the appropriate method to rate a policy based on the requestor's needs, and an Order agent can decide the appropriate pricing algorithm when the customer submits an order.

Another function within the Determine Action step could be to determine the appropriate goal for further consideration. For example, an Inventory agent would detect each time a product was pulled from a warehouse bin, and for each such instance it might need to first decide if the product should be reordered or, if it is selling too slowly, discontinue the product altogether. Each of these goals requires a different process. One might involve sending out and processing bids from other agents to refill the bin; the other might notify customer agents that the product will no longer be available, and await responses.

The Determine Action process might involve a high degree of complex processing in its own right. Can this be accomplished using an OO approach? Absolutely. However, some agent platforms have mechanisms that support higher order models of decisions directly— for example using rule engines instead of having the programmer do extra work in design, construction, testing, and maintenance.

## Invoke Action

Once selected, the appropriate action needs to be invoked. The action execution may involve actions internal to the agent, in which case, message events can be sent directly to the agent's own detectors. If the action involves other agents, the message events need to be sent to them. The agent controls its autonomy by using its own resources or having them provided by other agents. It determines what it can do and what it must delegate. In this sense, the agent manages itself—rather than just being managed.

In addition, some agents can determine when their internal actions are not functioning as expected. The agent can also communicate to itself that the situation needs to be remedied—by sending itself a message and letting some Determine Action step determine which action should be taken next. In other words, the agent can have its own self-aware processes. In a business process management system, such mechanisms can be handled in a distributed manner using events and agents, rather than by some centralized controller that will not scale under large processing volumes.

### Effectors

When messages need to be sent or events posted outside the agent, effectors are the connection with the agent's environment. It is the mechanism an agent uses to interact with and mobilize within the environment. This could involve sending messages though a message bus or activating a hardware device such as a printer or robot arm.

## Agents Can Do Multiprocessing

Agents can be single threaded or designed to process inputs concurrently (Figure A.3). Agents that can support concurrency might also have a process controller that coordinates the various internal actions in some manner.

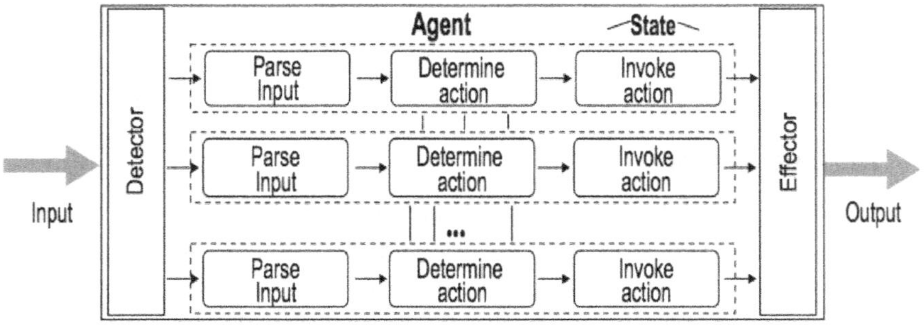


Figure A.3 – Concurrent processing within the agent.

## Reasoning, Planning, and Scheduling

A common approach for agents can involve reasoning, planning, and scheduling. (Figure A.4) In this approach, an agent can determine the appropriate action by having a *reasoner* step consider what it knows about its state and the state of its environment (including that of the service requestor). Additionally, the agent reasoner can identify the appropriate goals for acting based on the detected input and state knowledge. Here, the agent may optionally weigh the importance of certain goals (when there are conflicting goals to choose from). For example, a Scheduling agent may have a goal to ensure that all the tasks in its care are executed on time. Another goal might be that certain priorities must be given to important tasks. The two goals, however, may conflict when priority tasks cause the delay of other tasks. Here, the agent may have to weigh the cost of both and determine which service it intends to perform under a given constraint.

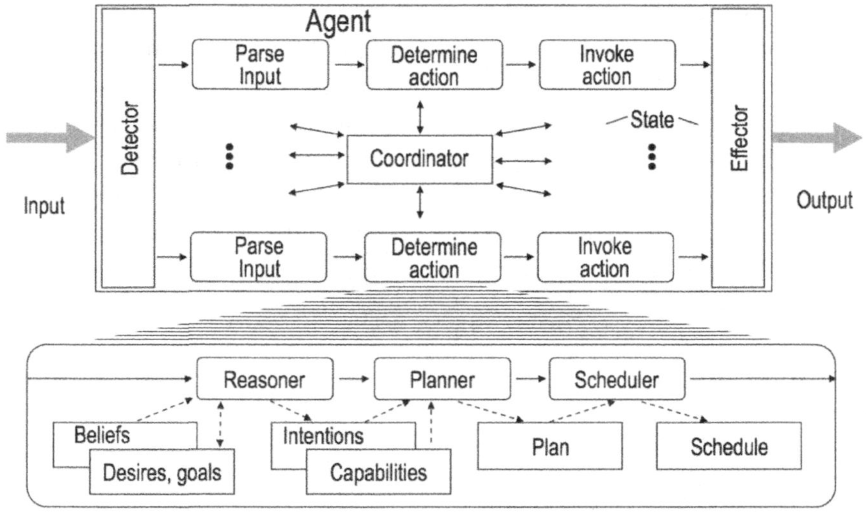


Figure A.4 – Determining the appropriate action can involve reasoning, planning, and scheduling.

A *planner* then determines the actual steps needed to execute the agent's intention. For example, the scheduling agent may need to ensure a particular product is created for given order. The agent may need a make-or-buy decision resulting in a process that either fabricates the product in-house or purchases a fabricated item from an external source. Some agent planners dynamically assemble the planned set of steps to fit each occasion; others have a library of prefabricated processes from which to choose.

The planned process is then sent to the agent's *scheduler* to determine which resources will be assigned and when the process will be scheduled.[2]

In addition to this (Figure A.4), an agent may also employ a *coordinator* that ensures that the agent's concurrent processing works harmoniously: managing conflicts and optimizing the overall functioning of the agent.

## Conclusion

Agent-based systems do not require complex forms of agents like those described above. For example, ant colonies have been very successful for a long time (7 million years). An estimated 10% of the Earth's animal biomass is composed of ants. (Much more than humans). An ant has about 250,000 brain cells; humans have about 10 billion. Ants can lift 20 times their own body weight; they may be small, but they're efficient. What if it were as hard to get your deliveries off-schedule, as it is to keep ants out of your kitchen? In other words, agent systems do not require sophisticated agents to yield impressive results. With simple rules and high fault tolerance, the colony thrives—a great first-system model.

---

[2] Agents using this approach are sometimes referred to as "BDI" agents, because they employ beliefs, desires, and intentions. *Beliefs* refer to what the agent "believes" the state of its environment and other agents to be; *desires* basically refer the goals the agent could attempt to achieve, and *intentions* refers to the set of goals the agent actually intends to achieve under a given circumstance.

# Appendix B. Agent Communication

## Introduction

Many of the early commercial agents were developed for information searches. Individual agents were launched on a tether to gather predefined kinds of information and return them to the human requester. In other words, these agents were solo operations that had very little—if any—interaction with other agents. Such an approach certainly has its many uses. However, if we look at the human world, such an approach *alone* could not build the societies or support the organizations that humans have come to enjoy. Instead, we set up networks of people that interact for various purposes. Interaction among agents, then, is not sufficient to build agent societies, we need agents that can coordinate—either through cooperation, competition, or a combination of both. These agent "societies" are called *multiagent systems* (MAS).

Multiagent systems, then, are systems composed of agents coordinated through their relationships with one another. For example in a kitchen, the toaster "knows" when the toast is done, and the coffeemaker "knows" when the coffee is ready. However, there is no cooperative environment here—only an environment with single agents. In a multiagent environment, the kitchen becomes more than just a collection of processors. The appliances would be interconnected in such a way that the coffeemaker and the toaster would ensure that the coffee and toast are ready at the same time.

Some of the rationales for multiagent systems are as follows:

- One agent *could* be constructed that does everything, but fat agents represent a bottleneck for speed, reliability, maintainability, and so on (i.e., there are no omnipotent agents). Dividing functionality among many agents provides modularity, flexibility, modifiability, and extensibility.

- Specialized knowledge is not often available from a single agent (i.e., there are no omniscient agents). Knowledge that is spread over various sources (agents) can be integrated for a more complete view when needed.
- Applications requiring distributed computing are better supported by MAS. Here, agents can be designed as fine-grained autonomous components that act in parallel. Concurrent processing and problem solving can provide solutions to many problems that, up until now, we handled in a more linear manner. Agent technology, then, provides the ultimate in distributed component technology.

To support multiagent systems, an appropriate environment needs to be established. MAS environments:

- provide an infrastructure specifying communication and interaction protocols.
- are typically open and have no centralized designer or top-down control function.
- contain agents that are autonomous, adaptive, and coordinative.

Clearly, single-agent environments are much simpler, because designers do not have to deal with such issues as cooperation, negotiation, and so on. However, the large-scale requirements of industry necessitate approaches that employ coordination and distribution. As such, FIPA and the OMG Agent Special Interest Group are focusing primarily on multiagent systems rather than single agents.

## Multiple-Agent Systems

As we discussed in the main body of the book, agents are autonomous entities that can adapt to, and interact with, their environment. To accomplish this, agents must have some means by which they can perceive their environment and act upon those perceptions.

Useful systems can be built involving multiple agents that act on their own behalf, yet do not communicate or interact with each other. For example, a pricing system can use agents to determine the price of some commodity, or an insurance policy rate estimator agent can provide a quote for obtaining an insurance policy based on the insured's needs. Such agents are able to provide the service for which they were programmed, yet have no need to interact with other agents. These kinds of systems are called *multiple-agent systems* (which are different than multiagent systems).

However, for more complex systems, agents typically need to communicate and interact with other agents to accomplish their goals. For example, in an agent-assisted service-oriented architecture, a Service Requestor agent seeks a service to satisfy a particular need, and a Service Provider agent offers to provide a particular service. Each agent has something the other needs. To bring the two together, some form of communication and interaction is required. In some cases, a requestor agent may already have a reference to the provider agent it needs, so it negotiates directly with the provider agent. Service directories provide another means for requestors to locate providers that register their services. Once an appropriate provider is located (its directory listing contains the provider's address) then the requestor can negotiate directly with the provider agent. Also, a Service Broker agent can be added to the mix that enables requestors and providers to communicate and negotiate.

When many agents communicate and interact in a system, this is known as a *multiagent system (MAS)*. This appendix discussed the ways in which agent communication and interaction can be accomplished in multiagent systems.

## The Semantics of Communication and Interaction

If every designer developed a different means of communication between agents, our agent systems would be become an agent-based tower of Babel. Not only would the content and meaning of a communication likely be different, but the mechanism of communication could occur in a variety of ways. For small, local agent systems, the communication content and mechanism can be specialized to the particular group of agents. The communication content and mechanism would still need to be carefully defined, but would not require great elaboration.

However, in sophisticated agent environments, agents can employ both simple and complex means of communicating with other entitles in their environment—including software, machines, and humans.

Furthermore, agents can employ interactive mechanisms that enable agent coordination, cooperation, persuasion, negotiation, competition, coalition, and so on. Without interaction, agents would not be able to reach joint agreements and work together to accomplish a business function.

Probably the most important feature of agent communication and interaction protocols is that they be both *machine readable* and *machine understandable*. This section discusses the basics required for machine-readable communication and interaction: agent communication languages (including message syntax and ontology) and agent interaction protocols.

## Agent Communication Languages

> *Agent communication* is the act of agents conveying facts or information.

When two people want to communicate, they need to choose a common language and interchange medium—though even then misunderstandings can occur. Simple gestures and a handful of words can communicate a great deal. Yet, to function as societies, we need to employ richer forms of communication.

The same is true of agents. Self-contained systems only need to communicate in a basic and non-standard manner. However, when agents interact widely and need to effectively communicate with agents in other systems and organizations, agents need a standard language—a language with a set of conventions that support agents in identifying, connecting and exchanging information with other agents. Agent communication languages (ACLs) enable agents to communicate in a clear and unambiguous manner. By standardizing these ACLs, different parties can build their agents to interoperate both within and between applications—and organizations.

An example of a simple point-to-point communication between two agents is illustrated in Figure B.1, where one agent is asking another for the current price of IBM stock. This message specifies: an ask *performative*, the sender's identity (Joe), the message content (PRICE IBM ?price), the address of the communication (stock-server), the name of the reply expected from the responding agent (IBM-stock), the language in which the content is specified (LRPROLOG), and the set of the agreed-upon terms, or *ontology*, that will be used in the content exchange (NYSE-TICKS). The responding agent replies with the requested stock price—along with its associated ACL parameters.

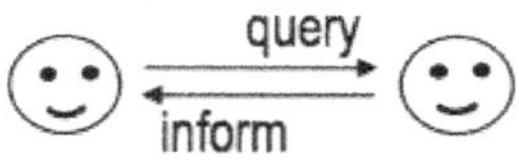


**FIPA ACL examples:**

```
(query                                (inform
:sender joe                           :sender stock-server
:receiver stock-server                :receiver joe
:content (PRICE IBM ?price)           :content (PRICE IBM 140)
:language LPROLOG                     :language LPROLOG
:ontology NYSE-TICKS                  :ontology NYSE-TICKS
:reply-with ibm-stock)                :in-reply-to ibm-stock)
```

Figure B.1 – Agent communication language (ACL) examples using FIPA ACL.

Currently, two primary standards for ACLs exist:

- *Knowledge Query and Manipulation Language (KQML):* Network environments that support plug-and-play processes are still quite rare. Most distributed systems are implemented with *ad hoc* interfaces between components. KQML is a language and set of conventions that support network programming specifically for knowledge-based systems and agents. It was developed by the ARPA-supported Knowledge Sharing Effort. (See www.cs.umbc.edu/kqml.)

- *Foundation for Intelligent Physical Agents (FIPA):* FIPA has been working to develop and promote *de jure* standardization in the area of agent interoperability since 1996. FIPA's ACL is a high-level agent communication language that is based on speech acts and is perceived by many as an improvement on KQML. (See www.fipa.org.)

Every FIPA ACL message has the following structure:

| **Element** | **Category of Elements** |
|---|---|
| performative | type of communicative act |
| sender | identity of the sender |
| receiver | identity of the intended recipient(s) |
| reply-to | recipient of subsequent messages |
| content | content of message |
| language | language in which the content is expressed |
| encoding | actual representation (such as XML) |
| ontology | names of ontology used in message |
| protocol | interaction protocol employed |
| conversation-id | identity of the ongoing conversation |
| reply-with | expression identifying response |
| in-reply-to | expression referencing earlier response |
| reply-by | latest expected response date |

The communicative acts that may be specified (such as ask and reply in Figure B.1) are defined by the ACL. Some examples of other FIPA, ACL and KQML communicative acts (called *performatives*) include:

- achieve or request - A wants B to perform a certain task.
- advertise - A registers as suitable for a particular request.
- ask or query - A requests information from B (ask-one or ask-all).
- broker - A wants B to find help to answer something.
- failure - A tells B that an action was attempted, but failed.
- not understood - A did not understand what B just did or said.

- recommend - A wants the name of an agent that supplies an answer.
- recruit - A wants B to request an agent to perform a given task.
- reply - A answers B.
- sorry or refuse - A cannot provide the requested information.
- subscribe - A wants any messages from B when they occur.
- tell or inform - A sends information.

Most of the ACL elements are self-explanatory. However, the language, ontology, and protocol parameters are particularly noteworthy.

## Language

Agent communication languages provide a high-level format for expressing communication acts among agents. The communication detail, however, is embodied in the content parameter, where the agent expresses the actual question, reply, or request. The format of the content must be agreed upon by both sender and receiver(s), otherwise effective communication will not be possible.

The *language* parameter helps to some extent, because it specifies a registered syntax form. For example, if Prolog or SQL were specified, the agent would know that the rules for content syntax must conform to the Prolog language. The Knowledge Information Format (KIF) is one standard for agent language syntax and was developed by a consortium at the University of Maryland. Another emerging trend is to use and extend XML, XML Schema, BPEL, and so on.

## Ontology

The syntax rules of a language are not enough to ensure clear communication; an agreed-upon set of terms is also required. Certainly, the syntax would define some terms, but there are also user-defined terms. For example, to ask for the number of clients that Fujitsu has could be expressed as: COUNT FUJITSU client ?integer. The syntax is well defined. But, if one agent uses the term "client" and the other knows only "customer," the two will not communicate effectively—even though both know that something is supposed to be tallied for Fujitsu. Agents can have different terms for the same concept and identical terms for different concepts. A common ontology, then, is required for representing the knowledge from various domains of discourse. The purpose of the *ontology* parameter in an ACL is to define the set of terms that will be used in an agent communication.

Although the need for terminology standards is not new, the dependence of agent communications on ontology makes such standards more critical than ever. Many organizations and consortia are now being set up to establish industry vocabularies. Common ontology representations using UML and XML schema are now being enriched with RDF, and OWL syntax.

## Protocols

Agent interaction involves *n*-way communications among agents for some purpose.

> *Agent interaction* is the action or influence of agents on each other.

The purpose of the protocol parameter is to enable a way for agents to interact in a clear – and machine-readable – manner. The *protocol* parameter specifies the name of a particular pattern of communication. Such conversational patterns are called *agent interaction protocols* (or sometimes just *protocols*). Each protocol specifies a pattern of interaction that is formally defined and abstracted from any particular sequence of execution steps. As such, *agent interaction protocols* enable a way for agents to interact in a clearly defined and machine-readable manner.

Common standard protocols already exist for the following kinds of interaction protocols: Contract Net (Negotiation), Iterated Contract Net, English Auction, Dutch Auction, Brokering, Recruiting, Publish/Subscribe, and Proposals.

Figure B.2 depicts a simple example of the *contract net* interaction protocols (using a modified UML Interaction Diagram). The process begins with the Buyer sending a request for proposal (RFP) to the seller (e.g., for some goods or services). The Seller then can decide to refuse the RFP for various reasons, including the fact that the offer is not understood for some reason. Or, the Seller could respond by sending a proposal back by the stipulated deadline. Once received, the Buyer can accept or reject the proposal. In response, the Seller can inform the Buyer that the contract is complete. If the contact has a cancellation clause, a cancel message may be sent to the Seller.

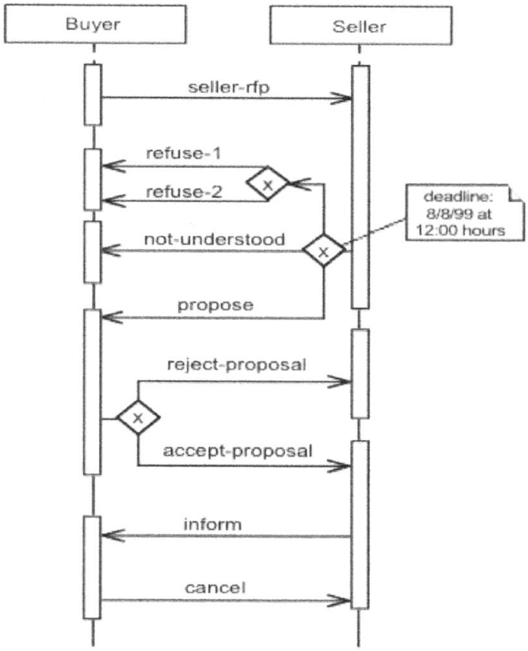


Figure B.2 – A "contract net" agent interaction protocol

## Objects and Messages

If agents use ACL and objects use message passing to communicate, then it is still not quite clear how agents and objects can coexist. In fact, this difference can be viewed as a defining characteristic of how agents and objects are different. Objects are objects if they can communicate via object messaging and agents are agents if they can communicate via agent communication language.

This observation holds a possible key to how to simultaneously permit both. Namely, some entities can be both objects and agents. This might permit a system to contain agents that use ACL to communicate with other agents, objects that use message passing to communicate with other objects, and some entities that can do both for they are simultaneously objects and agents, as the following diagram suggests:

agent --> | | ACL | object | | <-- object

There are several reasons why it is not simple to just model agents as objects directly.

## Expressive Limitations

When we model any software entity as an object, we focus on its interfaces and its state. In general, the single key characterization of an agent's behavior is that it accepts messages from other agents, performs some processing and (possibly) responds. This behavior, in terms of interface, may be represented in two forms. One would be to provide a method for every message that the agent is capable of processing. The other would be to provide a single method, AcceptCommunicativeString which would permit the agent to accept arbitrary messages. (A small set of multiple methods could be permitted, as well—particularly as separate channels for different roles. This can also be thought of as specialized ports for the agent.)

It is tempting to imagine providing an agent with a method for each message it can accept. However, we generally want every agent to be able to receive any message, then decide on its own how to process that message. Certainly, the messages it knows how to, and decides to process, can change over time.

On the other hand, the messages agents send and receive are not arbitrary. To be understood, they are described in a specific agent communication language with agreed upon semantics and structure. So it might actually make sense for objects that were also agents to be modeled as including the method AcceptACLString. At the same time, it is not satisfying to imagine a large application composed of agents implemented as objects each with one generic method just as it is not satisfying to imagine replacing object methods with a single agent method—too much is lost in this mapping in both directions.

## Autonomy

Method invocation also has the wrong basic connotations in terms of autonomy. In general, method invocation is done either on the caller's thread of control or, on the thread of a remote proxy for the caller, in the case of remote method invocation. Agents, on the other hand, aren't running as part of the caller, nor are they running with the caller's identity and privileges. In fact, it's quite the contrary. An agent runs on its own behalf, and with its own identity and privileges. While one can imagine doing things with access control such that the additional rights and proper identity were associated with each invocation, it adds steps that are outside the normal notions of method invocation.

Beyond identity and access control rights, we also run into the notion of autonomy. Unlike a normal object, where access control rights and visibility largely encapsulate notions of whether a method should run, an agent is an autonomous element of the software world. Thus, for every message that the agent receives, it may determine, based on its own goals and state, and the state of the ongoing conversation, whether to process the message and how to respond if it does. This implies that every method will, in effect, begin with the idiom of making such a determination, something which, in general, is beyond what the majority of objects do at method invocation time (parameter checking and comparison to internal state is fairly normal, but knowing the identity of one's caller, and basing decisions on that, is not).

Also, agents are active, not passive entities within a software system. Traditionally, an object is passive, with its methods being invoked under the control of another component of the system.

An agent, in general, can react not merely to specific method invocations, but to observable events within the environment. Further, as part of the basic structure of multi-agent systems, it is natural for agents to be engaged in multiple, parallel interactions with other agents.

### Conversations, and long-term associations

Another problematic issue for thinking of agent messages as method invocation is the question of long-term conversations and associations. Agents, unlike simple objects, may engage in multiple transactions concurrently, either through the use of multiple threads, or similar mechanisms. This is expressed naturally in a messaging environment, as each conversation can be assigned a separate identity, and either a unique message destination or a unique identifier can be used to sort out the threads of discourse.

Similar mechanisms can be built out of objects, of course, but they would bypass, or be in addition to, normal method invocation. One could imagine producing multiple cloned "copies" of the agent object and passing one reference to each counterpart, so as to provide separate communication contexts for each conversation. But the very need to invent in this kind of mechanism implies that the agent isn't acting as a simple object.

## Conclusion

As mentioned earlier, agents can employ both simple and complex means of communicating with other entitles in their environment—including software, machines, and humans. Additionally, agents can employ interactive mechanisms that enable agent coordination, cooperation, persuasion, negotiation, competition, coalition, and so on. Without interaction, agents would not be able to reach joint agreements, and work together to accomplish a business function.

The most important, however, of agent communication and interaction protocols is that they be *machine readable, understandable, and executable.* This Appendix primarily dealt with the basic notions of communication. The next Appendix continues by discussing ways that agents can interact using their communication abilities.

# Appendix C. Agent Interaction

## Mechanics of Agent Interaction

Many agent interaction mechanisms exist, such as point-to-point interaction, blackboards, agent mobility, and remote procedure calls. But, there are many more. This chapter describes the commonly used techniques employed by agents and agent systems.

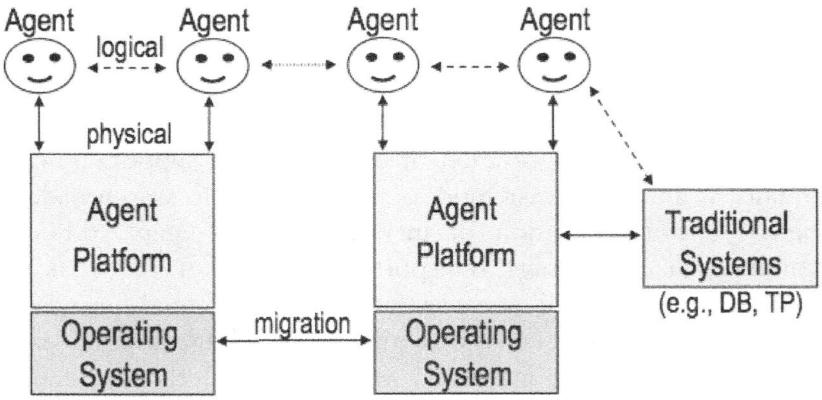


Figure C.1– Using the agent platform for communication and mobility.

## Point-to-Point Interaction

Agent communication can be achieved in two ways. The first way involves agents communicating directly with each other (*logical* connection). This approach provides flexibility and freedom but bypasses control and security. The other way involves agents communicating through an *agent platform* (Figure C.1). This resolves control and security problems but requires logical communications to be physically resolved via the agent-based software. Using an agent platform is especially important when communicating among different organizations or the agents are mobile.

Most agent systems use the second option, because the agent platform enforces control and security at a system level. With this approach, the look and feel of agents directly addressing other agents can still exist, even though all communications are still processed through the agent platform—even communications to traditional, or *legacy*, systems.

In agent environments, messages should be schedulable, as well as event driven. They can be sent in synchronous or asynchronous modes.

Furthermore, agents can know the addresses of the other agents with whom they wish to communicate, either because the agent has a record of them or because the agent uses a broker agent that has a record of them. However, a directory service should also be provided with the platform. With a directory service available, an agent can find another agent using techniques such as *white pages*, *yellow pages*, or some other approach.

Lastly, the transportation mechanism must support unicast, multicast, and broadcast modes, and such services as broadcast behavior, nonrepudiation of messages, and logging. Although commercialized message transportation does not yet exist for agent-based systems, it does exist in an object-oriented form. With some enhancements for the requirements of agent-based environments (directly or indirectly), the following technology could be used: CORBA, OMG Messaging Services, JAVA messaging service, RMI, DCOM, and Enterprise Java Beans Events.

## Blackboards

Generally speaking, a blackboard is a data-structure that stores information used by multiple different systems. Like a real-world blackboard:

- Anyone can read information from the blackboard at any time.
- Theoretically, anyone can write down some facts too.

For agent systems, the blackboard is ultimately a way for different agents to *communicate together*. The advantage of the blackboard is that it provides *modularity*; the various agents don't depend on each other, instead they just exchange the data via the blackboard. This reduces the level of coupling between the different behaviors, which makes the system easy to work with.

A *static* blackboard stores only certain types of information, and it cannot change at runtime (as opposed to a *dynamic* blackboard). The information within the predefined slots of blackboard can change at runtime of course, but no new facts can be added.

The structure of the blackboard is designed during development. The designers must go through an iterative process of figuring out what information is required to support intelligent selection of the behaviors and assets.

Using this approach has several advantages and disadvantages:

*Advantages:*

- Simple to create when the game isn't overly complex, the behaviors are well specified.
- Very efficient in terms of performance and storage requirements.
- Quick to build, and simple to implement in all programming languages.

*Disadvantages:*

- Can't store extra information without up-front design.
- Suffer from slow turn around times, as change to the knowledge structure requires a recompilation.

So, in essence, it's a trade-off between minimizing the time spent upfront on the blackboard, and the time required to create additional facts during development.

An agent system may communicate via one or more blackboards.

## Mobility and Remote Procedure Calls

Stationary agents exist as a single process on one host computer; mobile agents can pick up and move their code to a new host where they resume executing. Mobile agents are able to change platforms and environments; stationary agents are not. From a conceptual standpoint, such mobile agents can also be regarded as itinerant, dynamic, nomadic, wandering, roaming, or migrant. The rationale for mobility is the improved performance that can be achieved by moving the agent closer to the services available on the new host.

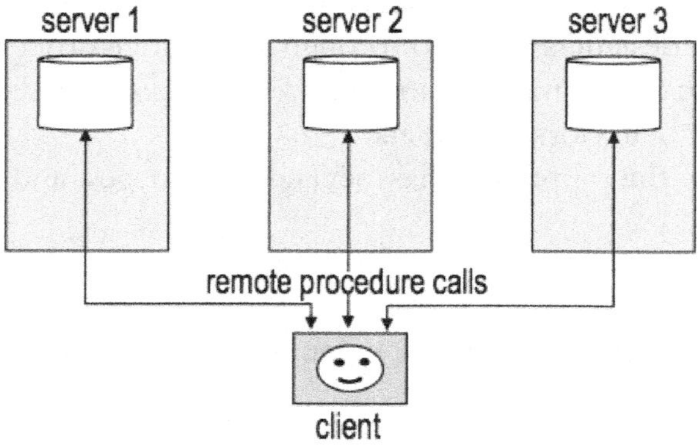


(a) Stationary agent uses RPC

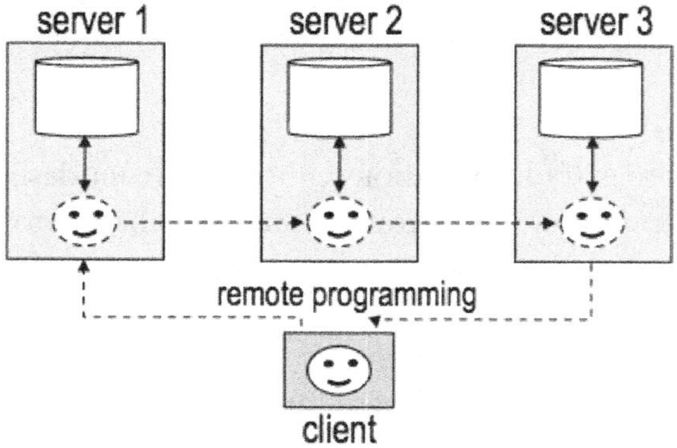


(b) Mobile agent uses RPC

Figure C.2– Stationary and mobile agents.

Stationary agents must use the network to exchange information primarily using the *remote procedure call* (RPC) as illustrated in

Figure C.2(a). When a stationary agent requires processing on a different platform, it must employ the services of another agent. Here, a communication (or request) conveys the intention to invoke a specific operation (via an RPC). The operation is then executed and the results (or reply) returned to the requesting agent. Using stationary agents has the following advantages and disadvantages:

*Advantages:*

- Reduces the complexity required for mobility.
- Encourages specialization within platforms.
- Employs well-established protocols.
- Supports closed-environment philosophy.

*Disadvantages:*

- Results in performance problems in those situations requiring high volume or frequency.
- Results in processing inefficiencies because having many specialized agents create more work than having a single mobile agent.
- Reduces effectiveness when a connection is lost.

In contrast, mobile agents use the network to exchange information primarily by changing platforms and environments using the *remote programming* (RP) technique. When a mobile agent requires processing on a different platform, it physically relocates to the desired server as illustrated in Figure C.2(b). This requires that all structural and behavioral properties of the agent must be transferred during migration and that any environmental differences be changed or accommodated. The big issues here are how much time is required to prepare for migration, how much data is actually transferred, and the performance of the transfer communication.

Migrations can be handled by the agent. While this reduces the complexity of the runtime environment, it increases agent complexity. In contrast, migrations can be transparent to the agent, which reduces agent complexity while increasing the complexity of the runtime environment. The advantages and disadvantages of mobile agents are:

*Advantages:*

- Reduces network load.
- Reduces network-related delay.
- Reduces resource usage of clients.
- Enables distributed problem solving.
- Supports asynchronous, autonomous processing.
- Promotes reconfigurable or customized services.
- Makes active behavior scenarios conceivable.
- Enhances decentralization options.

*Disadvantages:*

- Involves a number of security issues such as the identification and authentication of agents, protection from destructive agents, as well as the assurance of the agent's willingness and ability to pay.
- Requires transport/migration mechanisms be added to software environments—thus increasing their complexity.
- Has no industry standards for agent environments, migration approaches, or for measuring and billing resource consumption.
- Has not yet been used in an environment containing a large number of mobile agents.

## Basic Interaction Patterns Among Agents

As suggested in Chapter 6, *interaction* is a fundamental property of agents. To enable a group of interactive software agents to coordinate effectively and efficiently, several basic techniques can be used.

### Central Interaction Via a Single Agent

Figure C.3 depicts a star-wheel connection of agents. Such a pattern is very common for satellite and single-server networks. Agents can use them as well for a simple way of communicating and coordinating with each other through a global coordinator agent. The approach is particularly useful when agents require a level of interoperability based on a central knowledge base in order to secure task planning, resource allocation, execution control, monitoring, and intervention. Although depicted as agents, the entities in Figure C.3 could be a combination of objects and agents.

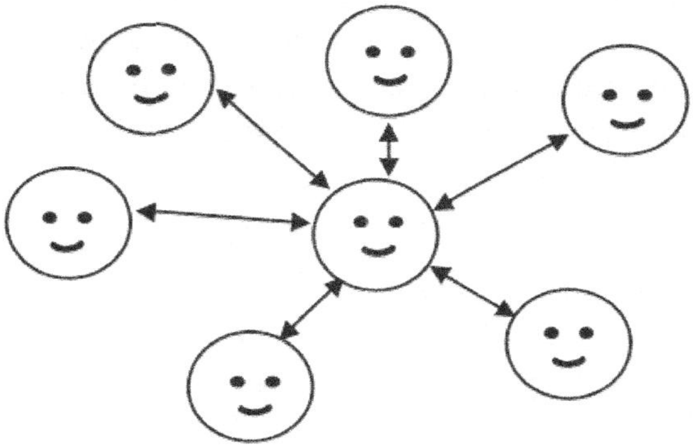

Figure C.3 – Centrally coordinated interactions.

The advantages and disadvantages of agents with centrally coordinated interactions include:

*Advantages:*

- It is fast because all agents are connected via one or two steps.
- Easy to understand, intuitive.
- Overall coordination is possible.
- Traceable. All coordination processing is in one place.

*Disadvantages:*

- Increased overhead to support overall coordination.
- Agents may not communicate directly.
- Very fragile. All communications go through the center.
- Not scalable. Raising the number of satellite nodes creates a bottleneck.

Overall, the feasibility of the central-coordination approach depends on the coordinator's ability and the number of satellite nodes. For small star-wheel agent networks with competent central agents, the technique can work. Otherwise, one of the remaining techniques should be chosen.

## Top-down Interaction Via Hierarchy

A common extension to the star-wheel approach is the hierarchy in which each outlying agent in a star-wheel can become a "hub" agent that centrally controls its own star-wheel. For example in Figure C.4, the top agent in the hierarchy provides a central hub for two agents, each of which becomes the hub for the agents "below" them, and so on.

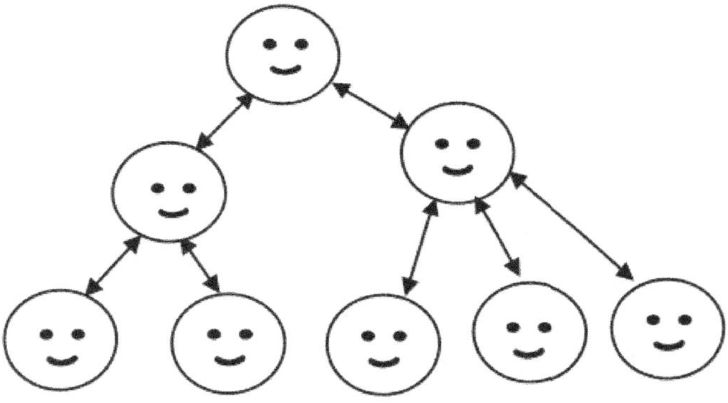

Figure C.4 – Interaction via hierarchy.

This technique of adding hierarchy extension has the following advantages and disadvantages:

*Advantages:*

- Ordered and traceable.
- Easy to understand, intuitive.
- Scalable. No one node in the network has to do too much.

*Disadvantages:*

- Not flexible. Cannot be reconfigured easily.
- Fragile. If one parent node becomes unavailable, the network below is cut off from the rest.
- Slow. Users must navigate up and down through the hierarchy

to reach most of the organization. Information exchanges that involve too many steps will be slow.

- Prone to distortion. The greater the number of steps in traversing the hierarchy, the greater the likelihood of compounding errors.

As one of the most common approaches in IT systems, hierarchies have been used in the development of OO software, business process definitions, supply chain structures, and Internet networks. This top-down centralized control proved useful for organizing and scaling software efforts.

The entities in Figure C.4 can be a combination of objects *and* agents. However, while agent-based systems can employ star-wheel and hierarchical techniques, they can *also* use distributed approaches. In other words, agent systems can offer *both* central and distributed approaches, whereas conventional approaches tend to limit themselves to star-wheel or hierarchical interaction.

## Community Coordination Via Hierarchy

The community (sometimes called *group)* coordination illustrated in Figure C.5 is almost identical to the top-down interaction via hierarchy, illustrated above. A *community* is just a collection of agents and may itself be an agent. Organizations, software components, and biological cells are some examples of communities. (See also Figure 11.6.)

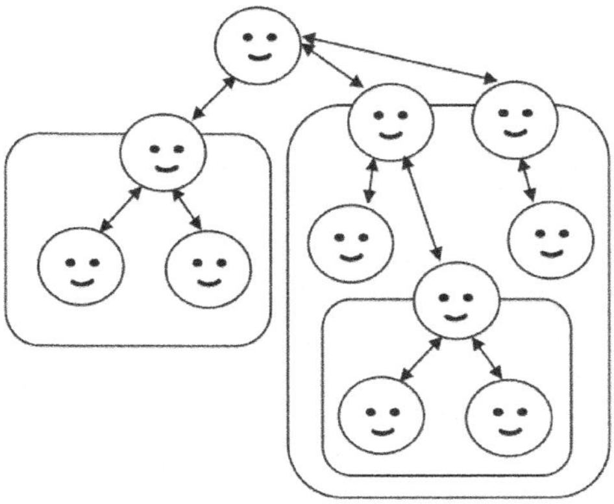

Figure C.5 – Interaction via community-based hierarchy.

Groups are encapsulated structures. To interact with a group, an external agent must communicate via an *interface agent.* An interface agent acts as the doorkeeper for the group, where only the doorkeeper can interact with the agents that are internal to the group. For example, for an external person to purchase a new computer from Apple, the transaction proceeds via an interface point in the Apple sales organization. For software components, you use the interface.

As indicated in Figure C.5, groups can have more than one interface agent, and groups themselves can contain groups. In this mode, group interactions essentially act like hierarchies. As such they have the same pros and cons as the top-down interaction via hierarchy, discussed above.

### Peer-to-Peer Interactions

The classical "me client, you server" architecture is too restrictive for agents. As illustrated in Figure C.6, the peer-to-peer metaphor is closer. Agents can *provide* resources at one moment and *request* resources at another. Furthermore, they can provide multiple services to multiple agents at the same time.

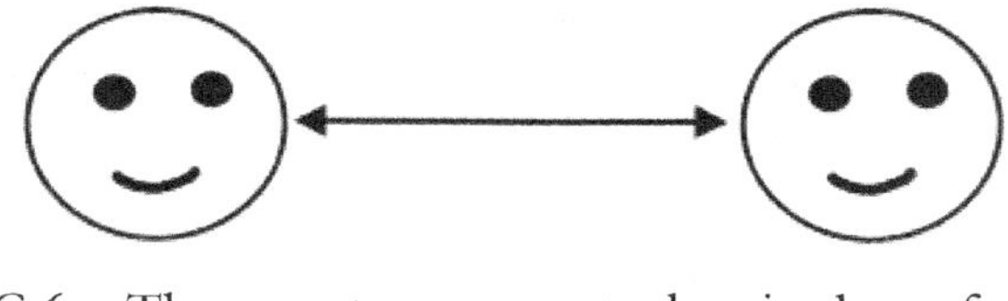

Figure C.6 – The peer-to-peer metaphor is closer for agents.

Interaction could simply involve two or more agents exchanging simple information such as ants do. Ants can communicate with other ants indirectly by leaving pheromones. As described earlier, if another ant detects a pheromone, it reacts by following the pheromones to food. People, on the other hand, communicate in many ways: through voice, writing, gestures, or just their general behavior.

## Individual Interaction Over a Network

Many examples of hierarchy can be observed in nature: the food chain, social groups, pecking orders, and reductionist views of decomposition. However, the predominant pattern in nature is a distributed—yet, interacting—network of entities: subatomic particles in an atom, electrical particles in a storm cloud creating lightening, flocking birds, ants searching for food, the stock market, and so on. This distributed approach in nature is very useful because it enables a degree of synergy that would not be possible otherwise. The interaction among the agents, then, is vital for certain kinds of IT systems, such as planning and scheduling, resource routing, logistics, and order-processing systems.

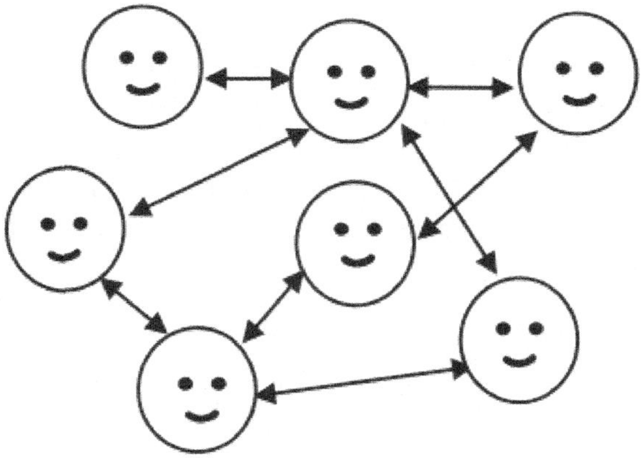

Figure C.7 – Individual interaction via a network using messages and dialogues.

Distributed networks may or may not require any kind of controlling authority. For example, ant colonies have no "controller ants" that manage food-gathering activities. In contrast, crowd-control personnel at football games are frequently useful. For agent-based systems, coordinators can be embedded as peer agents within the system if needed (Figure C.7).

The advantages and disadvantages of the network interaction approach include:

*Advantages:*
- Greater flexibility for each agent.
- No overhead caused by central points of control.

*Disadvantages:*
- Information exchange is limited.
- Information completeness is costly.
- Overall coordination is difficult.

## Individual Interaction Using Groups

Community interaction (mentioned above in community coordination via hierarchy) requires a certain degree of hierarchy because they must be accessed via interface agents. However, the agents that are part of a community group can interact in a network form. If the community has a sub-community (like that depicted in Figure C.8) the sub-community, then, has its own encapsulated boundaries and interface agents. Therefore, the agents that are part of a sub-community can interact in a network form. Only interface agents are permitted to cross boundaries to the next higher aggregation level.

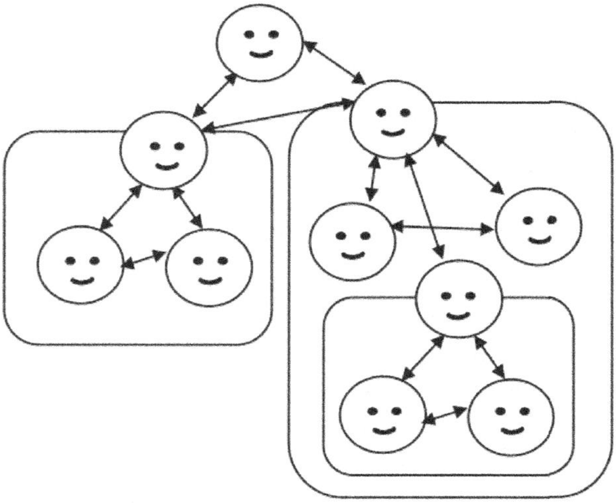

Figure C.8 – Individual interaction within agent communities, but *not* across communities.

By their nature, group interactions are hybrid. It certainly requires a hierarchical approach for inter-community communication. However, within a community any of the above forms can be used, as well. In other words, the internal group could be constrained to be centrally coordinated, hierarchical, or in this case networked.

## Individual Interaction Using a Blackboard

In the previous interaction techniques, messages exist only transiently, as they travel over the network. However, interacting agents may record messages so that they may persist for a period after they are sent. The term *blackboard* refers to a common work area where one or more agents can post and retrieve shared data. Using a network approach would be intensely interactive and time consuming if all the agents needed to be properly informed. In the blackboard approach, shared information can be immediately available for each agent (Figure C.9). Blackboards can be used for many kinds of situations. They can provide a short-term data persistence between two agents; they can also provide a long-term common work area for many agents simultaneously.

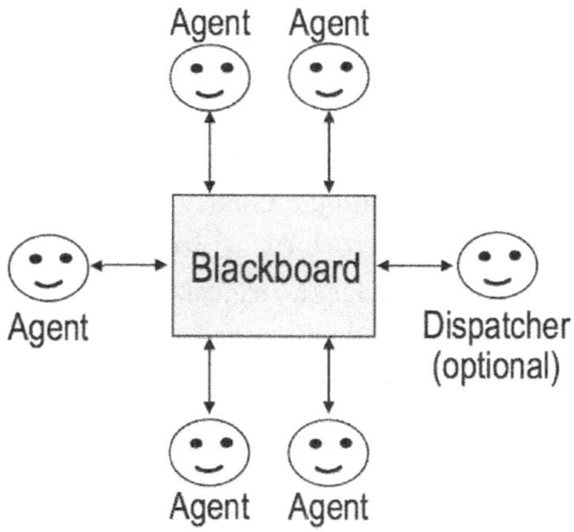


Figure C.9 – Individual interaction via blackboard.

In the ant example, the environment can be considered a kind of blackboard, where pheromones become the information that is posted and queried. Whereas, in the flocking-bird example, no common work area was employed—network interaction was all that was necessary.

Multiple blackboards are possible and can be implemented using a variety of techniques, including shared memory and database management systems. Additionally, dispatchers can be added to inform agents of changes. The advantages and disadvantages include:

*Advantages:*

- Each agent has greater flexibility.
- Information exchange is facilitated by a central source.
- Information completeness is possible.
- Each agent determines what is posted or retrieved.
- No overhead to support overall coordination.

*Disadvantages:*

- Overall coordination is difficult.
- Agents may not communicate directly.
- Doesn't scale well: grows exponentially.

## Conclusion

Since each of the interaction approaches described above has its advantages and disadvantages, clearly no one approach will suit every need. Choosing a mixture of approaches is a common solution. For example, in most large organizations, the structure typically supports a management hierarchy, where a manager's employees often organize in networks.

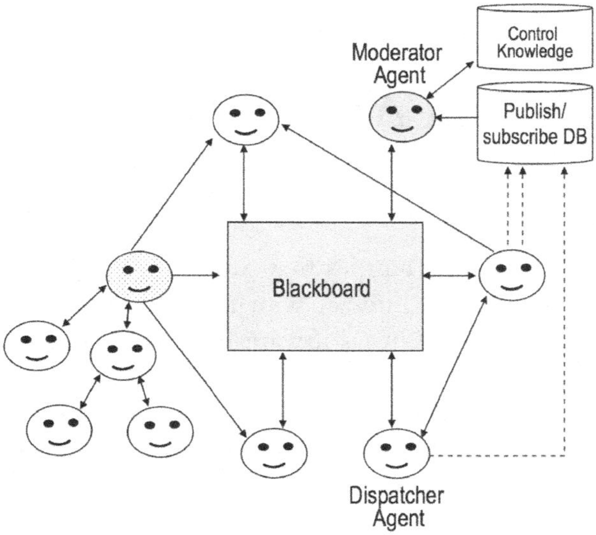


Figure C.10 – Interaction using a variety of techniques.

For multiagent system designers, the situation is similar. In Figure C.10, the agent configuration contains elements of various techniques.

Agent interaction, therefore, is not limited in its techniques; many others are possible. For example, desktop agents can watch how a person interacts with a system and try to remember common usage patterns for the future. Behavior, then, is being communicated to the agent—either directly or indirectly. Eavesdropping agents listen in on the interactions of other agents without their knowledge or consent. *Agent interaction* is defined as the action or influence of agents on each other. Action and influence can come in many forms, through electronic messages, signaling devices, voice, visual observation, pheromone detection, and so on. They can be direct (messages between agents) or indirect (non-message interaction); they can be centralized or decentralized.

# Appendix D. Security and Architecture

## Agent Security

Agents are software entities that often run in a distributed computing environment and interact with many other software entities, including other agents. When software runs in a distributed environment, security issues are numerous. The possibility of encountering security problems increases in open environments, such as the Internet or a virtual private network, or in any environment where all the entities are not known, understood, and administered by a single group.

Various types of security risks are described below. Many of these risks are inherent to distributed computing environments, particularly when software passes messages that can be intercepted, modified, or destroyed. While this is a threat to agent systems, it is also a threat to any software system that depends on messages being passed reliably. Another risk centers on whether or not the software can assume that it is using trustworthy services.

In practice, security is usually applied only to somewhat valuable items, because implementing security has associated costs. This is true both in the everyday world, where we protect our cars or homes from theft and in the world of computing, where we may protect some, but not all, company resources.

*Security policy* refers to how access to valuable resources is controlled. For example, a company may have a policy about which groups can access what data, or when certain types of processing jobs can run, or whether outside entities can connect to the company network. Agent systems will also require security policies that may control where agents can run, what they can do, and with what other entities they can communicate.

Security policies are usually based on *identity*—which is simply something that serves to identify or refer to an entity. In this way, an agent could be referred to by its name, a role that it is playing, or the fact that it is a member of some organization, and so on. An agent, then, can have multiple forms of identity. For example, a particular agent could simultaneously be a purchasing agent working on behalf of user Rolf Smith; be playing the role of a bidder in a negotiation with E-Widgets; having its software composed of elements from company Exdeus; and having the serial number 98734501. Each of these identities might be important in different interactions.

Identity is based on a *credential*, which is a set of data that can be validated by a third-party to prove that the entity is what it says it is. For example, when a user logs into a computer system, he often enters both a username and a password, which is the credential that is validated to indicate that he really is that username. Other common mechanisms for identity and credentials are X5.09 certificates and PGP keys.

## Types of Security Risks

Here are some security threats that could happen in multiagent systems.

- *Unauthorized disclosure:* A breach in the confidentiality of an agent's private data or metadata. For example, an entity eavesdrops, or *snoops*, on the interaction between agents and extracts information on the goals, plans, capabilities, or other information that belongs to the agents. Or, an entity can probe the running agent and extract useful information.
- *Unauthorized alteration:* The unauthorized modification or corruption of an agent, its state, or data. For example, the content of messages is modified during transmission, or the agent's internal value of the last bid is modified.
- *Damage:* Destruction or subversion of a host's files, configuration, or hardware, or of an agent or its mission. Such *hacking* may even harm or destroy an agent.
- *Unauthorized copy and replay:* An attempt to copy an agent or a message and clone or retransmit it. For example, a malicious platform creates an illegal copy or a clone of an agent, or a message from an agent is illegally copied and retransmitted.

- *Denial of service:* An attack that attempts to deny resources to the platform or an agent. For example, one agent floods another agent with requests, and the second agent is unable to provide its services to other agents.
- *Repudiation:* An agent or agent platform denies that it has received or sent a message or taken a specific action. For example, a commitment between two agents as the result of a contract negotiation is later ignored by one of the agents. That agent denies the negotiation has ever taken place and refuses to honor its part of the commitment.
- *Spoofing and masquerading:* An unauthorized agent or agent platform claims the identity of another agent or agent platform. For example, an agent registers as a directory service agent and therefore receives information from other registering agents.

## Message Passing

In systems where agents pass messages, the importance of avoiding message alteration or disclosure is described above. If a message is altered, it might provide incorrect information or transmit a dangerous action. If a message can be read by or disclosed to other entities, the other entities may use the acquired data inappropriately.

Message alteration is usually avoided by providing a mechanism for authenticating the message. Most of the techniques for doing this are based on public/private key pair technologies, such as X.509 certificates. Additional information is sent with the message that allows the receiver to validate that the message has not been changed. Message disclosure is avoided by encrypting the message that again is based mostly on public/private key pair technologies.

For both threats, the authentication or encryption can occur either by encrypting the message itself or by sending it through a transport that provides authentication or encryption services.

Other threats related to message passing include: copy and replay, spoofing and masquerading, and repudiation. Both in copy and replay and in spoofing and masquerading, an agent may assume the identity of another agent. Using this false identity, it can communicate with another agent in order to request an inappropriate action. Many agent systems use relatively simplistic naming schemes (or *iden-*

*tities)* with no additional credentials. Therefore, a message claiming to be from "Joe" cannot be validated.

This set of problems can be solved in various ways. By tagging messages with credentials, the message can be sent in a way that ensures authentication. Thus, the message can be sent without the possibility of tampering by a third party. Tagging messages with credentials can also help avoid repudiation. If a message is signed using a credential, the signing agent can not later deny that it sent the message.

## System Components Dealing with One Another

Agents can use agent platforms to provide services. They can also interact with well-known services such as a *directory service* that helps them locate other agents or an *ontology service* that helps them look up ontologies. When two system components interact, several risks can occur—the two most likely being damage or spoofing and masquerading.

In the damage scenario, the agent may do malicious or inappropriate things to the host system, such as corrupting or deleting files. Therefore, the agent platform may want to control which agents can take which actions. Typically, the agent would offer a credential that identifies it to the agent platform. After validating the credential, the agent platform would use a security policy, based on the agent's identity to determine what actions the agent could take, and would enforce that policy. This is very much like the access control lists found in most operating systems. However, agent systems probably want to control much more than simply reading, writing and running files. They might want to control message sending, utilization of various resources, when and where an agent can move, and whether a moving agent can run on this platform.

Just as the agent platform may want to validate what entity it is dealing with, an agent may want to validate that it is dealing with an agent platform it knows to be genuine. Agent platforms and services can pretend to be "legitimate" but in fact have some dangerous behavior, such as recording message transmissions before encryption, cloning copies of the agent for its own purposes, or providing false information.

Let's consider other risks to which agents can be exposed. In constructing software for an agent, certain types of risks must be addressed—ensuring that the following things do *not* occur:

- Viewing the private security key of the agent.
- Viewing the private data of the agent (i.e., the highest bid an agent is willing to make on a product).
- Invoking private methods in the agent.
- Designing public methods in such a way that permits security risks.

## More Security Considerations

When designing agent systems, the following aspects of security, security policy, and identity should be considered:

- Agents and agent platforms can have multiple credentials. Multiple credentials reflect the reality that we have multiple roles. Users may have credentials as part of several organizations, as an individual, as the owner of multiple credit cards, and so on.
- Agents can have their own credentials. They may also have credentials for the user that they represent in an e-commerce application.
- Agents should not be created that can act anonymously. For example, a user may want to get data about drug or alcohol treatment without revealing his or her identity. Obviously, sites can choose to reject these agents, if their security policies do not allow interaction with anonymous entities.
- All aspects of security need to be managed.
- Traceability of actions can be useful.
- Techniques for backup and recover can be useful for recovering from security breaches that harm or destroy an agent.
- Using a lease model on any credential can be helpful. In a lease model, credentials expire after a certain period of time, but can often be renewed from a credential authority. This control can be a very effective way to clean up credentials in a system that uses relatively short-lived agents. Requiring long-lived agents to renew

their credentials is also useful, because when an entity with bad credentials is forced to renew, it will be rejected and shut down.

- Identity and credentials are also useful for building reputation services. Such services provide a way of determining whether a particular entity has behaved responsibly.

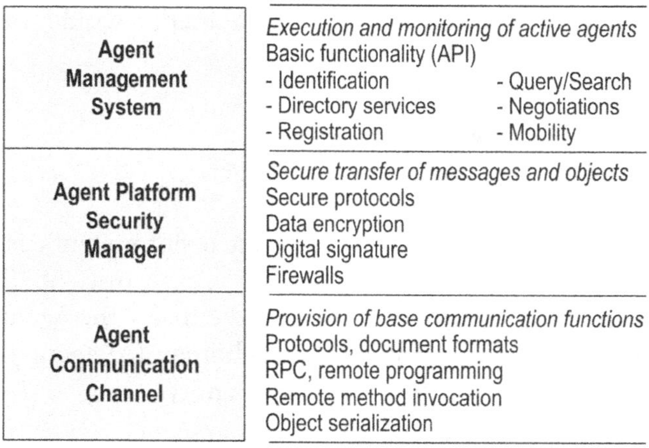


Figure D.1 The agent platform, an infrastructure for deploying agents.

## Agent Architecture

For the most part, agents will be deployed within conventional enterprises and will draw on the enterprise for many services. OMG's CORBA (see www.corba.org) provides a rich source of services and a proven architecture. This section provides a framework for considering how a system supporting agents might draw on CORBA services and facilities. The architectural basis for this discussion will be the IEEE FIPA architecture. [www.fipa.org] The *FIPA Agent Platform* provides a good construct from which to discuss the enterprise-related issues in agent deployment and is summarized in Figure D.1.

### Agent Platform

The key element to the enterprise architecture is the *agent platform* (AP) which provides an infrastructure in which agents can be deployed. An agent must be registered on a platform in order to interact with other agents on that or other platforms. Minimally, an AP consists of an *agent management system* and an *agent platform communication channel.*

FIPA does not specify the physical nature of a platform. However, two cases should be considered, that of a single host and that of multiple processors deployed as a "virtual" platform. If the platform is virtual, having it fulfill several requirements would be wise. It should have:

- High-speed communications.
- A single agent management system.
- A single agent platform security manager.

These last two requirements make the agent system easier to use. From the system perspective, the lifecycle and security of all agents in a given platform is controlled by a single entity—the agent management system. From the perspective of a human (or agent proxy), the platform should be controlled by a single entity.

## Agent Management System

The agent management system (AMS) can be implemented as a single agent that supervises access to, and use of, the agent platform. The AMS maintains a directory of logical agent names and their associated transport addresses for an agent platform. The AMS is responsible for managing the lifecycle of the agents on the platform and its actions include:

- Authentication.
- Registration.
- De-registration.
- Modification.
- Query platform profile.
- Search.
- Mobility requests.
- Control of agent lifecycle.

The AMS also provides two kinds of directory services to other agents: *white pages* and *yellow pages*. White page service is simply a way of locating individual agents. Yellow pages offer a way of locating agents for a given category. Agents may register their services with the directory or query it to determine what services are offered by other agents. For example, an agent might register itself as a rare art broker or punch press resource for other agents (including human) to contract its services.

## Agent Platform Security Manager

The agent platform security manager (APSM) is responsible for maintaining security policies for the platform and infrastructure. The APSM is responsible for run-time activities, such as communications, transport-level security, and audit trails. Security cannot be guaranteed unless, at a minimum, all communication between agents is carried out through the APSM.

The APSM is responsible for negotiating the requested inter- and intra-domain security services with other APSMs in concert with the implemented distributed computing architecture, such as CORBA, COM, and DCE, on behalf of the agents in its domain. The APSM is responsible for enforcing the security policy of its domain and can, at its discretion, upgrade the level of security requested by an agent. The APSM cannot downgrade the level of services requested by an agent but must inform the agent that the service level requested cannot be provided.

## Agent Platform Communication Channel

All agents have access to the agent platform communication channel, which provides a path for basic interchange between agents, agent services, AMS, and other agent platforms. It must at least support IIOP. Agents can reach agents on any number of other platforms through the Agent Communication Channel. Access to agents outside of the local namespace could be supported by the CORBA Trader Services.

# Appendix E: Agent Standards

## Introduction

Several of the agent standards from IEEE FIPA (Foundation for Intelligent Physical Agents) were introduced (www.fipa.org), and described in the Agent communication Language (ACL) standard and the FIPA architectural elements.

This specification introduces a standard that is currently in progress by the Object Management Group (OMG): the Agent Metamodel and Profile (AMP)[3]. The objective of AMP is to provide a metamodel and profile for extending UML with core capabilities to enable agents and agent-based software. At a minimum, these core capabilities include the notions of agent, role, and community—and the structural and behavioral patterns defined by such constructs. Given these capabilities, this submission attempts to:

- Clarify semantics concerned with modeling agents.
- Establish Agent modeling best practices utilizing OMG technologies.
- Develop a MOF-compliant agent metamodel to be used either as a standalone or via extending the existing UML metamodel with agent modeling capabilities.
- Enable agent model interchange between tools via XMI.
- Optionally facilitate modeling of Peer-to-Peer, Grid and Cloud computing, and other technologies in terms of a collection of Agents.

The primary goals that this submission fulfills are to provide a foundation to enable the use of agent technology that can:

---

[3] To review an initial standard, see: http://tinyurl.com/k6t69nb

- Model agents and agent-enabled constructs that can aid in the design of agent-based systems and emphasize how they will interact and collaborate.
- Be used in conjunction with existing and upcoming OMG technologies, such as: UML, the UML Profile and Metamodel for Services (UPMS) and the Event Metamodel and Profile (EMP).
- Be completed in a timely manner (approximately one year). Multiple follow-on agent-related RFPs can be planned and issued over time. Here, each RFP needs to be tangible and deliverable in a timely manner and carefully coordinated with the other agent-related RFPs

This submission, then, is expected to be the first in a series of agent-related submission. As such, it seeks to address those basic foundational elements of agent technology that are both commonly used and can be defined in a reasonable amount of time.

## Core Concept Overview

In general, agents can be software agents, hardware agents, firmware agents, robotic agents, human agents, and so on. While software developers naturally think of computer systems as being constructed of only software agents, a combination of agent mechanisms might in fact be used from shop-floor manufacturing to warfare systems.

These properties are mainly covered by a set of core aspects each focusing on different viewpoints of an agent system. Depending on the viewpoint of an agent system, various aspects are prominent. These aspects can be specified within the AMP metamodel

- *Agent aspect* – describes single autonomous entities and the capabilities each can possess in order to solve tasks within an agent system. In AMP, the stereotype Agent describes a set of agent instances that provides particular service capabilities.
- *Collaboration aspect* – describes how single autonomous entities collaborate within the multiagent system (MAS) and how com-

plex organizational structures can be defined. Collaboration can involve situations such as cooperation and competition.
- *Role aspect* – covers feasible specializations and how they could be related to each role type. The concept of a role is especially used in the context of agent service contracts and interactions. Like in agent systems, the role indicates which responsibilities an actor has to take on.
- *Interaction aspect* – describes how the interactions between autonomous entities or communities /organizations take place. Each interaction specification includes both the actors involved and the order in which messages are exchanged between these actors in a protocol-like manner.
- *Behavioral aspect* – describes how plans are composed from complex control structures and simple atomic tasks such as sending a message and specifying information flows between those constructs.
- *Organization/Community aspect* – Agents can form social units called communities. A community can be formed to take advantage of the synergies of its members, resulting in an entity that enables products and processes that are not possible from any single individual.

## Agents and Agent Classes

An *agent* is an autonomous, interactive entity. Agents have the following three important properties. They are:
- Autonomous
- Interactive
- Adaptive

An agent's foundational features are defined by an Agent Class. For example in Figure E.1 below, depicts individual agents (e.g., Agent1 or "Bob", Agent2 or "Betty" are Person agents; Agent3 is a neural network Manager agent called NN237, and Agent4 is a black-box Stock Trader processor called BB32).

The *agent class* is a classification of agents. In particular, each agent class provides the main foundational features, constraint, and semantics in common for a given set of associated agent individuals. The primary purpose of the agent class is to specify what a particular kind of agent will be—independent of its roles. While roles can change over the lifetime of an individual agent, its agent class does not. The purpose for this is to specify an immutable and defined structure. For example, the agent class Person would define an entity with certain structural and behavioral characteristics, which are independent of the roles played.

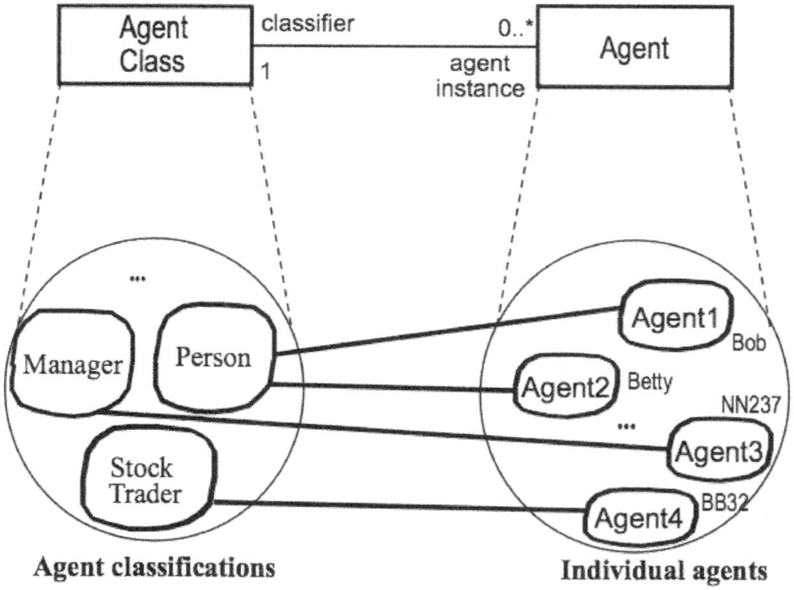


Figure E.1 – Agents as instances of Agent Classes

Three common approaches to defining agent classes exist:

- For software engineering, modeling Agents as instance of Agent Classes is useful because it can enable an MDA approach to creating the agents. For instance, a Cougaar Agent class would create agents that embodied the features that are associated with Cougaar Software agents. Similarly with other platforms, you could have JADE agents, JACK agents, Cybele agents, and so on. Although each platform produces agents, the agents will have different features for communication, internal processing, and so on.

- Agent classes are also used to specialize agents for application purposes. Instead of having generic agents, a Stock Trader or Manager Agent may be the "foundational" form. While Stock Trader and Manager can also be thought of as roles, agent designers are free to specialize their agents for any purpose. The disadvantage is that a Manager will always be a manager. If dynamic flexibility is not a design concern, then pre-defined role-based agents can be useful because they can be created and used immediately. If dynamic flexibility is a design concern, a more generic agent class can be defined and role association can be adopted (described further, below).
- A hybrid approach can also be employed so that the agent designer can specify Cougaar Manager or JADE Stock Traders. This approach is quite common, because it enables the MDA approach for creating agents from known agent software platforms and specializes the "role" for immediate deployment.

## Agents and Roles

The notion of *role* is fundamentally a thespian concept, and attention to how it functions in the theater can reinforce our intuitions and provide useful metaphors for application to multiagent systems (MAS).

As humans, we find the perspective and language of the theater a useful analogy for describing and understanding many of the same complex aspects of individual behavior. The *role* perspective consists of those factors presumed to be influential in governing human behavior. Since we commonly employ this device in real life for conceptualizing human behavior, it may also serve as a useful device for other kinds of individuals in a MAS—be they life forms, active software constructs, or hardware devices.

In the theater, an individual is assigned to play a part, or *role*. In a MAS, an actor is an agent. Roles define normative repertoires of behavior and other features for agents. They provide both major building blocks for agent social systems and the requirements by which agents interact. Each agent is linked to other agents by the roles it plays by virtue of the system's functional requirements—which are based on the expectations that the system has of the agent.

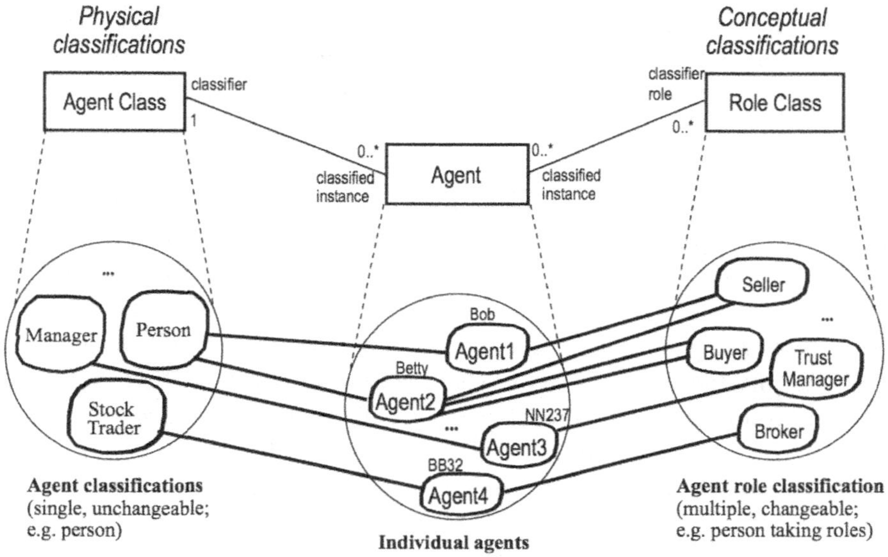


Figure E.2 – Individual agents have multiple ways for classification. Role classes provide multiple and changeable roles during the lifetime of an agent; agent classes are permanent classifications.

As depicted in Figure E.2, agents can be associated with more than one *role class* at the same point in time (multiple classification) and can change roles over time (dynamic classification). For example, Betty (Agent2) is a Person. Yet, dynamically, she has acquired the features to play multiple roles: Buyer and Seller. (Note she has two Buyer roles because she is a buyer for two different companies.) Later, she can take on additional roles or lose her current roles. The ability to acquire or dispose of roles is based on system requirements. For example, she could have been assigned or designated to play these roles by another agent with the ability to maintain roles. Or, she could have acquired the roles based on need, desire, or attained proficiency. In other words, role modification in the agent world can mirror (and document) the same approaches employed in the real world.

## Role Class and Role Assignment

A *role class* define a normative repertoire of behavior and other features that may be played by agents. In short, it is a social position that may be played by an agent; whereas the *agent class* specifies the physical definition of an agent. This figure depicts instances of role class (e.g., Broker, Buyer, Trust Manager, Buyer, etc.) and their general social relationship with agents – which also have the permanent foundational classifications via the agent class.

Each role class is a class, or a *kind* of role that may be played. As a class, a role specifies features, constraints, and semantics in common for a given set of associated agent individuals. For example, the Seller is a role class that would contain methods such as Request Bid Proposal (from a seller), Decline Seller Proposal, Buy Goods or Service, and so on. It also has attributes, such as Maximum Authorized Purchase and Buyer ID.

In contrast, a *role assignment* is an instance of a role class. Here, each role will have values, processes, and policy specifications associated with each feature. For example in Figure E.3, the role class of Buyer assigned to the Person Betty could have a Buyer ID of #9927, Maximum Authorized Purchase is $5,000, and plays role within the Think Box Corp, and so on. Since Better is a Buyer for Technika as well, she has different *role assignment* values where her Buyer ID of #63661, Maximum Authorized Purchase is $22,000, etc.

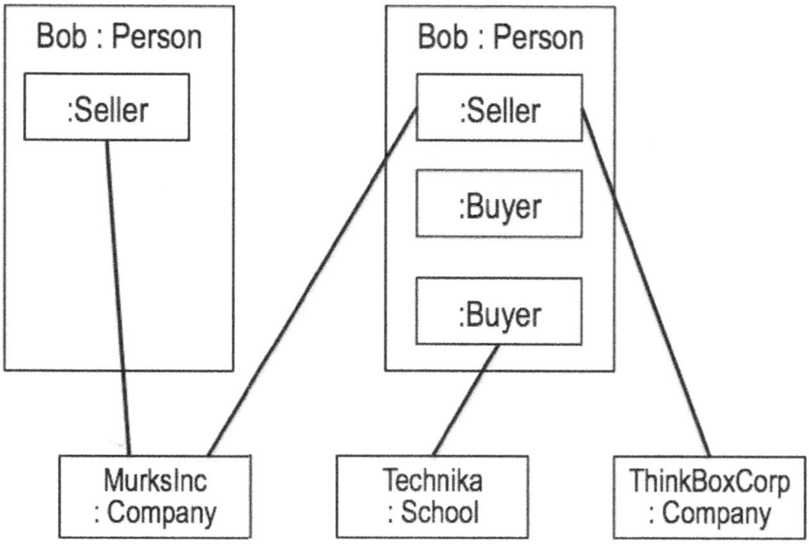


Figure E.3– A way of graphically representing multiple role assignments for an agent.

In Figure E.2, the assignment of roles is depicted using an association. Here, Betty has three associations to two different Role Classes. Bob has an association to the same class as Betty. Role Assignments, as illustrated in Figure E.3, clarify the actual role assignment to an agent by:

- Providing a separate entity to record the data for each role assignment.
- Enabling multiple role assignments for the same kind, by ensuring that each role assignment has its own unique existence and identification.
- Differentiating those apparently "identical" role assignments (e.g. Betty's two Buyer role assignments by distinguishing their context (e.g., Technika and ThinkBox organizations).

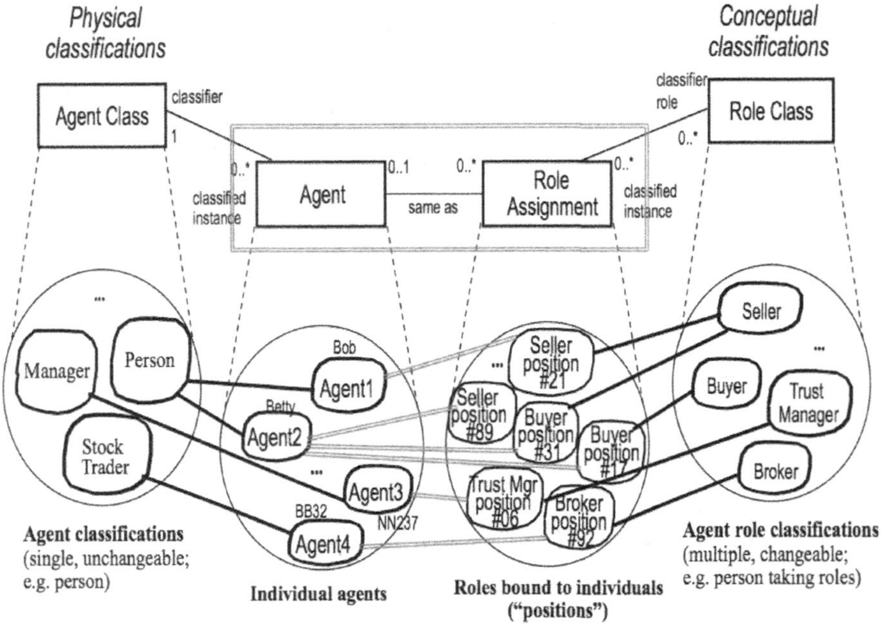


Figure E.4 – An agent and its roles are treated—together —as the same entity.

Figure E.4 expands and clarifies the initial depiction in Figure E.2 by inserting the role assignment between the Role Class and Agent. (While this could have been accomplished by associating a class with the association, a standard class with two associations was chosen for clarity.)

## Agent and Role Assignments – and the "Same As" Association

Agents and Role Assignments are technically different set of objects. Conceptually, however, the agent and the role assignments that it plays can be thought of as occurring within the same entity. For example, the Person Bob and the Seller role that he plays are not two separate things. Bob plays the role and the role is played by Bob. We do not think of the part that is playing Bob's role as not being Bob. Bob is taking the responsibility for playing the role assignment, as well as seen as being held responsible for how he plays his role. As such, the agent and its role assignments are related using a "same as" association. In Owl, the Same As association treats the linked entity as the same entity. In other words, Bob the Person and Bob playing the Seller position #21 are the same entity.

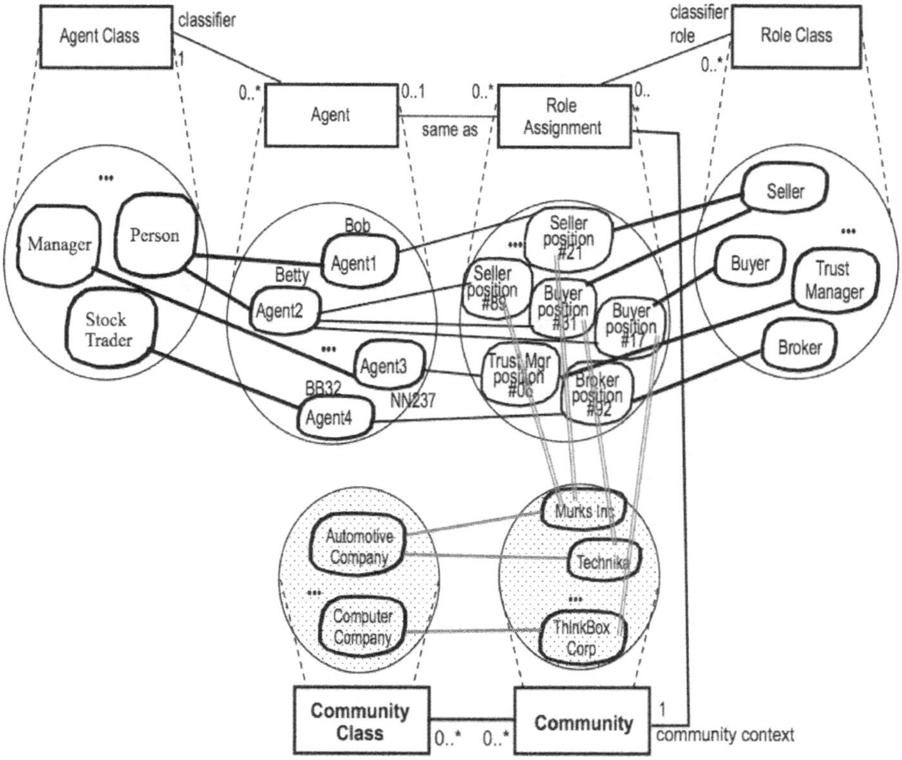


Figure E.5 – Using Community to provide role context.

## Community and Community Class

As a way to provide role context in the previous section, the role assignments are qualified by a community. A *community* is an individual community that comprises a collection of agents that are related via their roles. Each community can be treated as a composite structure—enabling a hierarchy of communities. A *community class* is a metaclass that defines the basic kinds of groups, or communities (e.g., Organizations, Institutions, Teams, Military, Manufacturing, Banking, and so on).

A useful property of community is that they are agents in their own right. For example in Figure E.5, Murks Inc is an agent because it is perceived as a legal entity that has its own autonomy and can interact with other agents. Yes, the community can and does consist of other agents (which themselves can be communities). However, from the outside world and the legal system, a community has its own rights, obligations, and prohibitions. It can be sued and subpoenaed. Due to these kinds of characteristics, communities are agents. And when communities can consist of any number of levels, a rich degree of scalability can be achieved. If agents were only atomic-level entities, the social structure of the world as we now know it would not be possible.

## Conclusion

Essentially, the AMP RFP requests a metamodel and profile for extending UML with capabilities applicable to agents and agent-based software. Submissions developed in response to this RFP will achieve the following: Clarify semantics concerned with modeling agents. Establish Agent modeling best practices utilizing OMG technologies. Develop a MOF-compliant agent metamodel to be used either standalone or via extending the existing UML metamodel with agent modeling capabilities. Enable agent model interchange between tools via XMI. Optionally facilitate modeling of Peer-to-Peer, Grid and Cloud computing, and other technologies in terms of a collection of Agents. It is expected that responses to this RFP will make good use of agent modeling capabilities already supported by the OMG.

# Index

# About the Authors

**Jim Sinur** is an independent thought leader in applying business process management (BPM) to innovative and intelligent business operations (IBO). His research and areas of personal experience focus on business process innovation, business modeling, BPM technology (iBPMS), process collaboration for knowledge workers, process intelligence and optimization, business policy and rule management (BRMS), and leveraging business applications in processes.

During his 20 years as Vice President at Gartner, Mr. Sinur was critical in creating the first Hype Cycle and Maturity Model, which have become a hallmark of Gartner analysis, along with the Magic Quadrant. He has been active in the rules, data and computing communities, helping shape direction based on practical experience. Mr. Sinur has vertical industry experience on the investment and operational sides of the insurance and financial services

Prior to joining Gartner, Mr. Sinur was a director of technologies with American Express, where he worked on a large, industrial-strength, model-driven implementation of a business-critical merchant management system. This system is still active in the merchant retention and support functions for American Express. His responsibilities there included architecture, advanced development technologies and data/database administration.

Before American Express, Mr. Sinur worked for Northwestern Mutual Life for 18 years, where he was involved in leading-edge projects like the Underwriting Workbench that employed many new and emerging methods and technologies. This was after he was involved with building and re-architecting many major applications on the investment and annuity side of NML's business.
jimsinur.blogspot.com

**JAMES J. ODELL** is a consultant, writer, and educator in the areas of agent-oriented and object-oriented systems, methodology, business process management (BPM), data and metadata modeling, applied ontology, metadata-driven service oriented architecture (SOA), event-driven development (EDA/CEP), and complex adaptive systems (CAS).

Throughout most of his forty-year career, Mr. Odell has been heavily involved in developing better methods to understand, communicate, and manage system requirements. In the mid 70s, he became one of the early innovators of data modeling and information engineering methodologies. In the early 80s, he was the principal consultant for KnowledgeWare, and James Martin Associates, where he pioneered and taught the concepts of data modeling, information strategy planning, and CASE technology application. In the late 80s, he became one of the first practical implementors of object-oriented analysis and design. Now working with the OMG and other major methodologists, he continues to innovate and improve development methods and techniques. In particular, he has been the chair of the OMG's Analysis and Design Task Force for 16 years and has participated in the development of standards such as UML, SoaML, SysML, Ontology Definition Metamodel (ODM), Agent Metamodel and Profile (AMP), and others. (The Activity Diagram was one of his primary contributions to UML.)

Most recently, Mr. Odell is involved in a mixture of ontology, metadata and metadata repositories, complex-event process (CEP), BPM, agent-based and complex adaptive systems—and their application to business systems. He is now participating in designing and building next-generation systems that enable their customers to dynamically manage multiple resources in changing and unpredictable environments. These systems serve several application areas, such as managing resources for inventory, manufacturing, call centers, green environments, financial application, and various large US Government projects.

Mr. Odell conducts seminars and workshops and provides consulting to major companies worldwide. He has co-authored five books with James Martin and published by Prentice-Hall. Additionally, he has co-edited five books on the topic of Agent-Oriented Software Engineering (AOSE) with Springer-Verlag. In additional, Mr. Odell has published many articles and papers. For more information on these publications, visit www.jamesodell.com.

**PETER FINGAR,** Executive Partner in the business strategy firm, Meghan-Kiffer Research, is one of the industry's noted experts on business process management, and a practitioner with over forty years of hands-on experience at the intersection of business and technology. As a former CIO and college professor, Peter is equally comfortable in the boardroom, the computer room or the classroom. Peter has taught graduate computing studies in the U.S. and abroad. He has held management, technical and advisory positions with GTE Data Services, American Software and Computer Services, Saudi Aramco, EC Cubed, the Technical Resource Connection division of Perot Systems and IBM Global Services.

Peter has developed technology transition plans for clients served by these companies, including GE, American Express, MasterCard and American Airlines-Sabre. In addition to numerous articles and professional papers, he is an author of twelve landmark books. Peter has delivered keynote talks and papers to professional conferences in America, Austria, Australia, Canada, China, The Netherlands, South Africa, Japan, United Arab Emirates, Saudi Arabia, Egypt, Bahrain, Germany, Britain, Italy and France.
www.peterfingar.com

# Companion Books ...

Co-requisite read for this book

Business Innovation in the Cloud
Executing on Innovation with Cloud Computing
Jim Stikeleather & Peter Fingar
Foreword by Derek Miers Forrester Research
This exciting and deeply insightful book offers a compelling vision of how the Cloud will rewrite the rules of business.
Gary Hamel
London School of Business, Author of What Matters Now

BPM Boots on the Ground
How to Implement Strategic Business Process Management
Lessons Learned from one of the World's Largest Organizations
Jim Boots

Time is the scarcest resource.—Peter Drucker
The COO Revolution
Reinventing Customer-Facing Processes for Moments of Truth
Rich Phillips & Kramer Reeves
With Peter Fingar
Forewords by
Jim Sinur & Phil Gilbert

The Business Process Ecosystem
Arthur C. Harris

SAMURAI BUSINESS
The way of the warrior for professionals in the digital century
By Joris Merks

The Novel That is Changing American Business
The Power of Process
Unleashing the Source of Competitive Advantage
Kiran K. Garimella

The PROCESS
Business Process Modeling Using BPMN
Alexander Grosskopf
Gero Decker, Mathias Weske
Includes a Pullout BPMN Reference Chart

Made in United States
North Haven, CT
04 November 2026

21730732R10153